STRATEGIES
FOR TEACHING
High School Band

MENC wishes to thank
Carolynn A. Lindeman for developing and coordinating this series;
Edward J. Kvet and John E. Williamson
for selecting, writing, and editing the strategies for this book;
and the following teachers for submitting strategies:

Linda Becker

William L. Berz

Lisa Boortz

David G. Branson

J. Bryan Burton

Elliot Del Borgo

Scott Emmons

Mark Fonder

Thomas W. Goolsby

George J. Hess

Dwight E. Leonard

David L. Mueller

Jeffrey T. Phillips

Mel Pontious

Marion K. Roberts

Margaret Schmidt

Elaine Schweller-Snyder

Darwyn (Tony) Snyder

Richard R. Tengowski

Molly A. Weaver

David Scott Zerull

YOUR KEY TO
IMPLEMENTING
THE NATIONAL
STANDARDS
FOR MUSIC
EDUCATION

STRATEGIES FOR TEACHING

High School Band

Compiled and edited by
Edward J. Kvet and John E. Williamson

MUSIC EDUCATORS NATIONAL CONFERENCE

Series Editor: Carolynn A. Lindeman
Project Administrator: Margaret A. Senko

Copyright © 1998
Music Educators National Conference
1806 Robert Fulton Drive
Reston, VA 20191-4348
Printed in the United States of America.
ISBN 1-56545-089-2

CONTENTS

PREFACE

The Music Educators National Conference (MENC) created the *Strategies for Teaching* series to help preservice and in-service music educators implement the K–12 National Standards for Music Education and the MENC Prekindergarten Standards. To address the many components of the school music curriculum, each book in the series focuses on a specific curricular area and a particular level. The result is eleven books spanning the K–12 areas of band, chorus, general music, strings/orchestra, guitar, keyboard, and specialized ensembles. A prekindergarten book and a guide for college music methods classes complete the series.

The purpose of the series is to seize the opportunity presented by the landmark education legislation of 1994. With the passage of the Goals 2000: Educate America Act, the arts were established for the first time in our country's history as a core, challenging subject in which all students need to demonstrate competence. Voluntary academic standards were called for in all nine of the identified core subjects—standards specifying what students need to know and be able to do when they exit grades 4, 8, and 12.

In music, content and achievement standards were drafted by an MENC task force. They were examined and commented on by music teachers across the country, and the task force reviewed their comments and refined the standards. While all students in grades K–8 are expected to meet the achievement standards specified for those levels, two levels of achievement—proficient and advanced—are designated for students in grades 9–12. Students who elect music courses for one to two years beyond grade 8 are expected to perform at the proficient level. Students who elect music courses for three to four years beyond grade 8 are expected to perform at the advanced level.

The music standards, together with the dance, theatre, and visual arts standards, were presented in final form—*National Standards for Arts Education*—to the U.S. Secretary of Education in March 1994. Recognizing the importance of early childhood education, MENC went beyond the K–12 standards and established content and achievement standards for the prekindergarten level as well, which are included in MENC's *The School Music Program: A New Vision.*

Now the challenge at hand is to implement the standards at the state and local levels. Implementation may require schools to expand the resources necessary to achieve the standards as specified in MENC's *Opportunity-to-Learn Standards for Music Instruction: Grades PreK–12.* Teachers will need to examine their curricula to determine if they lead to achievement of the standards. For many, the standards reflect exactly what has always been included in the school music curriculum—they represent best practice. For others, the standards may call for some curricular expansion.

To assist in the implementation process, this series offers teaching strategies illustrating how the music standards can be put into action in the music classroom. The strategies themselves do not suggest a curriculum. That, of course, is the responsibility of school districts and individual teachers. The strategies, however, are designed to help in curriculum development, lesson planning, and assessment of music learning.

The teaching strategies are based on the content and achievement standards specified in the *National Standards for Arts Education* (K–12) and *The School Music Program: A New Vision* (PreK–12). Although the strategies, like the standards, are designed primarily for four-year-olds, fourth graders, eighth graders, and high school seniors, many may be developmentally appropriate for students in other grades. Each strategy, a lesson appropriate for a portion of a class session or a complete class session, includes an objective (a clear statement of what the student will be able to do), a list of necessary materials, a description of what prior student learning and experiences are expected, a set of procedures, and the indicators of success. A follow-up section identifies ways learning may be expanded.

The *Guide for Music Methods Classes* contains strategies appropriate for preservice instructional settings in choral, instrumental, and general music methods classes. The teaching strategies in this guide relate to the other books in the series and reflect a variety of teaching/learning styles.

Bringing a series of thirteen books from vision to reality required tremendous commitment from many, many music educators—not to mention the tireless help of the MENC publications staff. Literally hundreds of music teachers across the country answered the call to participate in this project, the largest such participation in an MENC publishing endeavor. The contributions of these teachers and the books' editors are proudly presented in the various publications.

—*Carolynn A. Lindeman*
Series Editor

---

*Carolynn A. Lindeman, professor of music at San Francisco State University and president of the Music Educators National Conference (1996–1998), served on the MENC task force that developed the music education standards. She is the author of three college textbooks (*The Musical Classroom, PianoLab, *and* MusicLab) *and numerous articles.*

INTRODUCTION

The passage of the Goals 2000: Educate America Act in 1994 with the arts as one of the nine core subjects presents the music education community with a unique challenge. For years, educators have argued that music is a basic academic subject, not "curricular icing." At the same time, many in the arts field, especially the performing arts, have rejected the idea that study in the arts requires both a sequential curriculum and evaluation based upon skills and concepts found in the curriculum.

This rejection has been manifested most clearly in the traditional large-ensemble setting in the schools. How often have we heard ensemble directors state, either verbally or through their actions, that their curriculum is simply a performance at a festival and that their evaluation is the rating? While no one would argue that performance is one of the primary outcomes of a music education, is it not possible to maintain a high level of performance and also provide a comprehensive music education?

Many attempts have been made to address this concern. One of the earliest was the Hawaii Music Curriculum Program, which began in 1968. This project developed a statewide music curriculum for the public schools of Hawaii based upon the concept of Comprehensive Musicianship. A series of guides were developed, including *Comprehensive Musicianship through Band Performance* by Brent Heisinger (Menlo Park, CA: Addison-Wesley, 1976), which was designed so that:

> (1) musical understandings evolved from actual performance;

> (2) selected activities ensured the systematic introduction of a number of concepts; and

> (3) students were placed in varied musical roles—performing (small and large ensembles), improvising, composing, transcribing, arranging, conducting, rehearsing, and analyzing.

Other publications promoting a comprehensive musicianship approach for bands include *Blueprint for Band* by Robert Garofalo (Fort Lauderdale, FL: Meredith Music Publications, 1983) and *Teaching Musicianship in the High School Band* by Joseph A. Labuta (Fort Lauderdale, FL: Meredith Music Publications, 1996).

Large-scale implementation of a comprehensive musicianship approach for band performance has had little success, however, with the exception of the Hawaii Curriculum and the Wisconsin Comprehensive Musicianship Project. The National Standards for Music Education provide a unique opportunity and a model for developing specific strategies that can transform the traditional band rehearsal into a comprehensive band class in which specific musical concepts that are part of a planned, sequential curriculum can be integrated.

Strategies for Teaching High School Band was developed to provide high school band educators with sample lessons to begin implementing the National Standards during band rehearsals. These lessons should be especially helpful with Content Standards 3, 4, 6, 7, 8, and 9, which are often neglected in typical rehearsals.

Individual strategies have been provided for most standards, both proficient and advanced. The intent is to provide examples that can be used for bands at all levels. While some educators may wish to begin the process by directly implementing the suggested strategies, it is highly recommended that these strategies be used as models and adapted to fit the particular teaching situation.

The strategies in this publication represent the thinking and practice of high school band educators throughout the United States. They provide various approaches, methods, and literature to achieve the desired outcome for each standard. Therefore, specific texts or compositions suggested in this publication must not be considered as the only available or recommended source. Used with curriculum guides and other publications, such as the companion publication *Strategies for Teaching Beginning and Intermediate Band,* this document will serve as an aid to developing a comprehensive band program that is part of a districtwide preK–12 music program closely allied with the National Standards.

STRATEGIES

STANDARD 1B

Singing, alone and with others, a varied repertoire of music: Students sing music written in four parts, with and without accompaniment.

Objective

■ Students will vocalize a four-part chorale, following the conductor's cues while performing with appropriate balance and blend and with good intonation.

Materials

■ Four-part chorale from a chorale book

■ Transparency or chalkboard/markerboard

■ Overhead projector, if transparency is used

Prior Knowledge and Experiences

■ Students have experience singing with good breath control throughout their vocal ranges.

■ Students have experience reading a four-part score.

■ Students have studied aspects of musical composition such as voice leading, tonality, harmonic progressions, and suspensions.

Procedures

1. Have students play a four-part chorale as a warm-up exercise. Then ask every other student to play his or her part while the other students listen and follow their individual parts. Then have the students who were listening vocalize their parts on a neutral syllable, one part at a time, while the rest of the band accompanies them. Have the band members switch parts, giving the rest of the band the chance to vocalize their parts.

2. In turn, conduct each group of students as they sing all four parts of the chorale together on a neutral syllable with band accompaniment. Then have everyone sing the chorale a cappella. Challenge them to listen to all of the parts to achieve an appropriate balance, as they would while performing a similar composition on their instruments. Discuss with students what changes they need to make in their singing to improve the balance. Have them consider how they can alleviate any imbalance resulting from varying numbers of voices on each part. Conduct students in singing the chorale again, asking them to give special attention to balance.

3. Using a transparency or the chalkboard, lead students in outlining the chordal structure of the chorale. Then direct their attention to how their parts fit into that chordal structure, drawing attention to leading tones, suspensions, moving bass lines, and so on. Discuss with students the need for listening to their own parts as well as the other three parts in order to blend their voices and improve their intonation, just as they would use their listening skills in playing a composition on their instruments. Have them consider how they can apply their knowledge of the chordal structure and other compositional techniques to adjust their intonation in singing the chorale.

4. Lead students again in singing the chorale a cappella, first encouraging them to give special attention to their intonation. Stop at cadence points and play the pitches on the piano to assist students in maintaining the tonal center.

5. Repeat the a cappella singing, gradually allowing longer phrases or periods between playing chords for checking pitches. Eventually explain that you will play the first and last chord on the piano and

(continued)

ask them to identify whether they maintained the overall tonality or whether their singing became sharp or flat. Play the starting pitches and proceed in that manner. If students' singing becomes sharp or flat, repeat the exercise, having them work to improve their intonation.

6. Lead students in a final singing of the chorale, listening for accurate intonation and appropriate balance and blend. Remind students to watch you closely and follow your cues for attacks, releases, tempo variations, and dynamic nuances. [*Note:* High school students usually are capable of performing more softly with control when vocalizing than when playing on their instruments.]

7. Ask students to critique their performance. Discuss with them how they can transfer what they have learned about ensemble skills in a chorale ensemble to their playing in the band.

Indicators of Success

- Students sing the selected chorale with good ensemble balance and blend.

- Students demonstrate a keener sense of intonation as they sing the selected chorale and listen to the ensemble.

- Students accurately follow the conductor's cues for tempo and dynamics.

Follow-up

- Introduce a four-part arrangement of the hymn tune "Chester" and use steps similar to those above to teach students to sing it. Explain to students that this tune was the basis for the opening chorale to the band work "Chester," from *New England Triptych,* by William Schuman (Bryn Mawr, PA: Merion Music/Theodore Presser Company), Level 5. Then introduce the band work "Chester," either for performance study or through listening (e.g., Cincinnati College Conservatory of Music Wind Symphony, Eugene Corporon, Klavier KCD 11048). As they study the work, have students return to singing the hymn arrangement again, particularly listening to their singing to work on ways that will enhance expressive performance or listening.

STANDARD 2A

Performing on instruments, alone and with others, a varied repertoire of music: Students perform with expression and technical accuracy a large and varied repertoire of instrumental literature with a level of difficulty of 4, on a scale of 1 to 6.

Objective

- Students will perform with musical expression and technical accuracy a Level 4 composition for band.

Materials

- *Toccata for Band* by Frank Erickson (New York: Bourne Company), Level 4

Prior Knowledge and Experiences

- Students have experience reading and interpreting various expressive markings.

Procedures

1. Introduce *Toccata for Band*, pointing out to students the salient features that may present expressive and technical problems during initial performance, such as meter and tempo changes. Also, point out sections where individual sections are most exposed (e.g., first clarinets at measures 9 and 91; cornets at measure 38; horns and low brass/woodwinds at measure 81).

2. Conduct and rehearse the recurring tutti theme in measures 1–8, 30–37, and 123–30, working on appropriate articulations, balance, and rhythmic accuracy.

3. Conduct and rehearse the cornet theme—measures 38–55 and 131–48. Direct students' attention to the various components of musical expression and to the technical challenges, such as the lightness of the theme (the forte played in context); the contour and build of the line; balance; and the ending section, which begins with syncopation, then changes to 3/4 meter, obscuring the bar line.

4. Direct students' attention to the composer's manipulation of the tutti and cornet themes, rehearsing what may be considered variations on these themes. Specifically, rehearse measures 55–72, which use a theme similar to the tutti theme (down one step) in the upper woodwinds. Have woodwinds focus on expressive playing, and have all other instruments focus on technical accuracy in accompaniment figures. Then rehearse measures 9–29 and 91–114, which demonstrate how the composer uses augmentation of the cornet theme to create a flowing feeling or mood that is in extreme contrast to the other statements of the theme. Have students focus on expressive eight-measure phrases with controlled entrances and releases.

5. Use the final contrasting lyrical theme (measures 73–81, 81–90, and 188–95) to teach and demonstrate a type of call-and-response and tapering of short motives. Again, demand control and expressive playing.

6. Rehearse the band in the final nine measures of the composition, having them note the use of bits and pieces of all three themes—tutti, cornet, and lyrical—to create a growing and grandiose close.

(continued)

Also, have them note the composer's notation of specific articulations, so as to prevent harshness.

7. Direct students' attention to the transitions from one theme to the next. Note that each transition uses different performance practices, including decrescendos, crescendos, soft fermata/stop, and driving builds. Then conduct students in a run-through of the piece, encouraging them in an expressive and accurate performance.

Indicators of Success

- Students perform *Toccata for Band* demonstrating contrast between themes and variations through appropriate articulations, phrasing, expression, and rhythmic accuracy, including not dropping phrases.

- Students demonstrate an understanding of the construction of the work by performing similar sections in a similar way.

- Students accurately follow conductor's cues for tempo changes and dynamic nuances.

Follow-up

- In a subsequent rehearsal of *Toccata for Band,* record the band in a run-through of the composition. Play the tape of the run-through, asking students to critique the performance with regard to balance, articulations, rhythmic accuracy, pitch (intonation as well as notes), and expression. Lead students in a discussion of methods and techniques for improving the expression and technical accuracy.

- Introduce a Level 4 band composition from a different genre, such as a Mozart transcription, and use a similar process to teach it. Explain to students that structure in composition relates to the way it is put together. Lead them in performing contrasting or various sections accurately and appropriately. Guide them in understanding that the notations for articulations, dynamics, rhythms, and expressive devices are a start, but they must watch the conductor's gestures for interpreting the composition, as well.

STANDARD 2B

Performing on instruments, alone and with others, a varied repertoire of music: Students perform an appropriate part in an ensemble, demonstrating well-developed ensemble skills.

Objective

- Students will describe their role as players in the band and demonstrate their understanding of the function of their individual parts at specific points in the music and how those parts affect the balance, dynamics, and blend of the ensemble.

Materials

- Any composition for high school band
- Chalkboard/markerboard

Prior Knowledge and Experiences

- Students have studied and performed the selected composition.

Procedures

1. Using the selected composition as the basis for discussion, question students about the overall function of their individual parts in the music (that is, whether their parts are melodic, rhythmic, countermelodic, or harmonic; how they fit into the whole composition; and why they are important).

2. Have students identify where a particular melodic figure occurs in each section of the music. Ask students on each part to explain what role their parts perform at specific points and how that affects the balance, dynamics, and blend at those points in the music.

3. Ask each student to write a brief description of the role of an individual player in a large ensemble.

4. After students have completed their writing, ask individual students to read their descriptions for the class. Lead students in a discussion of the points that have been raised in the individual papers. Have students summarize the discussion as one student lists on the board the points that students identify.

Indicators of Success

- Students describe various roles of performers in a large ensemble.
- Students describe how the roles of their individual parts affect the balance, dynamics, and blend at various points in the music.

Follow-up

- Have students devise a performance chart or map as a visual representation demonstrating the relationship between the melodic elements (melody, countermelody) and the rhythmic and harmonic elements in a selected composition.

STANDARD 2C

Performing on instruments, alone and with others, a varied repertoire of music: Students perform in small ensembles with one student on a part.

Objective

- Students will demonstrate their understanding of their roles as individual performers and as ensemble members as they perform in a small ensemble.

Materials

- Any small-ensemble (trio, quartet, quintet, sextet) composition at the appropriate level
- Audiocassette recorder, microphone, and blank tape

Prior Knowledge and Experiences

- Students have had some experience performing in a small ensemble.
- Students have been practicing their individual parts for the music to be rehearsed.

Procedures

1. Have students rehearse a section of a small-ensemble composition. Engage them in a discussion of the interrelationships of the parts (that is, which instruments have melody, harmony, or particular rhythmic elements).

2. Ask individual students to demonstrate the roles of their individual parts, based on the discussion, by performing a selected passage of the music.

3. Lead a discussion of how balance, blend, and articulation enhance the ensemble performance. Have students discuss how their individual roles differ in a small ensemble from their roles in the band. Include some discussion of appropriate behaviors for working together, such as showing respect for each other's opinions.

4. To facilitate students' understanding, record their performance and play back the tape as needed. Guide them to discuss the improvements they discern in this performance over previous rehearsals of the composition.

5. Have students identify what work is needed to further improve the balance, blend, and articulation of the performance. Ask students to rehearse the composition again, incorporating the improvements they have suggested.

Indicators of Success

- Students demonstrate through discussion and performance an increased understanding of their individual roles as performers in a small ensemble.
- Students demonstrate improvements in balance, blend, and articulation of their performance of a small-ensemble composition.

Follow-up

- Prior to their rehearsal of a new small-ensemble composition, have students study their parts and discuss the interrelationships of the parts and the role that each part plays in the overall performance.

STANDARD 2D

Advanced

Performing on instruments, alone and with others, a varied repertoire of music: Students perform with expression and technical accuracy a large and varied repertoire of instrumental literature with a level of difficulty of 5, on a scale of 1 to 6.

Objective

- Students will accurately perform polyrhythms in a composition with a level of difficulty of 5, relating them to traditional African rhythm patterns.

Materials

- *Kilimanjaro: An African Portrait* by Robert Washburn (Miami: Belwin/Warner Bros. Publications), Level 5

- Recordings of traditional African music with polyrhythmic percussion, such as *Master Drummer of Ghana, Mustapha Tettey Addy,* Lyrichord LLCT 7250

- *All Hands On!: An Introduction to West African Percussion Ensembles* by Lynne Jessup (Danbury, CT: World Music Press, 1997)

- Transparency with selected polyrhythm patterns from *All Hands On*

- Charts (based on Jessup's notation) of polyrhythms in *Kilimanjaro*

- Overhead projector

- Audio-playback equipment

Prior Knowledge and Experiences

- Students have been rehearsing *Kilimanjaro.*

Procedures

1. Play a recorded example of traditional African music, asking students to listen particularly for the rhythms of the percussion parts. Lead a brief discussion of traditional African music, focusing on African polyrhythmic percussion.

2. Tell students that they will be hearing additional examples of the African polyrhythmic percussion tradition. Ask them to listen for and be prepared to identify characteristics of the African polyrhythmic percussion tradition in the music that they will be hearing. Play selected examples.

3. Using the transparency with selected patterns from *All Hands On!,* lead students in clapping polyrhythm patterns. Have them experiment with varied body percussion to obtain textural contrasts.

4. Using charts (based upon Jessup's notation) of polyrhythms in *Kilimanjaro,* have entire ensemble clap the rhythms until they can do so accurately. Have the ensemble perform rhythms on a designated single pitch on their instruments, transferring the skill they have mastered through the clapping exercise.

5. After students have mastered the rhythm patterns on single-note exercises, ask them to perform patterns for their instruments, as written in *Kilimanjaro.*

Indicators of Success

- Students accurately clap and perform polyrhythm patterns from *All Hands On!* and *Kilimanjaro.*

Follow-up

- Record students' performance of *Kilimanjaro* and ask students to listen to the polyrhythms and determine their relationship to the melodic content.

- Introduce students to more difficult polyrhythms in band music, such as the third movement ("Festival") from *La Fiesta Mexicana* by H. Owen Reed (Miami: Belwin/Warner Bros. Publications), Level 6.

STANDARD 3A

Improvising melodies, variations, and accompaniments: Students improvise stylistically appropriate harmonizing parts.

Objective

- Students will improvise harmony parts using chord tones for a given folk melody.

Materials

- Any appropriate collection of simple folk melodies

Prior Knowledge and Experiences

- Students have sung and played on their instruments several two- and three-chord folk melodies.

- Students have played simple folk melodies by ear on their instruments.

- Students have practiced singing roots of chords to folk melodies.

- Students have been introduced to "passing tones."

Procedures

1. Have students sing through a selected folk melody.

2. Ask students to play the folk melody by ear on their instruments. Give them the opportunity to play the melody several times, and make sure that everyone can perform the melody correctly before moving on.

3. Ask half the students in the ensemble to perform the melody on their instruments. Then ask the other half to figure out the chord changes by ear and softly sing the chord roots while other students perform the melody.

4. Repeat step 3, this time asking the second group to play the chord roots on their instruments instead of singing them.

5. Have students switch roles and repeat steps 3 and 4.

6. While half of the ensemble plays the melody, have other students improvise harmony parts by embellishing the chord roots using chord tones as passing tones from one chord root to the next. Switch groups and repeat this step.

7. Repeat step 6, having students on harmony parts add a characteristic accompanying rhythm. Then repeat, having students switch parts.

Indicators of Success

- Students improvise harmony parts for a given folk melody, embellishing chord tones with passing tones.

- Students add characteristic rhythms for their improvisations.

Follow-up

- Have students improvise harmony parts for melodies in a variety of styles.

STANDARD 3B

Improvising melodies, variations, and accompaniments: Students improvise rhythmic and melodic variations on given pentatonic melodies and melodies in major and minor keys.

Objective

- Students will improvise rhythmic and melodic variations on a selected blues tune.

Materials

- Melody of Duke Ellington's "C Jam Blues," in *In a Mellow Tone,* vol. 48, edited by Jamey Aebersold (Jamey Aebersold Jazz, PO Box 1244C, New Albany, IN 47151), transposed for all band members

- B-flat blues rhythm background generated from *Band-in-a-Box* (Buffalo, NY: PG Music), or from *Nothin' but Blues,* vol. 2 of *A New Approach to Jazz Improvisation,* Jamey Aebersold Jazz 1971; or similar rhythm background

- Audio-playback equipment

Prior Knowledge and Experiences

- Students have sung and played on their instruments the B-flat minor pentatonic scale (B-flat, D-flat, E-flat, F, A-flat).

- Students have learned the melody of "C Jam Blues."

Procedures

1. Have students perform the melody of "C Jam Blues" as a group with the B-flat blues rhythm background. [*Note*: Percussionists should all use mallet instruments.]

2. With the rhythm background playing, model for students ways of embellishing the given melody by altering the rhythm and by substituting different notes of the pentatonic scale for melody notes.

3. Ask half the students in the ensemble to perform the melody on their instruments using the recorded rhythm background as accompaniment. Ask the other half to improvise rhythmic and melodic embellishments in ways similar to those you modeled.

4. Have students switch roles and repeat step 3.

5. Ask individual student volunteers to improvise rhythmic and melodic embellishments while a small group of students plays the melody along with the recorded rhythm background.

Indicators of Success

- Students improvise rhythmic and melodic embellishments for the given melody, substituting different notes of the pentatonic scale for melody notes.

Follow-up

- After students have mastered improvising rhythmic and melodic variations on given pentatonic melodies, have them experiment with rhythmic and melodic variations on given melodies in both major and minor keys.

STANDARD 3C

Improvising melodies, variations, and accompaniments: Students improvise original melodies over given chord progressions, each in a consistent style, meter, and tonality.

Objective

- Students will improvise "blues licks" using notes from a minor pentatonic scale.

Materials

- Transparency of F minor pentatonic scale (F, A-flat, B-flat, C, E-flat), with transpositions for each band instrument
- F minor blues rhythm background generated from *Band-in-a-Box* (Buffalo, NY: PG Music), or from *Nothin' but Blues,* vol. 2 of *A New Approach to Jazz Improvisation,* Jamey Aebersold Jazz 1971 (Jamey Aebersold Jazz, PO Box 1244C, New Albany, IN 47151)
- Overhead projector
- Audio-playback equipment

Prior Knowledge and Experiences

- Students have studied the 12-bar blues form.
- Students can play melodies by ear on their instruments.

Procedures

1. Start the recorded background track for the blues in F minor. With a good swing feel, model short blues licks (two-to-four notes maximum length) using the notes F and A-flat concert. Have students echo them back immediately in correct tempo with the background music.

2. Repeat step 1, using a gradually expanding collection of notes. Add notes in this order: F, A-flat, E-flat, B-flat, C.

3. Ask students to improvise softly as a group to the background track using licks they learned in steps 1 and 2 as a model.

4. Have students improvise solos to entire choruses when they feel comfortable. Then have them "trade fours" or "twos"—that is, exchange, or trade, two- or four-measure performed solos.

Indicators of Success

- Students improvise blues licks using notes from the F minor pentatonic scale.

Follow-up

- Have students improvise blues licks in a similar way in other keys.
- Teach students various blues tunes by rote. Have them play a selected tune again and then improvise over the changes, imitating the styles of various professional blues or jazz performers.

Advanced

STANDARD 3E

Improvising melodies, variations, and accompaniments: Students improvise original melodies in a variety of styles, over given chord progressions, each in a consistent style, meter, and tonality.

Objective

- Students will improvise original melodies over a given chord progression in a consistent style, meter, and tonality.

Materials

- Chord progression for Pachelbel canon (transposed to key of choice for all band members)—see step 1

Prior Knowledge and Experiences

- Students have either listened to or played the Pachelbel canon.
- Students have studied triadic harmony, including performing the harmony as chords and as arpeggios.
- Students have improvised melodies over I-V-I and I-IV-V-I chord progressions.

Procedures

1. Have students play the Pachelbel chord progression:

2. Have students play an arpeggiated version of the Pachelbel chord progression (actually a chaconne) to this rhythm: ♩ ♩ ♩
   C-E-G, G-B-D, A-C-E, E-G-B, F-A-C, C-E-G, F-A-C, G-B-D (repeat or resolve to C-E-G)

3. Discuss with students and demonstrate stylistic resolutions of non-chord tones (i.e., seventh degree goes up, fourth and sixth degrees go down, second degree goes either up or down).

4. Have the ensemble start playing the block chord progression for the Pachelbel canon, and demonstrate for them an improvised solo based on the progression. Discuss with students the need for making the improvised melody consistent in style, meter, and tonality with the chord progression.

5. In order to give everyone a chance to improvise, have half the ensemble improvise melodies while other students play the chord progression. Repeat, giving the other half of the ensemble the opportunity to improvise.

6. Select two or three "soloists" to perform, either together or individually, while the band plays the Pachelbel chord progression.

Indicators of Success

- Students demonstrate consistency of style, meter, and tonality between their melodies and the given chord progression.
- Students improvise melodies over the given chord progression, making their melodies interesting throughout rather than static.

(continued)

Follow-up

- Continue the procedures outlined above over a sufficient number of rehearsals to give every member of the band an opportunity to improvise a solo over the Pachelbel chord progression. Have non-soloists use the chord progression as a warm-up for tone, intonation, and refinement of ensemble skills.

- Have students practice improvising on their own using a recorded loop of the Pachelbel chord progression on a tape recorder or a sequencer.

- Have students improvise on other chord progressions in different styles and tempos, such as I-vi-IV-V in a "du-wop" style and beat.

STANDARD 4A

Composing and arranging music within specified guidelines: Students compose music in several distinct styles, demonstrating creativity in using the elements of music for expressive effect.

Objective

- Students will compose melodies in two different styles and demonstrate their understanding of how to alter a melody to change the style.

Materials

- Manuscript paper
- Transparency with staff lines
- Overhead projector

Prior Knowledge and Experiences

- Students can identify the performing range of instruments in their own instruments' quartets (e.g., saxophone or brass quartet).
- Students can identify the key transpositions of instruments in their own quartets (e.g., saxophone: alto in E♭, tenor in B♭, and baritone in E♭; brass: trumpet in B♭, horn in F, nontransposing trombone and tuba).
- Students have studied basic music notation.
- Students have studied various articulation markings and have a common understanding of how these markings are interpreted.
- Students have studied characteristics of music in various styles (e.g., Romantic, Baroque).

Procedures

1. Ask students to compose two short melodies of two phrases each for their primary instruments in contrasting styles—for example, a Romantic melody and a Baroque melody. Tell them to write down their compositions, transposing them for other instruments in their own instruments' quartets.

2. Once the melodies have been written, ask each student to trade compositions with another student in the same section and have students play each other's melodies in the appropriate styles.

3. Move from one section to another, helping the players check the pitches, rhythms, and articulations as preferred by the student composers. Assist composers in refining the notation of rhythms and articulations so that it reflects the desired style.

4. Select several students' pairs of melodies, write them on a transparency, and discuss with the class (1) *what* in each melody of a pair must be altered in order to switch the styles of the two contrasting melodies; and (2) *how* those aspects of the melodies could most easily be notated as to enable others to perform the melodies in the "opposite" style.

Indicators of Success

- Students compose and accurately notate their own melodies.
- Students identify what needs to be changed in order to alter the style of a melody (e.g., rhythm, tempo, meter, articulation).
- Students play the melodies composed by other band members in the appropriate styles.

Follow-up

- Repeat the steps above, having students explore melodies in different genres, such as jazz or avant garde. Have them progress to composing melodies with characteristics of different style periods, such as Renaissance, Baroque, Classical, or twentieth century (e.g., twelve-tone music).
- As students become more experienced, give them opportunities to compose increasingly longer melodies that reflect a keener understanding of those elements of music that contribute to style and to develop an increased ability to evaluate their compositions.

STANDARD 4B

Composing and arranging music within specified guidelines: Students arrange pieces for voices or instruments other than those for which the pieces were written in ways that preserve or enhance the expressive effect of the music.

Objective

- Students will transcribe Baroque chorales for instrumental quartets.

Materials

- Manuscript paper
- Baroque chorale in the public domain (copies or transparency with notation)
- Overhead projector, if transparency is used

Prior Knowledge and Experiences

- Students can identify the performing range of instruments in their own quartets (e.g., saxophone or brass quartet).
- Students can identify the key transpositions of instruments in their own instruments' quartets (e.g., saxophone: alto in E♭, tenor in B♭, and baritone in E♭; brass: trumpet in B♭, horn in F, nontransposing trombone and tuba).
- Students have been introduced to chorale writing, style, and form.

Procedures

1. Distribute the copies of the selected chorale or project it from a transparency. Ask students to identify which instruments in their own instruments' quartets could possibly match each voice line (soprano, alto, tenor, and bass) of the chorale.

2. Have students write out the parts for the specific instruments in their own quartets. Explain that, to save time in transposing individual notes, they should begin by making sure that the key signatures are correct for the selected instruments. Encourage students to add expressive devices (e.g., dynamics and articulations) that would enhance the overall expressiveness of the performance of the chorale.

3. Ask several quartets to perform selected transcriptions.

4. Discuss with students difficulties in performing, such as lines out of range or challenges with control in certain registers.

5. Guide students in identifying characteristics of certain arrangements that maintain and perhaps enhance the musical expressiveness of the original chorale.

Indicators of Success

- Students select appropriate instruments for each chorale line, changing voicing of chords, if necessary, to keep the lines in comfortable ranges for certain instruments.
- Students determine which musical characteristics (compositional techniques) distract and which enhance the original chorale.

Follow-up

- After students have written several transcriptions using the steps above, have them arrange music from piano scores. Also, have them arrange music from condensed scores for small ensembles and then for large ensembles.
- Have students arrange for mixed groups of instruments, beginning with arrangements for instruments pitched in the same key (e.g., B♭ clarinet, B♭ trumpet, B♭ tenor saxophone, plus nontransposing bass and treble clef instruments). As students become more experienced, encourage them to take more liberties and enhance the musical expressiveness of the original composition.

STANDARD 4C

Composing and arranging music within specified guidelines: Students compose and arrange music for voices and various acoustic and electronic instruments, demonstrating knowledge of the ranges and traditional usages of the sound sources.

Objective

■ Students will arrange a short piano composition for a group of four to six instruments of their choice.

Materials

■ Variety of short, simple piano compositions in the public domain

■ Manuscript paper

Prior Knowledge and Experiences

■ Students can identify the performing range and key transpositions of various instruments.

Procedures

1. Explain to students that in this lesson, they will arrange a short piano composition for instruments. Have each student select a short piano composition from the materials provided.

2. Lead students in a brief discussion of how they might choose a specific group of four to six instruments that will be most appropriate for the character of the composition. [*Note:* Ask students to select instruments from those that are in their band so that groups of students will be able to play their arrangements.]

3. Tell students that they should transpose each part or musical line from the selected piano composition for a particular instrument. Have them consider how their selected instruments are traditionally used and how that use can help them determine which part of the original composition will be arranged for each instrument.

4. Ask students to begin by arranging the first four to eight measures of their selected compositions.

5. After students have completed their four-to-eight measure arrangements, select several arrangements and assign groups of students to play them for the class.

6. Have student groups play the selected arrangements for the class. If the class is familiar with a particular composition, ask whether they can identify it from the student arrangement. Also, ask the class to listen for correct transpositions for each instrument, whether the instruments chosen are suitable for the ranges of the parts, and whether they think the instruments selected are suitable for the character of the original composition. In a discussion following each performance, discuss their responses to these questions. For each arrangement, have them consider the student arranger's success in preserving or enhancing the expressive effect of the music.

7. Bring student arrangers into the discussion, asking them to consider changes they would make in completing their arrangements.

Indicators of Success

■ Students arrange the simple piano compositions for groups of four to six instruments.

(continued)

- Students select instruments for their arrangements that are suitable for the character of the original compositions.
- Students identify which instruments in their selected group of instruments are most appropriate in range and traditional use for each part of the original composition.
- Students make correct transpositions for instruments used in their arrangements.

Follow-up

- Have students complete their arrangements and ask student groups to perform them for the class. Ask the class to discuss the effect of each arrangement, exploring questions such as the following: Is the arrangement musically and stylistically as strong as, or stronger than, the original composition? Has the original composition been enhanced? How is the arrangement different from the original composition other than in the instrumentation? Does the arrangement stay true to the original? Ask student arrangers whether they achieved the desired effects.
- Have groups of students perform student arrangements in a concert.

STANDARD 4D

__Composing and arranging music within specific guidelines:__ Students compose music, demonstrating imagination and technical skill in applying the principles of composition.

Objective

- Students create, notate, and perform on their instruments eight-measure melodies featuring unity and variety.

Materials

- Manuscript paper
- Computers and music notation software (optional)

Prior Knowledge and Experiences

- Students can echo melodies by ear on their instruments.
- Students have basic notation skills and have experience recording their musical ideas.
- Students have studied unity and variety as a principle of composition through performance and analysis of various works.
- Students can identify the performing ranges and key transpositions of various instruments.

Procedures

1. Review with students the principle of unity and variety in composition.

2. Divide band into small ensembles and have students note the instrumentation of their ensembles. Review ranges and key transpositions as needed.

3. Ask each student to create and notate an eight-measure melody for his or her instrument using unity and variety as a principle of the composition. Explain that later, each student will create harmony parts for the instruments in his or her ensemble, and the ensemble will play the completed composition.

4. After students have completed their melodies, ask them to perform their melodies for their small ensembles so that the other ensemble members may replicate the melodies by ear in unison on their instruments. Encourage student composers to refine their melodies as needed to facilitate an unencumbered performance by ear and to maintain a manageable focus for the composition. Continue until all ensemble members can replicate accurately and easily the melodies created by their members.

5. Have selected ensembles play some of the student melodies in unison for the class. Lead a class discussion of how effective each student composer has been in using the principle of unity and variety in his or her composition.

6. Ask student composers to notate the final versions of their melodies for each instrument in their ensembles. Remind them to keep in mind the correct transposition for each instrument. If computers and music notation software are available, encourage students to use them.

Indicators of Success

- Students create, notate, and refine melodies for their instruments.
- Students in each small ensemble play by ear the melodies created by the members of their ensemble.
- Students demonstrate technical skill and imagination in using unity and variety as a principle of composition in their melodies.

(continued)

- Students accurately identify and describe the use of the principle of unity and variety in other students' compositions, as well as their own.

Follow-up

- Have students harmonize their melodies for instruments in their small ensembles, using keyboards or other harmonic media, if available. Encourage them to use unity and variety in the harmony parts.

- Have the small ensembles perform the compositions for the class, and have the class identify and describe with appropriate terminology the use of unity and variety, as well as the use of other principles of composition in each work. Also, have them discuss the form of each composition.

- Invite students to perform their compositions in a concert.

- Have students audiotape their performances for placement in their portfolios with the scores for their arrangements. If computers and music notation software are available, give students opportunities to create professional-quality scores and parts for their compositions.

- Have students create new arrangements of their compositions for instruments other than those for which the works were originally created.

STANDARD 5A

Reading and notating music: *Students demonstrate the ability to read an instrumental or vocal score of up to four staves by describing how the elements of music are used.*

Objective

- Students will accurately identify and describe the use of the elements of music in musical phrases of a given band composition.

Materials

- Full and condensed scores and full band arrangement of a selected composition for high school band

- Overhead transparencies of the condensed score

- Overhead projector

- Recording of the selected band composition

- Audio-playback equipment

Prior Knowledge and Experiences

- Students have studied the elements of music and have developed a music vocabulary for discussing them.

- Students have experience following the score of a band composition while listening to a recording of the composition.

- Students have been rehearsing the selected band composition.

- Students have conducted a simple band composition from a score during a band class.

Procedures

1. Display overhead transparencies of the condensed score and distribute individual parts for the selected composition. Lead students in guided listening, having them follow the condensed score as you play a recording of the composition.

2. Lead students through a complete performance of the composition, having them perform from their individual band parts.

3. Ask students to identify and describe in the score uses of pitch, rhythm, harmony, dynamics, texture, and form in the context of particular musical phrases.

4. After students identify and describe uses of particular elements, invite individual students to give appropriate performances of the particular musical phrases.

5. Have students again follow the condensed score for the composition as you play the recording. Ask them to direct their attention to the previously identified, described, and performed elements of music.

6. Lead students through a complete performance of the composition, with particular attention to playing expressively based on what they have learned about the uses of the elements of music in the composition.

Indicators of Success

- Students accurately identify and describe uses of pitch, rhythm, harmony, dynamics, texture, and form in the context of musical phrases throughout the selected composition.

- Students demonstrate understanding of uses of these elements of music by appropriately performing identified musical phrases.

Follow-up

- Lead students in a discussion, or ask them to write a short paper, about the value of identifying, describing, modeling, and performing the uses of elements of music in musical phrases as they relate to their understanding of, appreciation of, and ability to perform an entire composition.

STANDARD 5B

Reading and notating music: Students sightread, accurately and expressively, music with a level of difficulty of 3, on a scale of 1 to 6.

Objective

- Students will sightread, accurately and expressively, a band composition with a level of difficulty of 3.

Materials

- "Explorations" by Ed Huckeby (Oskaloosa, IA: C. L. Barnhouse), Level 3
- Chalkboard/markerboard

Prior Knowledge and Experiences

- Students have experience sightreading music with a level of difficulty of 2.
- Students can perform music with a level of difficulty of 4.
- Students have used for sightreading the S*T*A*R*S checklist in *Essential Elements* by Tom Rhodes, Donald Bierschenk, and Tim Lautzenheiser (Milwaukee: Hal Leonard Corporation, 1991).

Procedures

1. Review with students the S*T*A*R*S checklist, having a student note the following on the board: S = sharps and flats; T = time signature; A = accidentals; R = rhythms; S = signs.

2. Ask students to study their parts for "Explorations" using each area of the checklist. Have them find uses of particular items from the checklist; for example, have them note the sharps and flats and identify any changes to the key signature of the composition, note the opening time signature and any changes to the meter in the composition, and identify any accidentals.

3. Encourage students to tap or clap any difficult rhythms in their parts, particularly the change from 4/4 meter to 6/8 meter. Ask them to note other signs, such as dynamic and style markings, and locate the D.S. and Coda.

4. Have students sightread "Explorations," reminding them to think about S*T*A*R*S items.

5. Discuss with students the effectiveness of the S*T*A*R*S checklist as an aid for sightreading.

Indicators of Success

- Students identify items from the S*T*A*R*S checklist in "Explorations" before sightreading the composition.
- Students sightread "Explorations" accurately and expressively.

Follow-up

- Discuss with students what other items might be added to the S*T*A*R*S checklist, and have them incorporate those additions in preparing to sightread other band compositions.

Note: These procedures could be used with a Level 4 piece to accomplish standard 5E.

STANDARD 5C

Reading and notating music: Students demonstrate the ability to read a full instrumental or vocal score by describing how the elements of music are used and explaining all transpositions and clefs.

Objective

- Students will read a full instrumental score for a fugue, identify the form of the composition, and identify transposed melodic lines.

Materials

- "Ginger Marmalade" by Warren Benson (New York: Carl Fischer), Level 3—full score and full band arrangement
- Multiple copies of score

Prior Knowledge and Experiences

- Students have experience transposing parts for instruments in B-flat, E-flat, and F, as well as identifying those instruments that sound in a different octave from the printed note they are playing (e.g., string bass, piccolo).
- Students have studied the elements of music.
- Students have studied fugue form.
- Students have studied key transpositions for various band instruments.

Procedures

1. Have trumpets perform measures 4–6 of "Ginger Marmalade" as other students follow the score. Then have trombones play measures 16–18. Ask trumpets and trombones to perform their respective passages simultaneously. Discuss with students the transposition, and ask students to identify the form of the composition.

2. Have trumpets perform measures 4–6 again. Then have flutes and piccolos perform measures 7–9. Ask both sections to perform their respective passages simultaneously. Discuss with students the transpositions, and explain the transposition at the fifth (at concert pitch) as structured by the fugal procedure used at this location in the music.

3. Ask students at what measures a similar compositional procedure is found. [The obvious answer would be at measures 8–10 in the clarinets when compared to measures 11–13 in the flute, oboe, English horn, and bells.] Ask what the difference is between this motive and the one found in the beginning. [Answers might include the rhythmic development of the head of the motive, the change of melodic direction of the dotted-quarter, and the change of melodic material in the following measures.]

Indicators of Success

- Students identify the transposed melodic lines in the full score of "Ginger Marmalade."
- Students identify the form of the composition as a fugue and locate the various fugal entrances.

Follow-up

- Have students identify larger structural changes related to fugue form that occur in the score for "Ginger Marmalade," such as the location of various episodes between fugal statements.

STANDARD 5D

Reading and notating music: Students interpret nonstandard notation symbols used by some 20th-century composers.

Objective

- Students will interpret a composer's use of nontraditional instruments and notation in a 20th-century composition.

Materials

- "Crystals" by Thomas Duffy (Cleveland, OH: Ludwig Music Publishing), Level 4

- Crystal or glass goblets filled with water to produce particular pitches

Prior Knowledge and Experiences

- Students have performed musical compositions using nonstandard notation.

- Students have studied the use of "sounds" as musical effects in other compositions; for example, snare drum as machine guns and thunder sheet as gunfire in "Babi Yar," from *Holocaust Suite* by Morton Gould (New York: G. Schirmer), Level 5.

Procedures

1. Have students experiment with the level of liquid in the crystal or glass goblets to produce the desired pitches in unison with the flutes in "Crystals."

2. Ask students to vocalize the pitches indicated in the score for the goblets and flutes. Explain that glissandos are notated from initial pitch to final pitch. Have students experiment with glissandos to and from the indicated pitches.

3. Ask students to identify places in the score where the notation calls for a particular sound production.

4. Have students experiment with whistling the desired pitches for the prescribed duration.

5. Lead students in a performance of "Crystals," having them use the previously learned sound sources.

Indicators of Success

- Students interpret and perform the composer's intent in "Crystals," using nontraditional instruments and reading nonstandard notation.

Follow-up

- Have students explore the nontraditional sound sources and notation found in *Symphony no. 1: In Memoriam Dresden—1945* by Daniel Bukvich (Kansas City, MO: Wingert-Jones), Level 4.

- In a lesson you have developed cooperatively with the physics teacher, have students experiment with the properties of sound and acoustics.

Proficient

STANDARD 6A

Listening to, analyzing, and describing music: Students analyze aural examples of a varied repertoire of music, representing diverse genres and cultures, by describing the uses of elements of music and expressive devices.

Objective

- Students will analyze a selected example of music using a specific listening technique to identify the genre and describe the composer's use of the elements of music and expressive devices.

Materials

- Recording of a selected band composition
- Handouts with the following mnemonic device (learning tool): me, me, ha, me, ge (see step 1)
- Audio-playback equipment

Prior Knowledge and Experiences

- Students have studied the elements of music and have developed a music vocabulary for discussing them.
- Students have studied various expressive devices.

Procedures

1. Explain the following as a mnemonic device that students can use to help them remember how to describe a passage of music: me(dium), me(lody), ha(rmony), me(ter), and ge(nre).

2. Tell students that in the recording that they will hear, they should listen for the following:
   - medium (type of instrument or ensemble performing)
   - melody
   - harmony ("traditional" or "contemporary" and why)
   - meter (triple or duple, compound, etc.)
   - genre (symphony, concerto, ballet, etc.)

3. Play the selected example and then discuss with students each of the items listed above, asking them to define each item and describe it in relation to the selected composition.

4. For a second listening, instruct students to listen for the following:
   - instruments used
   - expressive devices (e.g., use of terraced dynamics)

5. Based on what they have heard and discussed, ask students to speculate on the composer of the work. Ask them to justify their responses. Discuss with them any similarities and differences in the composer's music and that of the other composers they suggested.

Indicators of Success

- Students identify the genre of the selected composition.
- Students describe the uses of the elements of music and expressive devices in the selected composition.

Follow-up

- Have students contribute additional terms that can be added to the listening procedure, such as compositional form, rhythmic devices, and orchestration.

STANDARD 6B

Listening to, analyzing, and describing music: Students demonstrate extensive knowledge of the technical vocabulary of music.

Objective

■ Students will identify a chaconne theme and label the compositional techniques used to create variations of the theme.

Materials

■ Recording of *First Suite in E-flat for Military Band,* such as Central Band of the Royal Air Force, Wing Commander Eric Banks, EMI Classics CDM 565122 2

■ Audio-playback equipment

Prior Knowledge and Experiences

■ Students have performed *Suite no. 1 in E-flat,* rev. for band, by Gustav Holst (New York: Boosey & Hawkes), Level 4.

■ Students have been introduced to chaconne and passacaglia forms.

■ Students have been introduced to the compositional techniques of augmentation, diminution, inversion, and retrograde.

Procedures

1. Review with students the chaconne and passacaglia forms as related to ground bass, as well as the differences between these closely related forms.

2. Discuss variations above the chaconne theme that are based on a specific harmonic progression.

3. Play the recording of "Chaconne" from *First Suite in E-flat for Military Band,* asking students to determine the number of variations of the theme.

4. Review with students how a composer can vary a theme using inversion.

5. Have students identify the ninth and tenth variations in the movement "Chaconne" as variations in which the theme is stated in inversion.

6. Have students, using appropriate technical vocabulary (such as augmentation, diminution, and retrograde), label other compositional techniques found in the variations.

Indicators of Success

■ Students identify the variations above the chaconne theme in *First Suite in E-flat for Military Band.*

■ Students use appropriate technical vocabulary to label the various compositional techniques, such as inversion of the theme, used in the movement "Chaconne."

Follow-up

■ Have students listen to the second and third movements of *First Suite in E-flat for Military Band* and identify the motives based on the first three notes of the chaconne theme.

STANDARD 6C

Listening to, analyzing, and describing music: Students identify and explain compositional devices and techniques used to provide unity and variety and tension and release in a musical work and give examples of other works that make similar uses of these devices and techniques.

Objective

- Students will identify and explain the use of theme and variations form in a musical work.

Materials

- "Thematic Variations on Dona Nobis Pacem" by James Sudduth (San Antonio, TX: Southern Music Company), Level 3

- Worksheets with "Dona Nobis Pacem" theme and variations in unison (see step 3)

Prior Knowledge and Experiences

- Students have been introduced to theme and variations form and the techniques used to alter a theme.

- Students have performed "Thematic Variations on Dona Nobis Pacem."

Procedures

1. Have the band perform the unison theme "Dona Nobis Pacem" found in "Thematic Variations on Dona Nobis Pacem."

2. Review some of the techniques used to alter or vary a theme, such as augmentation, diminution, alteration of the meter, alteration of the style (e.g., legato to staccato), inversion, or alteration of the key.

3. Have the band perform each variation of "Dona Nobis Pacem" from the worksheet, and ask students to describe how the melody was altered in each variation.

4. Have students examine their own parts from "Thematic Variations on Dona Nobis Pacem" and locate the theme and places where the theme has been altered.

5. Have the instrument groupings that have the variations perform the variations and then determine what type of variation has been used.

Indicators of Success

- Students identify the theme and variations in "Thematic Variations on Dona Nobis Pacem" and, using appropriate terminology, explain how the composer has varied the theme.

Follow-up

- Ask each student to compose and notate a simple three- or four-measure theme (melody). Then direct students to vary the theme in several ways.

Advanced

STRATEGY 6D

Listening to, analyzing, and describing music: Students demonstrate the ability to perceive and remember music events by describing in detail significant events occurring in a given aural example.

Objective

- Students will describe significant musical events in a given aural example.

Materials

- Recording of *Second Suite in F for Military Band,* fourth movement, Central Band of the Royal Air Force, Wing Commander Eric Banks, EMI Classics CDM 565122 2

- Handouts with teacher-generated interview form (see step 2)

- Audio-playback equipment

- Chalkboard/markerboard

Prior Knowledge and Experiences

- Students have been rehearsing *Suite no. 2 in F,* rev. for band, "Fantasia on the Dargason" (fourth movement) by Gustav Holst (New York: Boosey & Hawkes), Level 5.

- Students are familiar with various compositional techniques and devices (e.g., fantasia, augmentation).

Procedures

1. Play a recording of "Fantasia on the Dargason" and have students listen for specific compositional devices found in their individual parts.

2. Have students pair up to participate in peer-group interviews using the interview form on the handouts. [*Note:* Interview questions should focus on discovering specific compositional devices used at particular places within the movement. Students should describe the compositional techniques or devices using appropriate music terminology.]

3. After students have completed their interviews, lead them in creating a master list of their findings and document it on the board.

4. If some students have missed several significant events, have the class listen again to the recording to discover the correct answers. If they still have not discovered all the events, do not reveal the answers immediately. Encourage students to discover the events.

Indicators of Success

- Students identify and describe significant musical events in a movement from *Second Suite in F for Military Band.*

- Students use appropriate music terminology in describing significant musical events.

Follow-up

- Have students rehearse "Fantasia on the Dargason," and ask them to find additional significant events from your use of musical descriptions and terminology rather than rehearsal letters or measure numbers.

STANDARD 6E

Listening to, analyzing, and describing music: Students compare ways in which musical materials are used in a given example relative to ways in which they are used in other works of the same genre or style.

Objective

- Students will compare and contrast the use of thematic material in given examples.

Materials

- "Chorale and Shaker Dance" by John Zdechlik (San Diego: Neil A. Kjos Music Company), Level 4
- Recording of "Appalachian Spring" by Aaron Copland
- Audio-playback equipment

Prior Knowledge and Experiences

- Students have been rehearsing "Chorale and Shaker Dance."
- Students can recognize the Shaker theme in "Chorale and Shaker Dance."

Procedures

1. Remind students of the Shaker theme they have been performing in "Chorale and Shaker Dance." Play the recording of Copland's "Appalachian Spring," and have students listen and discover how the composer uses the Shaker theme, whether it is the central theme of the composition, whether it is performed in variation, and how the composer varies the theme.

2. Have students perform "Chorale and Shaker Dance," and ask them to listen for the use of the Shaker theme. Lead them in a discussion comparing and contrasting its use with the Shaker theme in "Appalachian Spring."

3. Have students write a summary of all descriptive comparisons.

Indicators of Success

- Students locate the Shaker theme in "Appalachian Spring."
- Students compare and contrast the use of the Shaker theme in "Appalachian Spring" and "Chorale and Shaker Dance."

Follow-up

- Ask students to participate in a scavenger hunt for other uses of the Shaker theme. When they find examples, ask them to bring them to class. Discuss with students how the theme is used in their findings.

Advanced

STANDARD 6F

Listening to, analyzing, and describing music: Students analyze and describe uses of the elements of music in a given work that make it unique, interesting, and expressive.

Objective

- Students will identify specific compositional techniques in a given musical work and describe how those techniques make it unique, interesting, and expressive.

Materials

- "Liturgical Dances" by David Holsinger (San Antonio, TX: Southern Music Company), Level 5
- Chalkboard/markerboard

Prior Knowledge and Experiences

- Students have performed "Liturgical Dances."
- Students have studied the elements of music.
- Students have studied compositional techniques.

Procedures

1. Rehearse a section of "Liturgical Dances," asking students to listen for techniques the composer used to create variety and expressiveness.

2. Have students describe what they have heard. List the various compositional techniques on the board as they identify them—for example, use of melodic sequences and pairing various combinations of instruments. Discuss with students the uses of these techniques, asking the following: What effect is the composer trying to produce? How do these effects contribute to the overall expressive content of the composition?

3. Have students discuss the various layers produced by different combinations of instruments in "Liturgical Dances." Ask the following questions: What instruments make up each layer? What is the relationship between the layers? Which layers are most important musically?

4. Have students summarize the compositional techniques that make this composition unique, interesting, and expressive.

Indicators of Success

- Students describe the compositional techniques used in "Liturgical Dances" and discuss how they make the composition unique, interesting, and expressive.

Follow-up

- Have students determine other elements of music the composer used to make "Liturgical Dances" unique, interesting, and expressive, such as the form of each liturgical dance.

- Have students discover other band compositions that are based on various dance forms—for example, *Suite of Old American Dances* by Robert Russell Bennett (Milwaukee: Chappell/Hal Leonard Corporation), Level 5; *Four Scottish Dances* by Malcolm Arnold and John Paynter (New York: Carl Fischer), Level 5; or various dances by Gordon Jacob.

STANDARD 7A

Evaluating music and music performances: Students evolve specific criteria for making informed, critical evaluations of the quality and effectiveness of performances, compositions, arrangements, and improvisations and apply the criteria in their personal participation in music.

Objective

- Students will develop a list of criteria for evaluating the quality of a performance and apply the criteria to a specific performance.

Materials

- Audiotape of a recent concert performance
- Audio-playback equipment
- Performance Evaluation Form worksheets (see figure)
- Chalkboard/markerboard

Prior Knowledge and Experiences

- Students have studied the terms "tone quality," "intonation," "accuracy," "articulation," "style," and "dynamics."

Procedures

1. Lead a discussion of areas students believe are important to a quality performance—for example, "playing the correct notes," "playing the correct rhythms," "staying together," "playing in tune," "following dynamic markings," and "using the correct articulation." Guide students to identify the skills that have been emphasized in their ensemble playing, encouraging them to use appropriate music terminology. Distribute the Performance Evaluation Form worksheets and have each student write down the criteria under the heading "Performance Skill," as you write them on the board.

2. Discuss with students the rating system listed on the worksheet for evaluating the overall quality of each performance skill on the list (see figure).

3. Tell students that you will be playing a recording and that they should rate each performance skill under the heading "Observed Performance." Also, under the heading "Reason for Rating," they should note why the rating was assigned—for example, "the lack of ensemble precision."

4. Have students listen to the recording again and review their ratings and comments on each performance skill.

5. Lead a discussion of students' ratings and comments in each area. Guide students in arriving at a consensus on each rating, playing excerpts from the recording again, as needed.

Indicators of Success

- Students develop a list of criteria for evaluating the quality of a musical performance.
- Students evaluate a musical performance using a rating system and explain the reasons for their ratings.

Follow-up

- Make an audiotape of the band's performance during rehearsal, and have students evaluate their performance using the criteria they developed.

(continued)

Performance Evaluation Form

Rating System: 1 = much above average; 2 = above average; 3 = average; 4 = below average; 5 = much below average.

Performance Skill	Observed Performance	Reason for Rating

STANDARD 7B

Evaluating music and music performances: Students evaluate a performance, composition, arrangement, or improvisation by comparing it to similar or exemplary models.

Objective

- Students will evaluate their own performance of a selected composition and a performance of the same composition by a professional ensemble and compare the performances.

Materials

- Student- and teacher-designed performance evaluation form (see form on page 34, for example)

- "English Folk Song Suite" by Ralph Vaughan Williams (New York: Boosey & Hawkes), Level 4

- Recording of "English Folk Song Suite," such as *Stars and Stripes: Marches, Fanfares & Wind Band Spectaculars,* The Cleveland Symphonic Winds, Frederick Fennell, Telarc Records DC 80099

- Audiotape recording of the high school band performing "English Folk Song Suite" in rehearsal

- Audiocassette recorder

Procedures

1. Distribute performance evaluation forms developed in a previous class. Briefly review with students music vocabulary related to items on the form and rating techniques.

2. Play the recording of the first movement of "English Folk Song Suite." Ask students to evaluate their performance by assigning ratings to criteria on the evaluation form and making appropriate comments on the form about their reasons for giving particular ratings.

3. Tell students that they will be hearing a recording of professional musicians playing the same composition. Ask them to evaluate the professional performance using the procedure described in step 2. Play the first movement of the composition on the selected recording.

4. Lead students in a discussion of evaluations of the two performances, having them identify strengths and weaknesses in each performance.

Indicators of Success

- Students identify strengths and weaknesses in their own performance and an exemplary performance.

- Students compare the performances using a performance evaluation form and specific criteria.

- Students use appropriate music vocabulary in describing the performances.

Follow-up

- Have students recommend rehearsal strategies that will improve the ensemble's performance, using the exemplary group's performance as a guide. Then have them repeat the performance evaluation process as needed.

(continued)

Prior Knowledge and Experiences

- The band has been rehearsing "English Folk Song Suite" and has made an audiotape of its performance of the first movement.

- Students have participated in designing a performance evaluation form.

- Students have participated in practice evaluations to develop appropriate evaluative skills.

- Students have developed a music vocabulary for discussing the elements of music and music performances.

STANDARD 7C

Evaluating music and music performances: Students evaluate a given musical work in terms of its aesthetic qualities and explain the musical means it uses to evoke feelings and emotions.

Objective

■ Students will describe the musical means used to evoke feelings and emotions in a given composition.

Materials

■ "Let the Spirit Soar" by James Swearingen (Oskaloosa, IA: C. L. Barnhouse), Level 3; or recording of "Let the Spirit Soar," such as *Music of Swearingen,* Washington Winds, Edward Peterson, Walking Frog WFR 102

■ Audio-playback equipment, if transparency is used

■ Chalkboard/markerboard

Prior Knowledge and Experiences

■ Students have studied the elements of music.

■ Students have studied basic musical concepts, such as dynamic contrast.

■ Students have been rehearsing "Let the Spirit Soar."

Procedures

1. Have students play through "Let the Spirit Soar," or listen to a recording, asking them to pay particular attention to the techniques the composer used to evoke various feelings and emotions.

2. Ask students to take special note of the title of the composition. Have them describe the feelings they experienced when performing, or listening to, the selection—for example, softer passages evoke feelings of sadness, melancholy, or thoughtfulness; climaxes evoke the feeling of majesty. List their comments on the board.

3. Have students give examples of things that "soar." List their ideas on the board. Ask them what the word "spirit" means to them.

4. Ask students to look at the music and determine what contributes to the "soaring" feeling. Lead them in looking at the melodic line (write it on the board if a recording is used) and noting how it rises and rises and then floats downward. Guide them in noting the dynamic changes as well as changes in the number of instruments performing at any given time. Also direct their attention to how the composer modulates to a higher key in the middle of the composition.

5. Ask students to match the musical elements and concepts they have described in "Let the Spirit Soar" with the list on the board of feelings and emotions evoked by the composition.

Indicators of Success

■ Students describe how the composer of "Let the Spirit Soar" used various musical elements and concepts to evoke feelings and emotions.

Follow-up

■ Have students, individually or in groups, use some of their feelings and images about "Let the Spirit Soar" to write a description of the composition for use in program notes. Have students, as a class, combine their ideas to write program notes for their concert performance.

STANDARD 8A

Understanding relationships between music, the other arts, and disciplines outside the arts:
Students explain how elements, artistic processes (such as imagination or craftsmanship), and organizational principles (such as unity and variety or repetition and contrast) are used in similar and distinctive ways in the various arts and cite examples.

Objective

■ Students will explain how composers and poets use elements, concepts, and devices in similar and distinctive ways.

Materials

■ "Babi Yar," from *Holocaust Suite,* by Morton Gould (New York: G. Schirmer), Level 5

■ "Babi Yar," poem by Yevgeney Yevtushenko, in *Holocaust Poetry,* compiled by Hilda Schiff (New York: St. Martin's Press, 1995)

■ Photographs from history texts that depict the geographical setting of "Babi Yar"

Prior Knowledge and Experiences

■ Students have been rehearsing *Holocaust Suite.*

■ Students have a basic musical vocabulary.

■ Students have studied musical concepts and harmonic devices, such as dissonance.

Procedures

1. Have students perform "Babi Yar" from *Holocaust Suite.* Ask them to listen for the various musical concepts and effects used in the composition (e.g., use of a thunder sheet to symbolize gunfire, the use of dissonance).

2. Ask students to visualize or picture the physical setting of the poem "Babi Yar" as you or a student reads the poem, which relates to the massacre of thirty-three thousand Jews in September 1941. In discussing the setting, refer to photographs from history texts.

3. Ask students to describe their individual perceptions of how the dynamics, harmonic devices (such as dissonance), and organizational principles (such as repetition) are used in *Holocaust Suite* to express or communicate the composer's perceptions of the Holocaust image.

4. Lead students in comparing Yevtushenko's use of artistic devices with Gould's in portraying an image of the Holocaust.

Indicators of Success

■ Students identify and compare the composer's and the poet's use of elements, processes, or principles in portraying an image of the Holocaust.

Follow-up

■ Provide an example of a Holocaust image in the visual arts by artist Kaethe Kollwitz, in *Prints and Drawings of Kaethe Kollwitz,* rev. ed., selected by Carl Zigrosser (Mineola, NY: Dover Publications, 1969). Have students compare the artistic elements used in the drawing with those in the music of "Holocaust Suite" and the poem "Babi Yar."

STANDARD 8B

Understanding relationships between music, the other arts, and disciplines outside the arts:
Students compare characteristics of two or more arts within a particular historical period or style
and cite examples from the various cultures.

Objective

- Students will discover relationships between music, visual art, and architecture of the Classical period.

Materials

- "Classic Overture" by Francois-Joseph Gossec, arr. Richard Franko Goldman and Roger Smith (Bryn Mawr, PA: Mercury Music/Theodore Presser Company), Level 4

- Photographs of the University of Virginia's rotunda (designed by Thomas Jefferson) and Sir Joshua Reynolds's painting *Jane, Countess of Harrington*; or other examples of architecture and visual art of the Classical period [*Note:* Small reproductions are available in *The Enjoyment of Music,* 7th ed., by Joseph Machlis and Kristine Forney (New York: W. W. Norton, 1995).]

- Photograph of the Parthenon, in *The Enjoyment of Music*

- Photograph of the painting *The Oath of Horatii* by Jacques-Louis David, in *Music! Its Role and Importance in Our Lives* by Charles Fowler (New York: Glencoe/McGraw-Hill, 1994)

- Audio-playback equipment

Procedures

1. Have students assist you in mapping the form of "Classic Overture" as they listen to their recorded performance of the piece. Play the recording again and then discuss the form of the composition with the students. At the end of the discussion, ask students to listen to the recording once more to check the form outlined on their maps.

2. Using "Classic Overture" as an example, lead students in a discussion of characteristics of music of the Classical period. Explain Gossec's place in music history, noting his long and prolific career as a composer from the mid-eighteenth century to the early nineteenth century and his fusing of Mannheim and French styles.

3. Show students photographs of the University of Virginia's rotunda and Sir Joshua Reynolds's *Jane, Countess of Harrington.* Have them identify characteristics of those works that correspond to the music they have been discussing (for example, the architecture's symmetry and the music's form; or the clarity of both the music and the painting).

4. Explain that during the Classical period, composers and artists espoused the ideals of classical antiquity. Show students the photograph of the Parthenon, built in Athens in the 5th century B.C., and ask them to identify characteristics that it has in common with the artworks of the Classical period they have been discussing. Also, show students Jacques-Louis David's *The Oath of Horatii,* and discuss with them how this painting reflects a return to classical ideals.

5. Ask students to consider how Gossec and his musical contemporaries were influenced by classical ideals in moving away from the musical style of the Baroque. Remind them of a composition in the Baroque style that they have played, such as "Baroque Suite" by Georg William Telemann, arr. William Hill (Ruidoso, NM: TRN Music Publishers), Level 3.

Indicators of Success

- Students identify characteristics common to various art forms of the Classical period.

(continued)

Prior Knowledge and Experiences

- Students have been rehearsing "Classic Overture" and have recorded their performance during a rehearsal.
- Students have had experience "mapping" the form of a composition.

- Students describe how composers and artists of the Classical period reflected the ideals of classical antiquity in their works.

Follow-up

- Have students demonstrate their knowledge of the style of the Classical period by identifying other music and visual artworks of the same period from a collection of examples of artworks from various style periods. Ask them to identify the characteristics that the selected works have in common with Classical period artworks that they have been studying.

STANDARD 8C

Understanding relationships between music, the other arts, and disciplines outside the arts: Students explain ways in which the principles and subject matter of various disciplines outside the arts are interrelated with those of music.

Objective

■ Students will describe how similar subject matter has been represented by a composer, a novelist, and a cinematographer.

Materials

■ Score for *Symphony no. 1: In Memoriam Dresden—1945* by Daniel Bukvich, (Kansas City, MO: Wingert-Jones), Level 4

■ Selected passages from novel *Slaughterhouse Five* by Kurt Vonnegut, Jr.

■ Video recording of *Slaughterhouse Five* (Universal City, CA: MCA/Universal Music and Video Distribution, 1989)

■ Videocassette recorder

■ Video monitor

Prior Knowledge and Experiences

■ Students have performed Bukvich's *Symphony no. 1.*

■ In history class, students have studied World War II. The history teacher has introduced the class to the controversy surrounding the Dresden firebombing (e.g., the use of prisoners of war as clean-up crews after bombing).

Procedures

1. Ask students to read aloud, from the novel *Slaughterhouse Five,* selected passages in which Vonnegut described the firebombing of Dresden.

2. As you lead them in performing musical passages from *Symphony no. 1,* ask students to listen to how Bukvich portrayed the same event in sound. Guide students in identifying the use of specially adapted instruments (brake drums, "gong drum," etc.) and nontraditional expressive techniques (shouting, whistling, movement) that can be used musically to portray the sounds of airplanes, bombs, explosions, and panic among people in Dresden.

3. Have students compare the techniques used by the novelist and the composer to portray the event, such as graphic descriptions of the bombing by the novelist and extreme dissonance used by the composer to portray the bombing and explosions.

4. Show students brief excerpts from the film *Slaughterhouse Five.* Then have the class discuss cinematic presentation of the event and explain how techniques used in the film (color, special effects, music score) compare to techniques and principles used in the music and literature. Invite students to comment upon the effectiveness of these techniques—for example, comparing the shouting and whistling special effects in the music to the special effects in the film.

Indicators of Success

■ Students identify and describe the musical, literary, and visual techniques used to depict the firebombing of Dresden in *Symphony no. 1* and the novel and movie *Slaughterhouse Five.*

(continued)

- In English class, students have studied *Slaughterhouse Five.* The English teacher has selected passages from the novel that describe the fire-bombing of Dresden and scenes from the movie based on the novel that portray the bombing and aftermath.

- Students have studied the elements of music.

Follow-up

- In cooperation with history and English teachers, have students prepare an integrated presentation for a public concert and exhibition. The program might include a display of artworks, a display of archival photographs and articles, and selected readings from the novel *Slaughterhouse Five* prior to the performance of each movement of *Symphony no. 1.*

STANDARD 8D

Understanding relationships between music, the other arts, and disciplines outside the arts: Students compare the uses of characteristic elements, artistic processes, and organizational principles among the arts in different historical periods and different cultures.

Objective

- Students will compare how painters and composers of the Romantic Era and of the 20th century have used elements, processes, and principles of their arts to represent or convey elements of warfare.

Materials

- *Military Symphony in F* by Francois-Joseph Gossec, arr. Richard Franko Goldman and Robert L. Leist (Bryn Mawr, PA: Theodore Presser Company), Level 3

- *Music for Prague, 1968* by Karel Husa (Milwaukee: Associated Music Publishers/ Hal Leonard Corporation), Level 6

- Slides or prints of Picasso's *Guernica* and Delacroix's *Liberty Leading the People*; or similar Romantic Era painting glorifying war or patriotism

- Worksheets for Visual and Musical Counterparts Comparison (see figure)—two per student or list outline twice on page

- Slide projector, if slides are used

Procedures

1. Distribute the worksheets for Visual and Musical Counterparts Comparison and ask students to record their responses as you lead them through steps 2–5.

2. Show students the 20th-century painting *Guernica*. Ask them to identify and describe key visual elements (line, space, color and form) of the painting. To guide the discussion as you continue through step 5, ask students the following questions:

   - Are any linear or melodic/rhythmic elements unconventional or exaggerated? Why do you think the artist/composer chose to do this?

   - Is the activity in the painting/music better characterized as clear or dense?

   - What palette of colors or instrumentation did the artist/composer choose to convey his thoughts?

   - What elements of unity and variety (form) did the artist/composer choose to convey his thoughts?

   - Which elements were most emphasized?

3. Have students identify and describe key musical elements (melody, rhythm, harmony, texture, and form) in the 20th-century musical composition *Music for Prague, 1968*.

4. Show students the Romantic Era painting *Liberty Leading the People*. Ask them to identify and describe key visual elements of the painting.

5. Have students identify and describe key musical elements in the Romantic Era musical composition *Military Symphony in F*.

6. Lead students in a discussion comparing the artistic processes used by the 20th-century artists and composers with those of the Romantic Era artists and composers in representing elements of warfare in their works.

Indicators of Success

- Students describe how a composer and an artist of the same era used characteristic elements, artistic processes, and organizational principles in their work to symbolize a similar event.

(continued)

Prior Knowledge and Experiences

- Students have been rehearsing *Military Symphony in F.*
- Students have been rehearsing *Music for Prague, 1968.*
- Students have studied how composers convey unity and variety with the elements melody, rhythm, harmony, texture, and form.
- In art class, students have studied how artists convey unity and variety with the elements line, space, color, and form.

- Students identify differences and similarities in how composers and artists of the 20th century used these elements, processes, and principles and how composers and artists of the Romantic Era used them.

Follow-up

- Have students write a brief report comparing elements of Romantic Era music and artworks with those used in 20th-century music and artworks.
- Have students explore other comparative relationships between the arts, such as absolute/descriptive music and representative/abstract art.

Visual and Musical Counterparts Comparison

Name of Artwork:

Name of Composition:

Artist:

Composer:

Describe the following as they relate to this artwork—

Describe the following as they relate to this music—

Line:

Melodic/rhythmic flow:

Space:

Clarity/density of melody/harmony:

Color:

Timbre/texture:

Form:

Form:

Advanced

Understanding relationships between music, the other arts, and disciplines outside the arts:
Students explain how the roles of creators, performers, and others involved in the production and presentation
of the arts are similar to and different from one another in the various arts.

Objective

■ Students will compare and contrast the roles of a composer in creating music and a choreographer in creating dance.

Materials

■ "Russian Sailors' Dance," from *The Red Poppy*, by Reinhold Glière, arr. James Curnow (Milwaukee: Hal Leonard Corporation), Level 4

■ Video recording *Moiseyev Dance Company—A Gala Evening*, V.I.E.W. Video (34 East 23rd St., New York, NY 10010), 1989

■ Video recording *Soviet Army Chorus, Band, and Dance Ensemble*, Kultur International Films (195 Highway 36, West Long Branch, NJ 07764), 1981

■ Videocassette recorder

■ Video monitor

Prior Knowledge and Experiences

■ Students have been rehearsing "Russian Sailors' Dance."

Procedures

1. Explain to students that "Russian Sailors' Dance" is an excerpt from the music for the ballet *The Red Poppy*. Provide them with a description of the scene: Sailors from many nations are fraternizing in port; as evening progresses, each group performs a dance representing its ethnic culture in a friendly competition; the Russian dance is humorous in that accents, steps, and so on, are "misplaced" because of the sailors' tipsiness.

2. Discuss with students the Ukrainian folk dance *gopak* and explain the competitiveness of many such performances. Show the video of "Ukrainian Gopak" from *Moiseyev Dance Company*. Discuss with students the types of movements of the dancers and how these reflect the style of each musical section.

3. Show the video of "Soldiers' Dance" from *Soviet Army Chorus, Band, and Dance Ensemble*. Guide students in relating competitiveness among the dancers to the scene in *The Red Poppy*.

4. Have students identify ways in which composers and choreographers work to create music and dance for ballets such as *The Red Poppy* and compare and contrast them. The discussion should include the following ideas:

   ■ *Similarities:* Both create works to depict specific scene, action, emotion; both create works that are typically performed or interpreted by others (musicians and dancers); both use symbolism (music/movement) to express, communicate, and portray an actual event.

   ■ *Differences:* Composers work with sounds—choreographers work with movement; composers' works may readily be transferred to other media (e.g., from orchestra to band), while dances may not be readily transferred. The music to a specific ballet remains constant over many years, while choreography may change dramatically to reflect new preferences in technique, costuming, and so on.

Indicators of Success

■ Students compare and contrast the processes by which the composer and choreographer for *The Red Poppy* created music and dance for the ballet.

(continued)

Follow-up

- Have students attend a ballet rehearsal to observe the roles of composer, choreographer, conductor, producer, musician, and dancer in preparation of a production.

- Prepare band for a performance of "Russian Sailors' Dance," and work with a dance teacher in the school or community to have dance students prepare a scene using the band's performance as accompanying music.

STANDARD 9A

Understanding music in relation to history and culture: Students classify by genre or style and by historical period or culture unfamiliar but representative aural examples of music and explain the reasoning behind their classifications.

Objective

- Students will classify cultural origins of selected aural examples and explain characteristics and elements of each selection, providing rationale for their identification.

Materials

- Recording of H. Owen Reed's *La Fiesta Mexicana,* such as Cincinnati College Conservatory of Music Wind Symphony, Eugene Corporon, Klavier KCD 11048
- Recording of the high school band's performance of second movement of *Kilimanjaro: An African Portrait* by Robert Washburn (Miami: Belwin/ Warner Bros. Publications), Level 5
- Recording of *Gaelic Rhapsody* by Elliot Del Borgo (Kansas City, MO: Wingert Jones), available by request with band arrangement
- Audio-playback equipment
- Blank Listening Guide form (see figure; omit sample responses listed)

Procedures

1. Distribute blank Listening Guides and explain to students that these sheets are to be used for identifying and noting characteristics, genre, and culture of each aural example.

2. Play the following excerpts, identifying them only by number as 1–3 and allowing approximately two minutes following each excerpt for students to complete writing of notes about each example:

   Kilimanjaro: "Masai Dance" (second movement)

   La Fiesta Mexicana: "De La Negra" from third movement

   Gaelic Rhapsody: "Irish Washerwoman"

3. Identify each selection and excerpt by name for the students. Have them place this information in the "Title, excerpt" column of the Listening Guide.

4. Lead students in a discussion about each excerpt, first asking them to identify the culture each composition represents. Ask them to explain their responses, describing what characteristics of the style led them to that conclusion. Encourage them to use appropriate music vocabulary. Have students identify the genre of each excerpt. [*Note:* See sample responses in Listening Guide figure.]

Indicators of Success

- Students classify the cultural origin and genre of selected music examples, providing a rationale for their decisions.
- Students identify and describe characteristics of selected music examples.

Follow-up

- Prior to the performance of each composition on a concert program, have students prepare information about the characteristics, genre, and origin of the compositions to be performed. Then select students to inform the audience about each selection.

(continued)

Prior Knowledge and Experiences

- Students have been performing music representative of various cultures throughout the academic year.

- Students have learned basic style characteristics of music of various cultures.

- Students have developed a music vocabulary for discussing the elements of music and style characteristics.

Listening Guide

Title, excerpt	Culture	Selected Characteristics	Genre
1. *Kilimanjaro* "Masai Dance" 2d movement	African	1. layered poly-rhythms 2. ethnic instruments 3. modal melodies	ethnic dance
2. *La Fiesta Mexicana* "De La Negra," from 3d movement	Mexican	1. hemiola rhythmic effects 2. Latin percussion instruments 3. parallel thirds/ sixths	mariachi song/ dance
3. *Gaelic Rhapsody* "Irish Washer-woman"	Irish	1. drones (imitation of pipes) 2. 6/8 meter 3. regular phrases	jig

STANDARD 9B

Understanding music in relation to history and culture: *Students identify sources of American music genres, trace the evolution of those genres, and cite well-known musicians associated with them.*

Objective

- Students will describe the contributions of George Gershwin to musical theater and the significance of his musicals in the history of musical theater.

Materials

- "Selections from Porgy and Bess" by George Gershwin, arr. Robert Russell Bennett (Milwaukee: Chappell/Hal Leonard Corporation), Level 4

- Bulletin board display (prepared in cooperation with general music teacher) with copies of photographs of Gershwin, scenes from various productions of his musicals, and brief articles about musical theater in general and about Porgy and Bess in particular.

- Recording of Gershwin's *Rhapsody in Blue, An American in Paris,* or "Cuban Overture"

- Recording of a song from *Funny Face, Strike Up the Band, Of Thee I Sing,* or another Gershwin musical

- Video recording *Porgy and Bess* (Woodland Hills, CA: EMD Music Distribution, 1993)

- Audio-playback equipment

Procedures

1. Give students information about Gershwin's life and his contributions to American musical theater from approximately 1920 to 1938. Refer to items on the bulletin board display. Note that his major theater works include *Funny Face, Strike Up the Band, Of Thee I Sing* (the first Broadway musical to be awarded the Pulitzer Prize in music), as well as numerous annual Ziegfield Follies productions.

2. Play the recording of a song from one of these works, noting that it is an early example of musical theater. Ask students to listen for differences in the style of the song and the songs they know from today's musical theater. Discuss with students how today's musical theater has evolved from the musical theater of Gershwin's time.

3. Explain to students that in Gershwin's symphonic works, such as *Rhapsody in Blue, An American in Paris,* and "Cuban Overture," he attempted to create a bridge between "classical" and "popular" styles. Illustrate this point with a recording of one of these compositions and ask students to listen for and identify aspects of each style in the work.

4. Explain that, because of its subject matter (murder and betrayal among the poor Black population of Charleston) and extensive use of the harmonies and forms of popular music, *Porgy and Bess* was controversial when it was first performed (1935) as a Broadway musical. Show students excerpts from the video *Porgy and Bess.*

5. Note that since a revival of *Porgy and Bess* was staged in Germany in 1955, it has been accepted as a major American folk opera and is performed by opera companies and musical theater groups around the world. Ask students why they think the subject matter of *Porgy and Bess* was controversial in 1935.

6. Continue the discussion of Gershwin and his music, asking questions such as the following: "Have any of you performed other works by Gershwin?" "What are the differences between opera and musical theater?"

7. Have the band continue rehearsing sections of "Selections from Porgy and Bess."

(continued)

- Videocassette recorder
- Video monitor

Prior Knowledge and Experiences

- Students have been rehearsing "Selections from Porgy and Bess."
- In general music class, students have been studying American musical theater.

Indicators of Success

- Students describe the bridge between "classical" and "popular" styles in Gershwin's symphonic music.
- Students describe the significance of *Porgy and Bess* and other Gershwin musicals in the development of Broadway musical theater.

Follow-up

- Have students prepare a written outline listing characteristics of Broadway musical theater and characteristics of opera. Then have them compare the genres.
- Have students view the Public Broadcasting Great Performances Series' documentary *Porgy and Bess: An American Voice* by Ed Apfel and Gloria Naylor, narrated by Ruby Dee, produced by James L. Standifer (aired nationally in February 1998). For related teaching materials, contact Burrelle's Transcripts, PO Box 7, Livingston, NJ 07039-0007; telephone 1-800-777-8398. Then have students present a debate: "Is *Porgy and Bess* opera or musical theater?"

Proficient

STANDARD 9C

Understanding music in relation to history and culture: Students identify various roles that musicians perform, cite representative individuals who have functioned in each role, and describe their activities and achievements.

Objective

- Students will describe the contributions of Patrick Gilmore in his roles as military band leader, composer-arranger, and concert promoter.

Materials

- "When Johnny Comes Marching Home," in *Great Big Book of Children's Songs* (Milwaukee: Hal Leonard Corporation, 1995)

- "Johnny, I Hardly Knew You," in *The Melody Book: 300 Selections from the World of Music for Piano, Guitar, Autoharp, Recorder and Voice*, 3d ed., by Patricia Hackett (Englewood Cliffs, NJ: Prentice-Hall, 1998)

- Video recording *A History of Bands in America* (Boca Raton, FL: SIRS, 1988)

- Videocassette recorder

- Video monitor

Prior Knowledge and Experiences

- Students have been rehearsing "American Salute" by Morton Gould, arr. Philip Lang (Miami: Warner Bros. Publications), Level 5—Gould's set of variations on Gilmore's "When Johnny Comes Marching Home."

Procedures

1. During a rehearsal of "American Salute," identify Patrick Gilmore, Irish-born musician and conductor, as the composer of "When Johnny Comes Marching Home." Briefly discuss with students Gilmore's 1863 adaptation ("When Johnny Comes Marching Home") of the Irish tune "Johnny, I Hardly Knew You" for this composition and the patriotic sentiments underlying its creation (end of war, victory over "the enemy," reuniting of family and nation).

2. Distribute the music for "Johnny, I Hardly Knew You" and "When Johnny Comes Marching Home." Play the songs on piano or guitar, or invite a student to play, and ask students to sing along. [*Note:* Singing the songs may be helpful in teaching melodic style to enhance students' playing of "American Salute."] Then lead a discussion comparing the songs, including the following points: changes in text and changes in tempo. Ask students for their ideas regarding Gilmore's rationale for each change.

3. Discuss with students Gilmore's service as bandmaster in the Union Army and guide them in a discussion comparing his role to the role of service band directors today in their mission of preserving America's culture. Show excerpts from the video *A History of Bands in America.*

4. Discuss Gilmore's post–Civil War activities, including his role as a concert promoter of Peace Jubilee celebrations in various cities across the nation. Note that, for each of these, thousands of singers and instrumentalists assembled to celebrate the restoration of the Union. Explain that the music for "When Johnny Comes Marching Home" was sold through mail order and music dealers, with the public invited to come to the site of "Jubilee" and participate in the performance. Have students compare this activity to similar celebrations and ceremonies today (e.g., return of veterans from the Gulf War, honoring veterans of World War II).

Indicators of Success

- Students describe the roles that Patrick Gilmore performed as bandmaster, composer, and concert promoter.

(continued)

Follow-up

- As a supplement to the band's performance of "American Salute," present a unit in which students study theme and variation form. Have them identify compositional techniques used during each variation. Ask students what other variations might have been used.

- If there is a military installation in your school's area, or if a military band gives a concert in your community, invite the band director to speak to your band about his or her responsibilities.

STANDARD 9E

Understanding music in relation to history and culture: Students identify and describe music genres or styles that show the influence of two or more cultural traditions, identify the cultural source of each influence, and trace the historical conditions that produced the synthesis of influences.

Objective

- Students will identify and describe European, African, and Native American influences on mariachi-style music in a given band selection.

Materials

- "Tres Danzas de Mexico" by William Rhoads (Ruidoso, NM: TRN Music Publishers), Level 4

- Recording of Leonard Bernstein's "America," performed by Chita Rivera, from *West Side Story*, Columbia 32603

- Recording of "La Negra," from third movement ("Festival"), of H. Owen Reed's *La Fiesta Mexicana*, Cincinnati College Conservatory of Music Wind Symphony, Eugene Corporon, Klavier KCD 11048

- Recordings of *Master Drummer of Ghana, Mustapha Tettey Addy,* Lyrichord LLCT 7250, and *African Heritage Tour,* WMI 005 (World Music Institute, 49 W. 27th Street, Suite 930, New York, NY 10001; telephone 212-545-7536); or other African polyrhythmic drum music

Procedures

1. During the band warm-up, distribute the rhythm exercise chart that includes birhythms found throughout "Tres Danzas de Mexico." Have students perform the exercise.

2. Explain that "Tres Danzas de Mexico" is in the style of mariachi music. Distribute the study sheet, which includes characteristics of mariachi music and defines aspects of mariachi music, such as *sesquialtera* (alternating rhythm, usually 6/8 and 3/4) and *ritmico colonial* (bimeter, usually 6/8 and 3/4 simultaneously). Explain that mariachi music uses European textures of fifteenth- and sixteenth-century Spain (parallel sixths and thirds in melodic lines, phrase structure) and African polyrhythm style. [*Note:* See texts in Materials for examples of polyrhythms.]

3. Introduce the mariachi style, using examples such as the following:

   - for *sesquialtera*—"America," from *West Side Story* and "Tres Danzas de Mexico" (measure 69 forward in third movement, for example)

   - for *ritmico colonial*—"La Negra" and "Tres Danzas de Mexico" (measures 31–38 in first movement)

   - for parallel thirds in melodic lines—"La Negra" and "Tres Danzas de Mexico" (measures 23–38 in first movement)

   - for polyrhythmic percussion style—"Tres Danzas de Mexico," music from *Master Drummer of Ghana* and *African Heritage Tour,* and written examples of African polyrhythms from texts

4. Using musical illustrations, identify and describe for students the following cultural influences on mariachi-style music:

   - African—polyrhythms, layered percussion, models for "Latin" percussion instruments

   - European—parallel thirds in melodic writing, regular phrase lengths, language

   - Native American—models for "Latin" percussion instruments, dance-step style of mariachi

5. Lead students in a discussion of historical influences on mariachi-style music, including the colonization of Mexico by the Spanish, the influence of African slaves and their music, and the influence

(continued)

- *All Hands On!: An Introduction to West African Percussion Ensembles* by Lynne Jessup (Danbury, CT: World Music Press, 1997)
- *Afro-Latin Rhythm Dictionary,* edited by Thomas A. Brown (Van Nuys, CA: Alfred Publishing Company, 1984)
- Rhythm exercise chart (see step 1)
- Study sheet (see step 2)
- Audio-playback equipment

Prior Knowledge and Experiences

- Students have been rehearsing "Tres Danzas de Mexico."
- Students have an in-depth knowledge of musical elements and terminology (e.g., bimeter and polyrhythms).

of Native Peoples. Note that October 12 is celebrated in Mexico as "Dia de la Raza"—Day of the Races—to commemorate the joining of the races of Europe, Africa, and America.

6. Ask students to identify and describe European, African, and Native American influences found in "Tres Danzas de Mexico." Have the band illustrate these influences by playing selected excerpts from the composition.

Indicators of Success

- Students identify and describe European, African, and Native American influences found in the mariachi-style composition "Tres Danzas de Mexico."

Follow-up

- Have the band perform musical selections based on African or Native American music—such as "Variations on an African Hymn Song" by Quincy C. Hilliard (Oskaloosa, IA: C. L. Barnhouse), Level 3; and "Sioux Variants" by William Hill (San Diego: Neil A. Kjos Music Company), Level 5. Guide them in identifying and describing diverse cultural influences upon this music.

RESOURCES

Band Music Referenced in This Text

"American Salute" by Morton Gould, arr. Philip Lang. Miami: Warner Bros. Publications. Level 5.

"Baroque Suite" by Georg William Telemann, arr. William Hill. Ruidosa, NM: TRN Music Publishers. Level 3.

"Chester," from *New England Triptych*, by William Schuman. Bryn Mawr, PA: Merion Music/Theodore Presser Company. Level 5.

"Chorale and Shaker Dance" by John Zdechlik. San Diego: Neil A. Kjos Music Company. Level 4.

"Classic Overture" by Francois-Joseph Gossec, arr. Richard Franko Goldman and Roger Smith. Bryn Mawr, PA: Mercury Music/Theodore Presser Company. Level 4.

"Crystals" by Thomas Duffy. Cleveland, OH: Ludwig Music Publishing. Level 4.

"English Folk Song Suite" by Ralph Vaughan Williams. New York: Boosey & Hawkes. Level 4.

"Explorations" by Ed Huckeby. Oskaloosa, IA: C. L. Barnhouse. Level 3.

Four Scottish Dances by Malcolm Arnold and John Paynter. New York: Carl Fischer. Level 5.

"Ginger Marmalade" by Warren Benson. New York: Carl Fischer. Level 3.

Holocaust Suite by Morton Gould. New York: G. Schirmer. Level 5.

Kilimanjaro: An African Portrait by Robert Washburn. Miami: Belwin/Warner Bros. Publications. Level 5.

La Fiesta Mexicana by H. Owen Reed. Miami: Belwin/Warner Bros. Publications. Level 6.

"Let the Spirit Soar" by James Swearingen. Oskaloosa, IA: C. L. Barnhouse. Level 3.

"Liturgical Dances" by David Holsinger. San Antonio, TX: Southern Music Company. Level 5.

Military Symphony in F by Francois-Joseph Gossec, arr. Richard Franko Goldman and Robert L. Leist. Bryn Mawr, PA: Theodore Presser Company. Level 3.

Music for Prague, 1968 by Karel Husa. Milwaukee: Associated Music Publishers/Hal Leonard Corporation. Level 6.

"Russian Sailors' Dance," from *The Red Poppy,* by Reinhold Glière, arr. James Curnow. Milwaukee: Hal Leonard Corporation. Level 4.

"Selections from Porgy and Bess" by George Gershwin, arr. Robert Russell Bennett. Miami: Chappell/Hal Leonard Corporation. Level 4.

"Sioux Variants" by William Hill. San Diego: Neil A. Kjos Music Company. Level 5.

Suite no. 1 in E-flat, rev. for band, by Gustav Holst. New York Boosey & Hawkes. Level 4.

Suite no. 2 in F, rev. for band, "Fantasia on the Dargason" (fourth movement) by Gustav Holst. New York: Boosey & Hawkes. Level 5.

Suite of Old American Dances by Robert Russell Bennett. Milwaukee: Chappell/Hal Leonard Corporation. Level 5.

Symphony no. 1: In Memoriam Dresden—1945 by Daniel Bukvich. Kansas City, MO: Wingert-Jones. Level 4.

"Thematic Variations on Dona Nobis Pacem" by James Sudduth. San Antonio, TX: Southern Music Company. Level 3.

Toccata for Band by Frank Erickson. New York: Bourne Company. Level 4.

"Tres Danzas de Mexico" by William Rhoads. Ruidoso, NM: TRN Music Publishers. Level 4.

"Variations on an African Hymn Song" by Quincy C. Hilliard. Oskaloosa, IA: C. L. Barnhouse. Level 3.

Recordings Referenced in This Text

African Heritage Tour. WMI 005. World Music Institute, 49 W. 27th Street, Suite 930, New York, NY 10001; telephone 212-545-7536.

Band-in-a-Box. Buffalo, NY: PG Music.

Bernstein, Leonard. *West Side Story.* Carol Lawrence, Larry Kert, Chita Rivera. Columbia 32603.

Holst, Gustav. *First Suite in E-flat for Military Band.* Central Band of the Royal Air Force. Wing Commander Eric Banks. EMI Classics CDM 565122 2.

———. *Second Suite in F for Military Band.* Central Band of the Royal Air Force. Wing Commander Eric Banks. EMI Classics CDM 565122 2.

Master Drummer of Ghana, Mustapha Tettey Addy. Lyrichord LLCT 7250.

Music of Swearingen. Washington Winds. Edward Peterson. Walking Frog WFR 102.

Nothin' but Blues. Vol. 2 of *A New Approach to Jazz Improvisation.* Jamey Aebersold Jazz 1971. Jamey Aebersold Jazz, PO Box 1244C, New Albany, IN 47151.

Reed, H. Owen. *La Fiesta Mexicana.* Cincinnati College Conservatory of Music Wind Symphony. Eugene Corporon. Klavier KCD 11048.

Schuman, William. "Chester," from *New England Triptych.* Cincinnati College Conservatory of Music Wind Symphony. Eugene Corporon. Klavier KCD 11048.

Stars and Stripes: Marches, Fanfares & Wind Band Spectaculars. The Cleveland Symphonic Winds. Frederick Fennell. Telarc Records DC 80099.

Methods and Other Books Referenced in This Text

Aebersold, Jamey, ed. *In a Mellow Tone.* Vol. 48. Jamey Aebersold Jazz, PO Box 1244C, New Albany, IN 47151.

Brown, Thomas A., ed. *Afro-Latin Rhythm Dictionary.* Van Nuys, CA: Alfred Publishing Company, 1984.

Fowler, Charles. *Music! Its Role and Importance in Our Lives.* Mission Hills, CA: Glencoe/McGraw-Hill, 1994.

Garofalo, Robert. *Blueprint for Band.* Fort Lauderdale, FL: Meredith Music Publications, 1983.

Great Big Book of Children's Songs. Milwaukee: Hal Leonard Corporation, 1995.

Hackett, Patricia. *The Melody Book: 300 Selections from the World of Music for Piano, Guitar, Autoharp, Recorder and Voice,* 3d ed. Englewood Cliffs, NJ: Prentice-Hall, 1998.

Heisinger, Brent. *Comprehensive Musicianship through Band Performance.* Menlo Park, CA: Addison-Wesley, 1976.

Jessup, Lynne. *All Hands On!: An Introduction to West African Percussion Ensembles.* Danbury, CT: World Music Press, 1997.

Labuta, Joseph A. *Teaching Musicianship in the High School Band.* Fort Lauderdale, FL: Meredith Music Publications, 1996.

Machlis, Joseph, and Kristine Forney. *The Enjoyment of Music,* 7th ed. New York: W. W. Norton, 1995.

Rhodes, Tom, Donald Bierschenk, and Tim Lautzenheiser. *Essential Elements.* Milwaukee: Hal Leonard Corporation, 1991.

Schiff, Hilda, compiler. *Holocaust Poetry.* New York: St. Martin's Press, 1995.

Zigrosser, Carl, ed. *Prints and Drawings of Kaethe Kollwitz,* rev. ed. Mineola, NY: Dover Publications, 1969.

Videocassettes

A History of Bands in America. Boca Raton, FL: SIRS, 1988.

Moiseyev Dance Company—A Gala Evening. V.I.E.W. Video, 34 East 23rd St., New York, NY 10010. 1989.

Porgy and Bess. Woodland Hills, CA: EMD Music Distribution, 1993.

Slaughterhouse Five. Universal City, CA: MCA/Universal Music and Video Distribution, 1989.

Soviet Army Chorus, Band, and Dance Ensemble. Kultur International Films, 195 Highway 36, West Long Branch, NJ 07764. 1981.

Additional Resources

*Boardman, Eunice, ed. *Dimensions of Musical Thinking.* Reston, VA: Music Educators National Conference, 1989.

Bordagni, Marco, and Joannes Rochut, eds. *Melodious Etudes for Trombone.* 3 vols. New York: Carl Fischer, 1928.

Boroff, Edith. *Music in Europe and the United States.* New York: Ardsley House Publishers, 1990.

Brass Anthology. Northfield, IL: The Instrumentalist Company, 1991.

Colwell, Richard, and Thomas Goolsby. *The Teaching of Instrumental Music,* 2d ed. Englewood Cliffs, NJ: Prentice Hall, 1992.

Cook, Gary. *Teaching Percussion,* 2d ed. New York: Macmillan/Simon & Schuster, 1997.

Farkas, Philip. *The Art of Brass Playing.* Bloomington, IN: Wind Music, 1989.

————. *The Art of French Horn Playing.* Miami: Summy-Birchard/ Warner Bros. Publications, 1956.

Garofalo, Robert. *Rehearsal Handbook for Band and Orchestra Students.* Fort Lauderdale, FL: Meredith Music Publications, 1983.

Gordon, Philip. *Forty-Two Chorales for Band.* New York: Bourne Company/International Music Company, 1962.

Grunow, Richard, and Edwin Gordon. *Jump Right In: The Instrumental Series.* Chicago: GIA Publications, 1993–94, 1996.

Holloway, Richard, et al. *Guide to Teaching Percussion.* Columbus, OH: William C. Brown/McGraw-Hill, 1996.

Hunt, Norman. *Guide to Teaching Brass.* Columbus, OH: William C. Brown/McGraw-Hill, 1993.

Kleinhammer, Edward. *The Art of Trombone Playing.* Miami: Summy-Birchard/Warner Bros. Publications, 1963.

Lisk, Ed. *The Creative Director: Alternative Rehearsal Techniques.* Fort Lauderdale, FL: Meredith Music Publications, 1991.

Marzano, Robert, et al. *Dimensions of Thinking: A Framework for Curriculum and Instruction.* Alexandria, VA: Association for Supervision and Curriculum Development, 1988.

Maxwell, Roger. *Fourteen Weeks to a Better Band.* Oskaloosa, IA: C. L. Barnhouse, 1974.

McBeth, W. Francis. *Effective Performances of Band Music.* San Antonio, TX: Southern Music Company, 1972.

Morello, Joe. *Master Studies.* Milwaukee: Modern Drummer Publications/Hal Leonard Corporation, 1986.

*Music Educators National Conference. *Teaching Wind and Percussion Instruments: A Course of Study.* Reston, VA: Author, 1991.

National Band Association. *Selective Music Lists for Bands,* rev. ed. Nashville, TN: National Band Association, 1997.

Putnik, Edwin. *The Art of Flute Playing.* Miami: Summy-Birchard/ Warner Bros. Publications, 1970.

Randel, Don Michael, ed. *The New Harvard Dictionary of Music.* Cambridge, MA: Belknap Press of Harvard University Press, 1986.

Rousseau, Eugene. *Practical Hints on Playing the Saxophone.* Miami: Belwin/Warner Bros. Publications, 1985.

Sawicki, Carl J. *The Oboe Revealed.* Carl J. Sawicki, PO Box 101, Fredericksburg, TX 78624; telephone 830-997-1994. 1988.

Smith, Claude T. *Symphonic Warm-ups for Band.* Milwaukee: Jenson/Hal Leonard Corporation, 1982.

Smith, Leonard B. *Treasury of Scales.* Miami: Belwin/Warner Bros. Publications, 1985.

Smith, Norman E., and Albert J. Stoutamire. *Band Music Notes.* Lake Charles, LA: Program Note Press, 1982.

Spencer, William. *The Art of Bassoon Playing.* Revised by Frederick Mueller. Miami: Summy-Birchard/Warner Bros. Publications, 1986.

Sprenkle, Robert, and David Ledet. *The Art of Oboe Playing.* Miami: Summy-Birchard/Warner Bros. Publications, 1961.

Teal, Larry. *The Art of Saxophone Playing.* Miami: Summy-Birchard/ Warner Bros. Publications, 1963.

Thurmond, James Morgan. *Note Grouping.* Fort Lauderdale, FL: Meredith Music Publications, 1991.

Voxman, Himie, and William Gower. *Rubank Method.* Milwaukee: Hal Leonard Corporation.

Westphal, Frederick. *Guide to Teaching Woodwinds,* 5th ed. Columbus, OH: William C. Brown/McGraw-Hill, 1990.

*Available from MENC.

MENC Resources on Music and Arts Education Standards

Aiming for Excellence: The Impact of the Standards Movement on Music Education. 1996. #1012.

Implementing the Arts Education Standards. Set of five brochures: "What School Boards Can Do," "What School Administrators Can Do," "What State Education Agencies Can Do," "What Parents Can Do," "What the Arts Community Can Do." 1994. #4022. Each brochure is also available in packs of 20.

Music for a Sound Education: A Tool Kit for Implementing the Standards. 1994. #1600.

National Standards for Arts Education: What Every Young American Should Know and Be Able to Do in the Arts. 1994. #1605.

Opportunity-to-Learn Standards for Music Instruction: Grades PreK–12. 1994. #1619.

Performance Standards for Music: Strategies and Benchmarks for Assessing Progress Toward the National Standards, Grades PreK–12. 1996. #1633.

Perspectives on Implementation: Arts Education Standards for America's Students. 1994. #1622.

"Prekindergarten Music Education Standards" (brochure). 1995. #4015 (set of 10).

The School Music Program—A New Vision: The K–12 National Standards, PreK Standards, and What They Mean to Music Educators. 1994. #1618.

"Teacher Education in the Arts Disciplines: Issues Raised by the National Standards for Arts Education." 1996. #1609.

Teaching Examples: Ideas for Music Educators. 1994. #1620.

The Vision for Arts Education in the 21st Century. 1994. #1617.

MENC's *Strategies for Teaching* Series

Strategies for Teaching Prekindergarten Music, compiled and edited by Wendy L. Sims. #1644.

Strategies for Teaching K–4 General Music, compiled and edited by Sandra L. Stauffer and Jennifer Davidson. #1645.

Strategies for Teaching Middle-Level General Music, compiled and edited by June M. Hinckley and Suzanne M. Shull. #1646.

Strategies for Teaching High School General Music, compiled and edited by Keith P. Thompson and Gloria J. Kiester. #1647.

Strategies for Teaching Elementary and Middle-Level Chorus, compiled and edited by Ann Roberts Small and Judy K. Bowers. #1648.

Strategies for Teaching High School Chorus, compiled and edited by Randal Swiggum. #1649.

Strategies for Teaching Strings and Orchestra, compiled and edited by Dorothy A. Straub, Louis S. Bergonzi, and Anne C. Witt. #1652.

Strategies for Teaching Middle-Level and High School Keyboard, compiled and edited by Martha F. Hilley and Tommie Pardue. #1655.

Strategies for Teaching Beginning and Intermediate Band, compiled and edited by Edward J. Kvet and Janet M. Tweed. #1650.

Strategies for Teaching High School Band, compiled and edited by Edward J. Kvet and John E. Williamson. #1651.

Strategies for Teaching Specialized Ensembles, compiled and edited by Robert A. Cutietta. #1653.

Strategies for Teaching Middle-Level and High School Guitar, compiled and edited by William E. Purse, James L. Jordan, and Nancy Marsters. #1654.

Strategies for Teaching: Guide for Music Methods Classes, compiled and edited by Louis O. Hall with Nancy R. Boone, John Grashel, and Rosemary C. Watkins. #1656.

For more information on these and other MENC publications, write to or call MENC Publications Sales, 1806 Robert Fulton Drive, Reston, VA 20191-4348; 800-828-0229.

MOTOR CITY *muscle*

MOTOR CITY *muscle*

Stan Fischler

Warwick Publishing
Toronto   Los Angeles

ISBN 1-895629-48-9

Published by:
Warwick Publishing Inc., 24 Mercer Street, Toronto, Ontario M5V 1H3
Warwick Publishing Inc., 1424 N. Highland Avenue, Los Angeles CA 90027

Distributed by:
Firefly Books Ltd., 250 Sparks Avenue, Willowdale, Ontario M2H 2S4

Design: Kimberley Davison
Editorial Services: Harry Endrulat
The photographs for this book come from three collections: The Harold
Barkley Archives, The Fischler Archives, and the personal collection of Max
McNab. For further information, please contact Warwick Publishing.

Printed and bound in Canada by Love Printing Services Limited.

Dedication

I first encountered Max McNab's name in a hockey story about the Red Wings in 1949. He worried me a great deal.

At the time I was a passionate Leafs' fan and anyone who appeared to strengthen the Detroit team was a threat to my mental well-being.

From that point on I followed McNab's career from Detroit to Vancouver and ultimately San Diego, where he emerged as one of hockey's brightest executives.

But I really got to know Max first-hand when he came to New Jersey as general manager of the Devils in November 1983. From the very beginning McNab was, as my dad would affectionately say, "a prince."

Nicer guys were not to be found. His presence was a tonic and he proved that it was not a prerequisite for managing to be a barracuda.

In more recent years when Max became a Devils' vice-president, we would spend many an evening "comparing notes" before a New Jersey home game. It was one of the true delights of the business and has remained so to this day.

Naturally, many of our moments of reminiscing included excursions into the Red Wings' past, discussing Jack Adams, Gordie Howe and Ted Lindsay.

Max was a well of information and invariably genial and cooperative. Max McNab always made hockey fun and it is to him that this book is dedicated.

Table of Contents

Introduction

When the Detroit Red Wings marched all the way to the 1995 playoff finals and threatened to win their first Stanley Cup in forty years, critics immediately began comparing Scott Bowman's club to the Motor City Musclemen of yesteryear.

Specifically, the analysts had in mind the Detroit club that spanned the years 1949-1955 when the likes of Gordie Howe, Red Kelly, Ted Lindsay, Terry Sawchuk and Marty Pavelich arrested hockey fans' attention with some of the most artistic, exciting and physical hockey ever played on a major professional level.

Of course, there was one major distinction between the 1995 Red Wings and their predecessors from the 1950s — Howe-Lindsay & Co. won Stanley Cups; Bowman Inc. was swept out of the finals in four straight games. Furthermore, the team representing the Motor City in the years after World War II earned a niche among the greatest hockey teams of all time; Bowman's club was a mere pretender to a throne that it never could grasp.

Whether or not the 1949-1955 Detroiters rank as a true hockey "dynasty" is a matter for debate and the conclusion is simply based on one's definition of the term. If dynasty is defined as a team that dominated the NHL over a relatively long period of time, then the club managed by Jack Adams certainly qualifies. However, if the dynastic bottom line is the club's ability to win no less than three straight Stanley Cups, then the Wings slip out of the picture.

This, of course, is all academic. What matters is that the Detroit Red Wings in that post-war period were a very special team both as personalities and performers. They boasted one of the best goalies of all time, one of the best defensemen and arguably the single most versatile player ever to grace the ice, Gordie Howe.

To best understand the flowering of this amazing hockey plant, one must first trace its roots to the original planting of the seeds and the man most responsible for their growth, Jack Adams.

After 1927 Adams orchestrated the franchise through 35 seasons, which included a dozen first-place finishes and no less than seven Stanley Cups. Adams singular claim to fame is precisely the same as the Red Wings' claim to dynasty status — from 1949 to 1955 Adams' club finished in first place seven successive years. It was an accomplishment that even surpassed that of the New York Yankees during their famed Murderers Row years.

In fact when the two teams were compared, Adams would recoil in mock horror. "We are not the Yankees of hockey," Adams would bellow. "The Yankees are the Red Wings of baseball!"

And, furthermore, he meant it.

The Beginnings

Jack Adams was the Red Wings and the Red Wings were Jack Adams. The two entities were inextricably intertwined, not unlike Jackie Robinson and the Brooklyn Dodgers or Conn Smythe and the Toronto Maple Leafs. Adams was there at the very beginning and remained in Detroit through the golden years. But before he arrived, Adams already had become a major hockey name as a player.

A center and eventual member of the Hockey Hall of Fame, Adams was born in Fort William, Ontario, on June 14, 1895, and would eventually star for several teams ranging from Toronto to Ottawa to Vancouver. Despite his acknowledged skills as a center, Adams would minimize his talents. Asked about his stint with the Vancouver Millionaires over three seasons in the early 1920s, Adams once said, "A bad hockey team, and I was one of its bad players."

Actually, he led the Pacific Coast Hockey Association in goals one year and once in penalties. The latter surprised no one who knew Jack even on a casual level. His combativeness was as much a part of his makeup as his scarlet nose. Once, during the 1918-19 season, when he was with the Toronto Arenas, Adams became engaged in a wild fight with Sprague Cleghorn, another ace not known for his delicacy. Canada's Governor General happened to be a front-row spectator that night

and had he taken a dim view of the proceedings, it could have meant Adams' expulsion.

"It was a real slugfest," Adams later recalled. "Funny, I never did hear what the Governor General thought about it, but I thought I saw a distinguished-looking man clapping his white-gloved hands."

Nothing Adams did was halfhearted, especially when he violated the laws of hockey. Alfie Skinner, a star for the Toronto Arenas, well remembered Jack's generous use of his stick. "Adams was an awful slasher," said Skinner. "Some fellows would slash and you'd hardly feel it through your pads. But when Adams swung his stick at a vulnerable part of your anatomy, he swung hard. He meant to hurt! On the other hand, he'd take punishment without a murmur. He'd never complain when anyone whacked him. A guy like that you had to admire."

You also had to admire Adams' timing. He managed to be the right man in the right place at the right time when it came to laying the cornerstone for Detroit's professional hockey team.

Adams had completed the 1926-27 season with the Ottawa Senators at a time when the National Hockey League was experiencing its most galvanic growth period in the United States. Boston, Pittsburgh and New York already had successful debuts in the major circuit and now Detroit was ready for its first big-league sextet.

Left: The Detroit Red Wings' dynasty of the early fifties was the work of general manager Jack "Jolly Jawn" Adams, who had once been a star player in his own right. Adams launched the careers of such Hall of Famers as Gordie Howe, Ted Lindsay and Red Kelly.

This was a relatively easy procedure because the Western League was folding and the Townsend-Seyburn interests of Detroit were able to purchase the WHL's Victoria Cougars for $100,000. The purchase price included some fine players, among them Jack Walker, Art Duncan, Frank Foyston, Clem Loughlin and Frank Frederickson. Foyston, Walker and Frederickson eventually were inducted into the Hockey Hall of Fame.

As a member of the Ottawa Senators during that 1926-27 campaign, Adams was in a position to examine the new Detroit club — originally nicknamed the Cougars — firsthand. Playing their home games at a temporary arena in nearby Windsor, Ontario, the Cougars hardly impressed Adams. They finished the 44-game NHL schedule with a dismal record of only a dozen wins and finished last in the American Division.

This did not sit well with some of the Cougars' ownership including members of the Ford Motor Co. family as well as others from the Fisher Body Company. They wanted a competitive club to play at the new Olympia Stadium which was opening at the corner of Grand River and McGraw. The owners commissioned club president Charles Hughes to find a manager that could make Detroit a hockey powerhouse.

Meanwhile, Adams had learned that NHL president Frank Calder had been asked by Hughes to help locate a dynamic personality to guide the Cougars. He phoned the league boss and requested an interview. "I'm the man for the Detroit job!" Adams brashly told Calder whereupon the president called Hughes and arranged an appointment for the two to meet.

Typically, Adams put all his cards on the table, telling the Detroiter that there was no need to look any further; his job search was over. "I'd been involved in winning the Stanley Cup for Ottawa," said Adams, "so I told Hughes that he needed me more than I needed him."

Hughes agreed. He signed Adams and Jolly Jawn, as he came to be known in Motor City circles, immediately rebuilt the team. From a dismal 12-28-4 record, the Cougars climbed to the .500 mark, winning 19, losing 19 and tying six games. It wasn't a good enough record for a Stanley Cup berth, but there was no question that the road to the Cup had opened for Detroit. The following season, Detroit, with a new nickname, the Falcons, finished third in the American Division.

There was only one problem — the Great Depression struck the continent and fans simply didn't have the cash to buy hockey tickets. "One night in 1930," Adams said, "we played an exhibition game for some charity run by Frank Murphy, the Detroit mayor. It was a cash collection, pay what you could. Just before the game started we

HIGH-SCORING HOCKEY ACE

Herb Lewis of the Detroit Red Wings says:
"I go for Camels in a big way!"

THE lightning-quick camera eye caught *Herb Lewis* (*above, left*) in this slashing set-to before the goal. Next split-second he scored! After the game (*right*), Herb said: "You bet I enjoy eating. And I'll give Camels credit for helping me enjoy my food. Smoking camels with my meals and afterwards eases tension. Camels set me right!" Camel smokers enjoy smoking to the full. It's Camels for a "lift." It's Camels again "for digestion's sake." Thanks to Camel's aid, the flow of the important digestive fluids–*alkaline* digestive fluids–speeds up. A sense of well-being follows. So make it Camels–the live-long day.

heard there was a guy driving up and down Woodward Avenue outside the Olympia. He had five bags of potatoes and wanted in. We took his spuds and gave him standing room."

To cut costs, Adams eliminated travel by sleeping cars on the train trips and limited his players to day coaches. Instead of traditional meals, the players had to make do with cheese sandwiches. "We were this depressed," Adams recalled. "If Howie Morenz, the great Montreal star, had been available for $1.98, we couldn't have afforded him."

Nevertheless the Falcons — renamed from Cougars as a result of a newspaper competition — finished first in the American Division of the NHL in 1933-34 and beat the Toronto Maple Leafs in the semifinal playoff to qualify for the Stanley Cup finals. However, the Chicago Blackhawks beat them and Detroit still was without a Stanley Cup of its own.

However, the Red Wings and Adams had turned an important fiscal corner thanks to the acquisition of the franchise by grain millionaire James Norris Sr. One of the continent's leading businessmen, Norris loved hockey and had the heritage to back it up. He had played hockey for the Montreal

The 1942 finals erupted in a classic melee after game four when Red Wings manager Jack Adams (wearing hat to the left of no. 11) punched referee Mael Harwood (obscured by Adams). The players are Eddie Wares of the Wings (11) and Wally Stanowski of the Maple Leafs. Adams was suspended for the duration of the series. Toronto won the next three games.

Amateur Athletic Association's famed Winged Wheelers. Norris suggested a new team name, the Red Wings, and an insignia symbolic of the industry which dominated the city.

A no-nonsense type, Norris laid it on the line with Adams: "I'll give you a year on probation with no contract."

In no time at all Adams gained Norris' confidence and the pair became virtually inseparable from that point on. Because of his love for a deal, Adams became known as "The David Harum of Hockey." He bought Syd Howe (no relation to Gordie) from the St. Louis Flyers for $35,000 and Howe eventually became a Hall of Famer in Detroit. Adams purchased Hec Kilrea from Toronto with equally satisfactory results.

During the 1935 playoffs Adams and his Boston counterpart, Frank

Patrick, got into a trading conversation. "If I had Cooney Weiland," Patrick said, mentioning Detroit's crack center, "Boston would be in this final."

To which Adams shot back, "If I had Marty Barry, Detroit would win the Stanley Cup."

A few minutes later the exchange was made. Weiland became the center between Dutch Gainor and Dit Clapper on Boston's Dynamite Line. Barry was placed between Larry Aurie and Herbie Lewis to form a set of forwards that would heavily influence the Red Wings' destiny.

The Lewis-Aurie-Barry line paced Detroit to a first-place finish in the American Division in 1935-36, although they had formidable reinforcements. Johnny Sorrell and Ebbie Goodfellow were splendid second-liners and, as one observer aptly put it, "Ebbie Goodfellow was Gordie Howe before Gordie Howe became a Red Wing."

In the spring of 1936, the Red Wings took a serious run at the Stanley Cup and began by dispatching the Montreal Maroons in the opening round. The highlight, by far, was the longest hockey match ever played in the NHL — exactly 116 minutes and 30 seconds of sudden-death overtime was required, almost two additional full games. The winning goal was scored by Modere (Mud) Bruneteau of Detroit at 16:30 of the sixth overtime.

The goaltending of Norm Smith and the defensive work from Bucko McDonald and Doug Young were instrumental in the victory and set the stage for the triumphant drive to the finals. Adams coached Detroit to a three games to one victory to annex the silver mug.

Winning two consecutive championships was considered a virtual impossibility in the highly competitive NHL of the mid-1930s. No less daunting to the Red Wings during the 1936-37 season was an unusual spate of injuries. Captain Doug Young suffered a broken leg and was lost for the season. He was soon followed to the sidelines by Orville Roulston, with another broken leg. When the Red Wings' leading scorer, Larry Aurie, broke his ankle early in March 1937, Adams wondered if and when the bad luck would ever end.

Despite the injuries, the Red Wings finished first in the American Division for the second consecutive year, winning 25 games, losing 14, and tying nine for 59 points, once again tops in both divisions. The Red Wings' superiority extended into the playoffs where they first disposed of the pesky Montreal Canadiens three games to two. The fifth game was another sudden-death classic, lasting until 12:45 a.m. when Hec Kilrea of Detroit beat Habs goalie Wilf Cude after 51 minutes and 49 seconds of overtime.

Although the defending champi-ons should have been favorites to defeat the New York Rangers in the 1937 Stanley Cup finals, an injury to goalie Norm Smith in the first game at Madison Square Garden left Detroit in the underdog role. New York won the opener, 5-1, forcing the Red Wings to start substitute goalie Earl Robertson in Game Two.

Robertson beat the Rangers 4-2 in the second game, lost 1-0 in the third, but then blanked the Rangers 1-0 to tie the series at two apiece. Responding nobly to the pressure, Robertson hit new heights in the finale on April 15, 1937, at Olympia Stadium. With goals by Marty Barry (twice) and Johnny Sorrell, Robertson stopped the Rangers cold for a 3-0 decision. Thus, Detroit became the first team to finish first and win the Stanley Cup in con-secutive seasons.

Adams then made one of the few errors of his administration and was the first to admit it. "I stood pat," he allowed, "and I should have been dealing."

His Red Wings not only failed to defend the Stanley Cup, they managed to miss the playoffs entirely. "This," said Adams, "was the bitterest blow of all."

Rebuilding the Red Wings into champions would require patience and fortitude. By the 1941-42 season the Red Wings were good enough to reach the Stanley Cup finals where they were underdogs against a powerful Toronto club. Ever the innovator, Adams devised a strategy which would tilt the series his way; at least in the beginning.

Instead of having his forwards carry the puck over the enemy blue line as was the custom in those days, Adams decided that the somewhat slower Toronto defensemen could be exploited if his scorers instead fired the puck into the corners of the Leafs' zone and then outraced the enemy defensemen to the rubber.

The plan thoroughly befuddled the Maple Leafs who lost Games One, Two and Three and appeared doomed to lose Game Four at Detroit's Olympia. In fact the Cup was within Adams' grasp as his stickhandlers led Game Four with 15 minutes to play. But the Maple Leafs rallied and, at game's end, with the score 4-3 for Toronto, Adams erupted at referee Mel Harwood.

This was no idle explosion. Jolly Jawn was under the impression that Toronto boss Conn Smythe exerted undue pressure on NHL president Frank Calder and, furthermore, Adams believed that the referees were against him. Adams struck referee Harwood amid a melee that featured several protesting Detroit players. When the dust had cleared, Adams was suspended by Calder for the duration of the finals while Don Grosso and Eddie Wares each were fined $100 for abusing Harwood.

Without Adams on the bench, the Red Wings proceeded to lose the next three games — 9-3, 3-0, 3-1 — in one of the ice game's classic reversals. Never before or since had a team lost the first three games of the Stanley Cup finals only to rebound and win the next four.

Bitterly, Adams blamed others for the disaster. "To me," Adams insisted, "the 1942 series was controlled by the Toronto papers and Conn Smythe. They influenced Calder into favoring the Leafs."

In Adams' eyes, justice triumphed the following season. Paced by crack forwards Carl Liscombe, Joe Carveth and Sid Abel, Detroit eliminated Toronto four games to two in the opening round — the clincher was a 3-2 sudden-death thriller decided at 9:21 of the first overtime — and moved up against the Boston Bruins in the finals.

Except for Game Two in which

Detroit rallied for three third period goals to win 4-3, it was a remarkably easy series. The Red Wings won in four straight and got 4-0 and 2-0 shutouts from goalie Johnny Mowers in the last pair of matches. But Mowers, along with several other Detroit players, went off to war and the decimated Red Wings lost to Chicago four games to one in the opening round.

A season later, the Red Wings regrouped, finished a respectable second and then participated in one of the strangest Stanley Cup tournaments ever to involve a Detroit team.

In the semifinals, the Red Wings opened against a Boston squad that

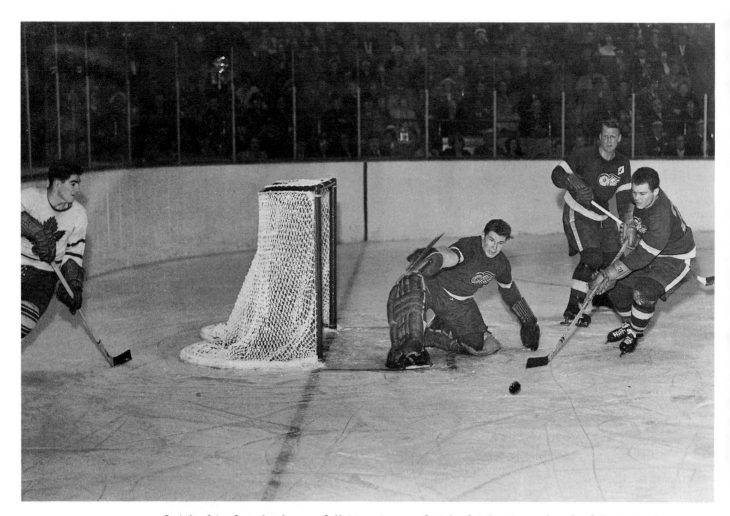

Fleming MacKell (left) has just tested Harry Lumley whose right pad just sent the puck to the side.

finished in fourth place, a full 31 points behind Jack Adams' team. Nevertheless, Boston won the first two games of the series at Olympia putting the Wings behind the eightball. However, Detroit responded by winning the next three straight before the Bruins tied the series at three apiece with a 5-3 win on April Fools' Day 1945. But there was no fooling around on the Wings' part when they returned home for the decisive seventh game on April 3, 1945. They topped the Hub team 5-3 and advanced to the finals against the hated Toronto Maple Leafs.

Although Adams was going with a 19-year-old goalie named Harry Lumley, his club was favored to take Toronto, especially since Detroit had

finished 15 points ahead of their rivals. When the series opened on April 6, 1945, at Olympia, Toronto coach Hap Day started an unusual character in goal. Frank McCool was afflicted with ulcers and frequently had to skate to the bench for antacid to calm his churning stomach. Despite his condition, McCool had beaten Montreal four games to two in the opening round and now was taking aim at the Stanley Cup.

His aim was good. McCool coolly beat Detroit 1-0 and 2-0 in successive games at Olympia. Frustrated, Adams couldn't understand why his scoring ace Joe Carveth had suddenly become unproductive. When the series moved to Toronto, nothing changed in the script. McCool posted another shutout and Gus Bodnar scored Toronto's lone goal.

Unlike the semifinal, when Detroit lost the first two games but at least scored goals, the Red Wings were now down three games and had scored absolutely nothing. "It doesn't look like the puck ever is going to go in for us," snapped a decidedly un-jolly Adams.

But the breakthrough finally occurred in Game Four. Flash Hollett opened the scoring for the Red Wings who rallied from a 3-2 deficit with three unanswered third period goals and a 5-3 triumph.

Having solved McCool at least once, the Wings returned home and this time got a pair of third period scores from Hollett and Carveth, giving them a 2-0 win. When the series returned to Maple Leaf Gardens for Game Six, McCool and Lumley were so outstanding over three periods that neither team scored. Finally, at 14:16 of the first overtime period, Ed Bruneteau beat Ulcers McCool and Detroit won its third straight game!

The seventh and final game would be played on April 22, 1945, at Olympia and, not surprisingly, Motor City fans were recalling that their favorite club was now in a position to do exactly what Toronto had done to

Below left: Far out of his crease, Toronto goalie Turk Broda smothers the puck while left wing Harry Watson (left) and defenseman Bill Barilko (5) surround Detroit's Ted Lindsay (behind Broda).

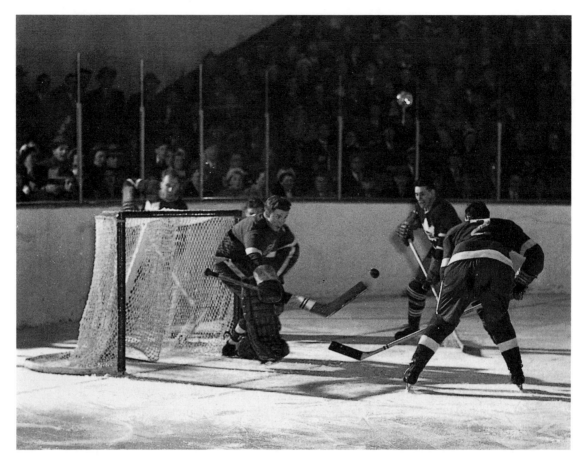

Detroit in the 1942 finals — lose the first three and then counterattack for four consecutive wins. All signs pointed to a win for the home club. They were on a roll; they were the better team during the regular season and McCool appeared to be cracking under the strain.

"I see by the Detroit papers that we are about to get beaten," said Toronto coach, Hap Day. "I don't believe it and I hope you don't believe it."

The Leafs got an early goal from Mel Hill and McCool nurtured the one goal lead into the third period. But at 8:16 of the third, Murray Armstrong scored on a rebound and the game was tied. The momentum should have shifted to the Red Wings but it didn't. Two minutes later referee Bill Chadwick whistled Syd Howe of

Detroit into the penalty box for high-sticking Gus Bodnar. Day sent his power-play unit out for the kill.

Pressing for the winner, Leafs' defenseman Babe Pratt passed the puck from the blue line to forward Nick Metz who was standing in front of the net. Metz shot, but Detroit's youthful goalie, Harry Lumley, anticipated the move and blocked it. The rebound skimmed to the onrushing Pratt who fired it into the net. For the next seven minutes, the Wings stormed McCool's crease, but they failed to get the equalizer and the game ended 2-1 for Toronto.

Sitting dolefully in the Red Wing dressing room was a young left wing who hated to lose more than most veterans. Ted Lindsay had been born to be a hockey player. His father, Bert

Lindsay, had been a first-rate goalie at the turn of the century and played alongside such legendary aces as Newsy Lalonde, Lester Patrick and Cyclone Taylor. Lindsay had arrived at the Red Wings' training camp in the fall of 1944, an unknown among 63 skaters auditioning for the NHL club. In no time at all he was discovered by Adams.

"There's a kid after my own heart," said Adams. "Look at the way he steps into those big guys."

Lindsay had played his first game for the Red Wings on October 29, 1944, and helped Detroit to a 7-1 victory over Chicago. In his second game he scored his first NHL goal as the Red Wings trounced the Rangers, 10-3. "I knew he had a lot of moxie," said Adams, "and I knew he'd do a good job. But he exceeded anything I had hoped for. He's just a natural and will be one of the NHL's great ones."

It wasn't apparent at first. In 1945-46 Lindsay played in 47 games, scored seven goals and 10 assists for 17 points. It was an offense-poor year for a Detroit club whose top scorer was Adam Brown with 20 goals and 11 assists. In fact the only area in which the Red Wings dominated was penalties — defenseman Black Jack Stewart topped the NHL with 73 minutes.

But Adams was building the nucleus for a post-war powerful team and it would be comprised of youngsters such as Lindsay and another promising youth who really should have been a New York Ranger had the Broadway Blueshirts been more alert and less callous.

In 1942, at the age of 14, Gordie Howe attended a Ranger tryout school at Winnipeg. "The rink was packed with better-developed boys," wrote Bill Roche of the *Toronto Globe and Mail*, "and when Gordie did not show anything exceptional in his few brief whirls on the ice, he was sent back to Saskatoon with no Ranger string on him."

It also has been noted that the youthful right wing was homesick and treated shabbily by some of the New York veterans. Whatever the case, the Rangers had their chance to nab Howe and they blew it. A year later Fred Pinkney, a Detroit scout, had Howe attend a Red Wings' training camp. Jack Adams would not make the same mistake the Rangers had committed.

"A bunch of knowns and unknowns were milling around on the ice in the customary loosening-up procedure," Adams remembered. "All of a sudden, I saw one big kid skate in on a net and shoot right-handed. Back he came on the next rush and had to move out of position from his wing. But he got the puck and fired another shot left-handed. I sat up and really began to take notice when that happened. I hadn't seen anything like it in years.

"Both of the shots had been good ones, too. Not just a powerful drive

Right: Famed Detroit defenseman Black Jack Stewart (2) charges at Toronto center Max Bentley as goalie Harry Lumley uses his stick to clear the Leafs' shot. Bentley's linemate Joe Klukay circles the net.

Bill Quakenbush

from one side and a weak one from the other. Neither had been a backhand lift. Good switch-hitters in baseball have become quite common, but capable switch-hitters in hockey are just as rare as they have always been. Young Howe had caught my eye right then and there, but I didn't know who he was. I called him over to the boards to tell me his name.

"Standing only a few feet away was Syd Howe, one of our veterans who was nearing the end of a fine career in the NHL. When Gordie told me his name, I thought to myself, 'If you turn out to be just half as good as old Syd, you'll be quite a hockey p l a y e r .' Gordo didn't burn up the ice or anything like that in t r a i n i n g

camp, but just his switch-shooting alone had sold me. I sent him back to Saskatoon with a solid Detroit string on him and instructions to come back to our camp next autumn."

There was no way of determining at that early date precisely how the gangly right wing would mature both physically and mentally. But Adams decided that the best way of gauging Howe's potential was through the normal Junior hockey progression so Gordie was invited back to his second Detroit training camp for evaluation.

"He had filled out considerably that next fall," Adams continued. "I wanted to have him develop on one of our farm clubs, so I sent him to the Galt Juniors of the Ontario Hockey Association. We were operating the Galt club that winter and little Al Murray, who had played for the New York Americans defense, was their coach. However, we ran into trouble. The Canadian Amateur Hockey Association would not give Howe a transfer from Saskatoon to Galt. Therefore, the kid had to stay out of organized hockey for an entire winter."

However, Adams was sufficiently impressed with Howe to begin discussing a possible contract. Young Howe was amenable to the terms mentioned by Adams, but added that he would not sign on the dotted line unless Adams included a windbreaker with the Red Wings' logo on the front. The Detroit boss readily

Leonard "Red" Kelly

Celebrating another win in 1952. (Left to right) Ted Lindsay, Sid Abel and Tony Leswick.

agreed, but soon forgot his promise.

Howe went to Galt but only participated in exhibition games. Nevertheless, his growth graph continued an upward climb and by training camp in 1945, Adams decided that the 17-year-old was ready to turn pro with the Red Wings' farm club at Omaha in the United States Hockey League. Tommy Ivan, who would have a profound effect on Howe's career — not to mention the Red Wings' fortunes — was coaching the Omaha Knights.

Now Adams presented the professional contract to Howe and expected no problems with the signing, but Howe was hesitant enough to inspire

Adams to inquire about the problem.

"What seems to be the matter?" Adams asked. "Why the hesitation about signing? You like that contract, don't you?"

Howe hesitated momentarily and then expressed his concern. "The salary is all right," Howe explained, "but what about that windbreaker you promised me when I signed last year's contract?"

"That was our first and last argument," Adams remembered.

After a season at Omaha, Howe was ready for the "show," as professionals like to call the NHL. He became a big-leaguer to stay in 1946-47 by which time all the World War II veterans had returned to their respective teams and the post-war NHL began to blossom. Detroit finished fourth in the six-team league with a 22-27-11 record. Nevertheless, they qualified for a playoff berth.

Pitted against their most disliked foes, the Maple Leafs, the Wings proved competitive in the first two games. They lost the opener in Toronto 3-2 in overtime and then rebounded for a 9-1 triumph also at Maple Leaf Gardens. But that was it for Adams' skaters. They went down 4-1, 4-1 and 6-1 to lose the series four games to one.

The defeat notwithstanding, Adams sensed that he had the core of a winner with strength at every position. Harry Lumley — known as "Applecheeks" to his chums — had become one of the NHL's best goaltenders while Bill Quackenbush, Leo Reise Jr. and Black Jack Stewart formed the foundation of a splendid defense. A redheaded youngster named Leonard Kelly also patrolled the back line, but Kelly added another dimension to his game — he went on the attack whenever the opportunity arose and, because of his expert skating ability, was able to quickly return to his own end if the occasion demanded.

By the 1947-48 season Howe began to display many of the skills that were suggested during his previous training camps. The slope-shouldered right wing was the perfect complement to Ted Lindsay on the left. Their center iceman would be Sid Abel, the tall, rugged leader who had played on the 1943 Cup winners and who was named club captain at the age of 24.

No three forwards ever jelled more successfully. As they began to pump goal after goal into the enemy nets it was rather appropriate that the city which developed the motor production line should name the Abel, Lindsay and Howe trio the Production Line. Each of the three played in all 60 games of the 1947-48 season. Lindsay led the NHL with 33 goals while Abel finished fifth on the league list in assists with 30. Lindsay's 95 penalty

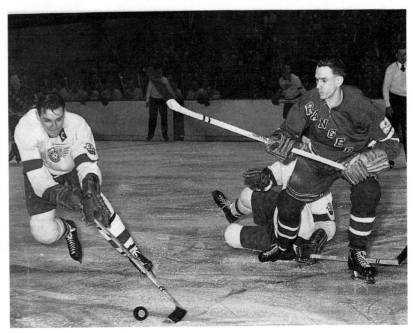

Sid Abel scoops up the puck.

minutes put him fifth in that department while Lumley topped all other netminders with seven shutouts; he was runner-up to Toronto's Turk Broda for the Vezina Trophy race. Lumley's goals against mark was 2.46 while Broda's was 2.38

Nothing said it better about the Detroit-Toronto rivalry than the homestretch race between the clubs. With two games remaining on the schedule Toronto held a one-point lead (73-72) for first place. The teams would play a home-and-home series on a Saturday and Sunday night which would determine the Prince of Wales (first place) Trophy winner. The Leafs won both ends, leaving Detroit five points behind at the close of the 60-game schedule.

The close race suggested that the teams were relatively equal in strength and when they collided in the 1948 Stanley Cup finals, experts expected a long and fascinating series.

It was fascinating but only because of the manner in which Day's Leafs thoroughly dominated Adams' Red

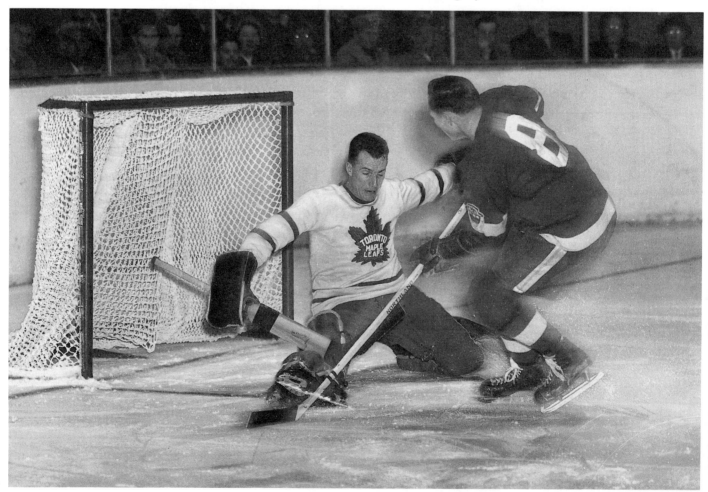

Wings. Except for Jimmy McFadden's goal which gave Detroit a 1-0 lead in Game One, Detroit never led again. They went down 5-3, 4-2, 2-0 and 7-2 but apparently benefited from the sweep for the Red Wings returned in 1948-49 stronger than ever.

"We were a close group," said Red Kelly, "all about the same age and all doing the same thing. None of us had married in those years, and hockey was our whole life."

That life took on new meaning in the 1948-49 season, one in which the outlines of Detroit's championship portrait were drawn but fell short of completion. As the two-time defending Stanley Cup champion Maple Leafs began slipping, the Red Wings powered forward. Although Howe was sidelined for 20 games because of an injury and Lindsay for 10, the Red Wings boasted such overall balance that they were able to move into first place and hold on to the top spot through season's end.

They finished nine points ahead of runner-up Boston and 18 points ahead of fourth-place Toronto. Abel's 28 goals were tops in the league while even in an abbreviated season Lindsay collected 30 assists, placing him third overall in that department. Harry Lumley's 34 wins led all goaltenders, and the Quackenbush-Stewart-Reise-Kelly defense looked more formidable than ever.

"We were coming on strong," said left wing Marty Pavelich. "There was a good balance up and down the lineup and we had the best goal-scoring record (195) in the league. There was a lot of optimism in our room as we headed for the playoffs."

And well there should have been as the Wings launched their quest for the Cup against third place Montreal which placed 10 points behind them. Once the playoffs began all bets were off. The Habs battled Detroit through three periods at Olympia, but all the Motor City skaters could show for it was a 1-1 tie. After two overtime periods, the score remained deadlocked only to be settled at 4:52 of the third sudden-death period when Detroit got the edge. Montreal rebounded to win the second match at Olympia at 2:59 of the first overtime, and the plot was laid out for a long and bitter series. It ended on April 5, 1949, at Olympia where the home club prevailed 3-1 but entered the finals exhausted.

By contrast, Toronto which had finished the regular season under .500, disposed of Boston in five games. Whether it was fatigue, overconfidence or weak goaltending, Detroit's excuses could not match the shock that reverberated from the crossroads of Grand River and McGraw once the 1949 finals began.

As had happened in the previous finals, the Red Wings jumped into an early lead. George Gee beat Turk Broda at 4:15 of the first period to set off a thunderous ovation at Olympia but few would be heard thereafter. Hap Day's Leafs fought their way back and by the end of regulation time, the score was knotted at two.

Three of the least likely players — defenseman Jim Thomson, third-line forwards Ray Timgren and Joe Klukay — combined to score the sudden-death winner at 17:31 as the red light was lit by Klukay.

The Red Wings would never recover from the shock. In Game Two at Olympia, the visitors picked up three goals before Detroit was heard from in the third period. The final score: Toronto 3, Detroit 1. When the series moved on to Maple Leaf Gardens, the Leafs repeated the 3-1 count two more times and, incredibly, had annexed the series in another four-game sweep.

Adams could not have been more humiliated. Now the Leafs had beaten his club in the playoffs five times in eight years. And Toronto had won the last 11 games in a row!

This hardly was an auspicious start for a dynasty but it actually was the turning point for the Red Wings.

"Sometimes," said the insightful Pavelich, "a team has to lose in the playoffs before it learns what it takes to win. By the start of the 1949-50 season, we knew what we had to do in order to become champions."

Adams tinkered here and there with his lineup, like a master mechanic fine-tuning a race car, and finally developed the proper horsepower for a team that could go the distance.

In October 1949, the dynasty was born.

The Dynasty

As the 1940s moved to a close it became obvious that two teams had come to dominate the National Hockey League. Conn Smythe's Toronto Maple Leafs won consecutive Stanley Cups in 1947, 1948 and 1949 and finished first overall in the 1947-48 season.

The Detroit Red Wings, second-place finishers in 1947-48, finished on top in 1948-49 and reached the Stanley Cup finals both seasons. But the difference between the two power-houses could best be measured by the playoffs. Coach Hap Day's Torontonians defeated Tommy Ivan's Detroiters four games to none in consecutive spring tournaments.

"There were two things that kept Jack Adams optimistic," said Marty Pavelich, who had become one of the most effective Red Wings and one of the NHL's foremost defensive forwards, "and they were the relative youth of our team and the fact that the big guy [Gordie Howe] was beginning to come into his own."

That Howe had the makings of a superstar became more evident during the 1949 semifinals between Montreal and Detroit. He scored eight goals against the Habs in the seven-game series and he continued to sparkle in 1949-50. Perhaps it would be more accurate to say that the Production Line — Abel, Lindsay, Howe — as a triumvirate as well as individually, dominated the scoring.

What made this more remarkable was a back ailment that bedeviled Lindsay even while he led the NHL in scoring. Then, in an unprecedented move, Jack Adams took advantage of a February 1950 schedule break and sent Lindsay to Hot Springs, Arkansas, for a vacation.

"We felt that we had to do something," said Adams. "Ted wasn't well. He had a bad back and a rotten cold. We tried to get him to ease up, but he wouldn't. He said he'd work out by playing. We figured that we had to get him where there was no ice and plenty of heat if we wanted to keep him off skates and cure his back. So we sent him away."

Lindsay spent five days in Arkansas, missing only one regular scheduled game, and then returned to the lineup. During that era the NHL provided $1,000 and $500 bonuses to the scoring champion and runner-up, respectively; a fact that could have resulted in selfish play among the linemates0, each of whom was a contender for top scorer.

"If we finish one-two-three we'll split the awards," said Abel. "We're not going to jeopardize the team's chances by competing against each other."

As captains go, Abel was one of the most commanding. He had a strong personality which was a necessary ingredient when working with young-sters such as Lindsay and Howe. The latter two had become particularly adept at working give-and-go plays, but Abel ensured that he was cut in on the passwork.

"Abel is one of the finest athletes I've ever handled," said Adams. "He's a smart hockey man and a real team player. Lindsay is the finest left-winger Detroit ever had and as game a boy as they come. Howe — what can I say — he's going to be one of the greatest players in history."

On March 6, 1950, the captain was further honored when Mayor Albert Cobo of Detroit officially proclaimed

"Sid Abel Day" in the Motor City. That night before the Red Wings game, the mayor presented Abel with a scroll signed by all members of the Common Council. Abel's hometown of Melville sent a plaque and, naturally, he received a long list of gifts from admiring fans, owner Jim Norris and the Abel Fan Fund. The captain put the finishing touches on the evening by taking a pass from Howe and beating Gerry McNeil in the Montreal goal to tie the score at one apiece.

The reincarnation of Abel was one

Toronto's legendary Walter "Turk" Broda.

of the season's best stories, especially after Ole Bootnose scored three goals in a 5-3 victory over the Bruins on November 2, 1949. It was the first time in his career that Abel managed a hat trick in an NHL game. "It took me 10 years to do it," he laughed, "but it was sure worth the wait."

Only twice in NHL history had players from the same team finished one-two-three in the scoring race. The first unit was Boston's Kraut Line, one of the best lines ever to grace the NHL. The Krauts (Bobby Bauer-Milt Schmidt-Woody Dumart) did it in 1939-40 and Montreal's Punch Line (Maurice Richard-Toe Blake-Elmer Lach) did so in the 1944-45 season.

Paced by The Production Line, Detroit won its second straight Prince Of Wales Trophy, finishing 11 points ahead of runner-up Montreal. Detroit had a record 88 points and scored 229 goals, of which Howe-Lindsay-Abel totaled 92. Most interesting was the fact that Howe's 35 goals topped his linemates. Abel had 34 and Lindsay had 23. What's more, Howe finished only eight goals behind the red light leader, Maurice Richard, who was selected the NHL's First All-Star right wing for the sixth consecutive season.

Howe, who edged Richard in the scoring total by three, was picked right wing for the Second All-Star team. "As great as The Rocket was," said Marty

Pavelich, "the word around the league even then was that it only was a matter of time before Gordie passed him."

What mattered most to Pavelich, Howe, Lindsay and even the stick boy at that point in time was the upcoming playoffs. Jack Adams had not sipped champagne from the Stanley Cup since 1943 and he was getting antsy. He knew his club would face perennial nemesis Toronto in the first round, but he also took solace in his lineup which was better than any he'd had in years.

"If we can keep free of injuries," Adams declared on the eve of the playoff opener, "we can do it this year. We've got the team."

But did they have the ability to deliver in the clutch? Certainly, Toronto proved that it did, finishing fourth the previous year with a below-.500 mark while still reaching their peak in the playoffs. Adams wasn't so sure about the clutch ability of his club.

"We led all the way during the season," he recalled, "so Abel and the two kids were never under what you would

Below: Members of the Red Wings rush Gordie Howe from the ice after a near-fatal collision with the end boards.

call real pressure. But the tougher it is, the better they like it."

It certainly did not look that way on the night of March 28, 1950, at Olympia Stadium. With Turk Broda starring in goal, the Maple Leafs stopped every shot The Production Line and friends hurled at him. But the 5-0 final score was overshadowed by one of the most horrifying episodes ever to blemish the face of big-league hockey.

With Toronto clearly in control and time winding down, Maple Leafs' captain Ted (Teeder) Kennedy carried the puck toward the Detroit blue line. The Toronto center was being pursued by two opponents. Defenseman Black Jack Stewart was coming up from behind Kennedy while Howe cut

across at an angle to head him off at the pass. Peripherally, Kennedy spotted Howe an instant before contact and pulled up quickly enough to avoid his check.

Unable to stop his momentum, Howe plunged headfirst into the boards and lay there, unconscious, blood streaming from his nose and eye. "That he was badly injured was evident," said Toronto journalist Ed Fitkin who wrote a biography of Howe, Lindsay and Abel. "First reports were that he might lose the sight of an eye."

Howe was rushed to the hospital, where it was immediately apparent that his condition was extremely serious. In an era before television had yet taken hold, newspapers were the prime

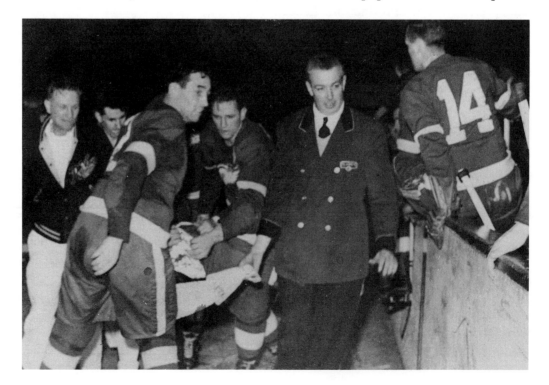

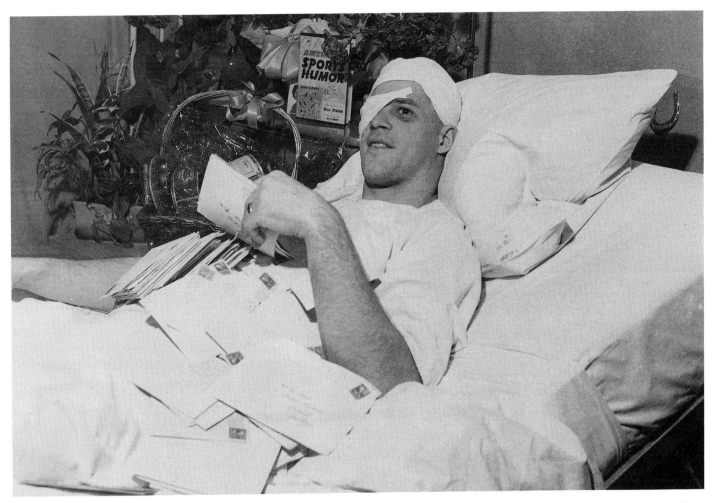

Howe recovers from his near-death experience under a blanket of fan mail.

source of information. In this case the Detroit dailies — the *Times, Free Press* and *News* — rushed "Howe Extras" into the streets. Among the reports were those that stated Howe had suffered a fractured skull, broken nose and cheekbone.

A prominent brain surgeon was summoned and his examination determined that Howe had suffered an injury similar to one that resulted in the death of a boxer not long before. That is, presuming it was an accident and there was

no presuming in Detroit. Making no bones about their position, the Red Wings accused Kennedy of butt-ending Howe as he attempted to elude the Detroiter. This prompted even more charges and counter charges from the Toronto camp.

Meanwhile, Howe's life hung in the balance. His diagnosis included a brain concussion, a fractured nose and cheekbone. Medics already had done surgery to remove fluid causing pressure on the brain. Although his condi-

Dapper coach Tommy Ivan was respected for his insights and his calm. He's standing behind (left to right) Alex Delvecchio, Johnny Wilson and Gordie Howe.

tion was still listed as "serious" some 24 hours after the collision, he was reportedly out of danger and the prognosis was for a recovery.

Nevertheless, Howe's mother and sister were flown to Detroit from Saskatoon because of the gravity of the injury. When the women walked into the hospital room, Howe was taken by surprise.

"Why, Mom," he said, "what are you doing here?"

"Just came down to look after you," she replied. "How are you feeling?"

"I'm fine," said the patient. "Just have a headache, that's all. Don't worry about me. I'm all right."

But Adams wasn't so sure that his team was all right; not without the sharpshooting Howe. En route to the club's playoff base in Toledo, Ohio, Adams was the picture of gloom on the team bus as was everyone else connected with the contenders. At that point

in time there were many rumors suggesting that the injury had ended Howe's career or, at the very least, he never again would be able to reach his former standard of excellence.

"We were a mighty sick bunch all the way to Toledo," coach Tommy Ivan said. "I've never seen any of the boys that low before. There wasn't one of us who thought about going to bed until we found out that Gordie was okay."

Early the next morning word was received in Toledo that the right wing had sufficiently improved to allow the Red Wings to re-focus on Game Two at Olympia. Actually, there was a double-focus. First, coach Tommy Ivan had to figure a way of winning now that his club had lost nine straight playoff games to Toronto. Second, there was a matter of revenge. In the minds of most players was a conviction that Kennedy had played dirty; this despite a probe by NHL president Clarence Campbell which thoroughly exonerated the Leafs' captain.

"I don't play hockey that way," said Kennedy in his defense before Game Two, but the Red Wings were not listening. They targeted the Toronto center at almost every turn and, finally, late in the second period — with Detroit leading 3-1 — a Pier Six brawl erupted involving virtually every player on both teams.

"We were all keyed up anyway over the playoffs," Lindsay remembered, "and the injury to Gordie sort of set off the explosion. We blew our tops, but believe me, when there's so much at stake out there, you sometimes get out of control."

The prime target, of course, was Kennedy who emerged battered but unbowed, although serious injury was just barely averted as sticks were flying amid the fists and uppercuts. When the dust had cleared the Red Wings had a 3-1 win and both teams received an ultimatum from Campbell; play hockey or else!

To compensate for Howe's loss, Ivan gambled on Joe Carveth, one of the heroes of Detroit's last Stanley Cup championship but who was seeing less and less ice in his advanced NHL years. Carveth fitted snugly on the line with Abel and Lindsay, and suddenly the Red Wings were alive, if not well.

The veteran Turk Broda blanked Detroit, 2-0, in Game Three — the first at Maple Leaf Gardens — and held the Wings to a 1-1 tie through regulation time and the first sudden-death period of Game Four. A goal for Toronto would virtually seal the series for the defending champs.

Then, a strange thing happened. Before the second overtime was 40 seconds old, low-scoring Detroit defenseman Leo Reise Jr. took a feed from Lindsay and fired a long shot that fooled Broda; and Detroit had won the match 2-1, tying the series.

Once again Broda shut out Detroit

Few rivalries in professional sports have been as nasty as the one that existed between the Detroit Red Wings and the Toronto Maple Leafs in the late 40s and early 50s! Here Toronto captain "Teeder" Kennedy pulls a profusely bleeding Jimmy Morrison away from certain slaughter at the hands of Tough Tony Leswick (3).

A Ranger attack is thwarted by Red Kelly (leg raised) and other wingers in the 1950 Cup finals.

2-0, which meant that the Wings had to win two straight in order to reach the finals. This time Harry Lumley pulled a Broda and stole a 4-0 game to tie the series at three apiece, setting the stage for a climactic seventh game at Detroit. The first — and winning — goal was delivered by Marty Pavelich who had taken Lindsay's pass and found the hole.

Free of the early series histrionics, Game Seven settled into a scoreless defensive struggle through three periods of regulation hockey. Both Lumley and Broda seemed sharp and remained so until Detroit won a face-off in the enemy end with 8:30 consumed in the first sudden death. The puck wound up on Reise's stick and the defenseman dispatched a drive that beat Broda at 8:34. The Toronto jinx had been broken!

The Red Wings-Rangers Stanley Cup final of 1950 remains one of the strangest on record. For starters, New York was deprived of its Madison Square Garden home ice — pre-empted by a circus. Instead, the Broadway Blueshirts played two "home" games at Maple Leaf Gardens while the remaining five were held at Detroit's Olympia Stadium. Essentially, the New Yorkers lived through 21 consecutive days on the road during the playoffs, yet they gave the Red Wings a tremendous run for the Stanley Cup.

At first the series appeared to the Detroiters to be a breeze compared with the bitter semifinal. Tommy Ivan's stickhandlers gave up a first period goal to Buddy O'Connor and then rebounded with four straight second period scores to put the game away 4-1.

When Doc Couture gave the Wings a 1-0 lead in the second period of Game Two at Maple Leaf Gardens, visions of a four-game sweep swept across the Detroit bench. However, these dreams were destroyed when

New York responded with three consecutive goals and a 3-1 triumph.

Never one to stand pat, Jack Adams immediately summoned five players from Indianapolis — just in case!

A 4-0 Lumley shutout soothed Adams' mind after Game Three at Toronto, particularly since all remaining games would be played at Detroit. Whether the Wings were victims of overconfidence or simply were outplayed remains a moot point to this day, but the fact remains that New York simply took the series away in the next two games.

The combination of Chuck Rayner's goaltending and Don (Bones)

Raleigh's clutch scoring left Olympia spectators gaping in disbelief. Rallying with two third-period goals, the Rangers tied the count at three apiece and won it on Raleigh's sudden-death score at 16:26 of the first overtime.

With the series tied at two games apiece, the Rangers nursed a Dunc Fisher second- period goal through 18 minutes of the third before Lindsay beat Rayner on a passing play from Carveth and Abel. But Raleigh wasted no time icing the game at 1:38 of overtime and,

Above: After failures in the 1948 and 1949 playoffs, Red Wings' goalie Harry Lumley finally helped win a Stanley Cup over the Rangers in the spring of 1950.

Below: Rangers' forward Tony Leswick prepares a backhander against Harry Lumley in the 1950 Cup finals. Leo Reise Jr. is helping out.

Above: Coach Tommy Ivan congratulates defenseman Leo Reise who had earlier scored a sudden-death goal against Toronto in the 1950 semifinal round.

Right: Red Wings' defenseman Clare Martin (left) celebrates victory in the 1950 Stanley Cup finals with goalie Harry Lumley (center) and defensive forward Marty Pavelich.

suddenly, New York was only one game away from the Stanley Cup.

What's more, the confident Manhattanites scored the first two goals of Game Six. However, the Wings were not about to quit. Trailing 3-1 in the second period, they rallied and at 4:13 of the third period Lindsay beat Rayner to make it a 4-4 game.

Then, at 10:34 of the third period Abel broke free and unleashed a shot that Rayner stopped, but the rebound returned to Abel and he lifted the rubber over the fallen goalie to provide Detroit with a 5-4 victory.

So, it all came down to Game Seven, and the script was remarkably the same in the first period. A pair of early New York goals staked the visitors to a 2-0 lead, but

Detroit rebounded in the second, tying the score at 2-2. Undaunted, O'Connor put New York ahead again, but Jimmy McFadden got one for the Winged Wheelers at 15:57 and that's the way the score remained through the end of the third period.

The Stanley Cup would be decided by an overtime goal. By this time, Ivan had warned his players to keep an eye on the elusive Raleigh who already had twice killed his Red Wings. But once the sudden death was underway, Raleigh broke free once more.

Catapulted into the clear with a radar-like pass, Raleigh went one-on-one with Harry Lumley whose moves he had carefully studied. "I had him beaten," said Raleigh, "but the puck went over the top of my stick. It was like hitting a post; it was a sure goal."

Teammate Nick Mickoski, who followed Raleigh on the play, added, "Don had Lumley beat but the puck rolled over the top of his stick."

Saved by the rolling puck, the Red Wings regrouped and held New York at bay through the first overtime. The second overtime lasted through the eight minute mark before Detroit forced a face-off in the Ranger end. Rangers' coach Lynn Patrick considered a line-up change and then decided to go with his skaters on the ice. George Gee had five assists in the

playoffs and was rated one of the shrewdest forwards in the business. He was to get the biggest assist of his life. His left wing was Pete Babando who had one goal in his previous seven playoff games.

Before the puck was dropped, Gee noticed that Babando was not in precisely the position he wanted. He asked the linesman for time and whispered to Babando to move a few inches. To the packed Olympia, it seemed like an idle gesture; that is, until the puck was dropped.

Red Wing heroes, defenseman Bob Goldham (left) and captain-center Sid Abel (right), accompany victorious goalie Harry Lumley off the ice after Detroit defeated the New York Rangers to win the Stanley Cup.

Gee won the face-off cleanly and deposited the puck on Babando's stick. Babando took the puck in stride and fired a 15-foot backhander that Rayner never saw. The puck had eyes, finding its way through a labyrinth of legs and into the net at 8:31 of the second overtime.

Olympia rocked as it never had before. The thunderous ovation remained at its highest decibel count ever as president Clarence Campbell stepped on the ice and presented the Stanley Cup to Abel. Players made a human chair out of their arms and hoisted coach Tommy Ivan aloft while manager Adams doffed his fedora in triumph. Then came the piece de resistance; bandage-swathed Gordie Howe stepped on the ice and the roar was redoubled.

Pandemonium continued in the dressing room where reporters crowded around the jubilant winners. "Boy, it took us a long time to win the Cup," said Lumley, "but it sure was worth it."

Lindsay wrapped his arms around the goalie and added, "You can say that again; what a vacation this is going to be!"

Adams put it as succinctly as possible: "This is one of the great teams."

But Adams wanted to perpetuate the championship and he also knew there was considerable doubt about Howe's ability to return from his potentially career-threatening injury. Abel, despite his excellent playoff, was a concern simply because of his age; which meant there was only one thing to do — make the big trade.

Metro Prystai jams the puck past a sprawling goalie.

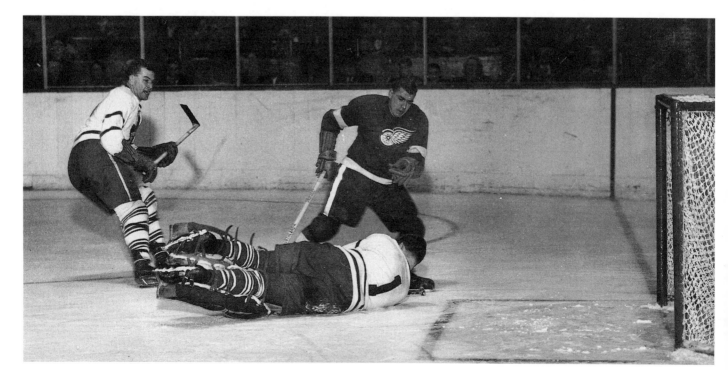

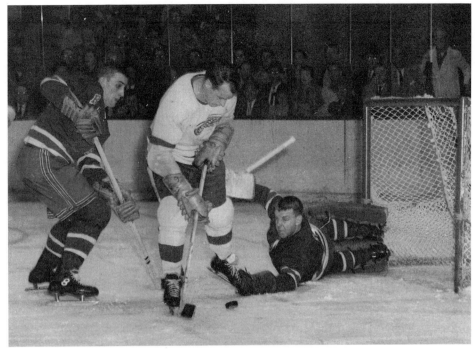

On July 13, 1950, Adams pulled the trigger. He sent Harry Lumley, Black Jack Stewart, Al Dewsbury, Don Morrison and Pete Babando to Chicago for goalie Sugar Jim Henry, defenseman Bob Goldham and forward Gaye Stewart.

By far the biggest gambles involved the departure of Lumley and Stewart each of whom had been a linchpin at his respective position. But Lumley was expendable because of an excellent prospect, Terry Sawchuk, who was buried in the minors and who, some experts believed, was even better than Applecheeks Lumley. Replacing Stewart would not be easy because of his leadership qualities. But he was aging and Goldham had proven a very capable backliner who could fit neatly into the Detroit system.

Metro Prystai was considered the true gem in Adams' eyes. He already had displayed star qualities with Chicago and loomed as heir apparent for Abel's position between Lindsay and Howe.

By the time the 1950-51 season was a month old, it seemed certain that Adams' gambles had paid rich dividends. Sawchuk was sensational in goal — Lumley was having an awful season in Chicago — Goldham had worked out perfectly on defense along with

Red Kelly, Marcel Pronovost, Leo Reise Jr. and Benny Woit, whereas Black Jack Stewart was limited by injury to only 26 games for the Blackhawks. More importantly was the win column; despite a gallant pursuit by the Maple Leafs, Detroit finished with a league-leading 44 wins, three more than second-place Toronto.

The reason? Gordie Howe was back, bigger, stronger, smarter and more menacing than ever.

L'Affaire Kennedy had made an indelible imprint on Howe's psyche and philosophy and it would have a pervasive effect on his game until his retirement.

Although rabid Detroit fans didn't want to hear such talk, Howe unequivocally exonerated Kennedy before returning to Saskatoon for his long recuperation. "Ted isn't the kind of player who would deliberately injure an opponent," said Howe

Having said that, Howe spent the summer playing golf and rounding

Gordie Howe is about to score on the Rangers' Gump Worsley with Lou Fontinato looking helpless.

himself into shape for the comeback year. When training camp opened, he weighed in at close to 195 pounds and seemed quite at ease on the ice, although Jack Adams insisted that he wear a protective helmet at the start.

Always tough, Howe now seemed even tougher and it appeared as if his modus operandi was not to allow any foe to get the better of him. There would be no repeat of the Kennedy episode even though it was an accident. Howe's elbows — like the shovel on a bulldozer — would see to that.

He scored a goal in the fourth annual All-Star game (won by Detroit 7-1, over the All-Stars) and helped Ted Lindsay to a hat trick. Skeptics suggested that he might have become "shy" as a result of his head injury, but there was absolutely no evidence to suggest that this was the case; certainly not on the scoring sheet nor on the ice.

Howe averaged a point a game in his first 15 games and took over the NHL scoring leadership at the 34-game mark. He pulled off two consecutive hat tricks against Chicago within a week and was on his way to a league-leading 43-goal season. He won the Art Ross Trophy and scored a total 86 points.

Runner-up in goals was

Maurice Richard who trailed by one. The Rocket was second in scoring but lagged 20 points behind Howe. Adams, who had feared that he had lost his prodigy in the spring was now claiming that Howe was the game's top player, better even than Rocket Richard. Howe's total of 83 points set a new NHL standard, bettering Herb Cain's old mark by a point. Underlining Howe's newfound greatness was his nomination as a First All-Star right wing, ending Richard's six-year reign.

"Howe is the greatest thing that has appeared in hockey in 25 years," Adams asserted.

This did not sit well with Montreal

Left: The classic form of Terry Sawchuk.

Below: Detroit defenseman Red Kelly is surrounded by Toronto's Howie Meeker (left) and Cal Gardner while goalie Terry Sawchuk's eyes are riveted to the rubber.

Ted Lindsay

Canadiens' coach Dick Irvin who swore by the Rocket. "When Howe scores as many goals as Richard has," said Irvin, "then I'll consider it time to start comparing them."

But Irvin couldn't stop other experts from making comparisons. One of the most controversial was launched by Toronto-based physical culturist Lloyd Percival who operated an outfit called "Sports College." Far ahead of his time, Percival studied athletes in a new and intensely scientific manner and published his findings in a series of "Sports College" bulletins.

After examining Howe and Richard in a number of categories, Percival concluded that Howe clearly was superior in all but one out of 17 categories. "He showed that Howe skated faster, had a better average speed, back-checked more often and showed more speed than Richard while doing so," noted Toronto journalist Ed Fitkin.

Richard came out on top in only one department; he accelerated faster on his skates than Howe. The result caused Dick Irvin to testily conclude, "It's obvious that this is an attempt to rob Richard of the right he deserves as the greatest right wing in hockey today."

There was no disputing Detroit's superiority in just about every other category. Sawchuk, playing every single game, finished with a league-leading 44 wins. His goals against average was 1.99, tops for any netminder who played more than 40 games, and he led the league with 11 shutouts.

Although he was a defenseman, Red Kelly had 17 goals and 37 assists for 54 points in 70 games which placed him among the league's leading scorers! In the regular season, at least, Detroit's defense didn't miss Black Jack Stewart a bit.

Nor was there any loss of toughness. This was amply demonstrated by Lindsay on the night of January 25, 1951, in a game at Olympia against Boston. Terrible Ted's longtime nemesis Wild Bill Ezinicki — now with the Bruins after having been traded from Toronto — clashed with the Detroiter and the result was a vicious brawl. It began with a seemingly harmless pushing bout which escalated into a stick-jabbing row and then a fistfight that twice had to be broken up before cooler heads prevailed.

According to one reporter, "Lindsay landed three hard rights, the last dropping Ezinicki. Lindsay landed on top and shot a couple more punches before noticing that Ezinicki was out cold. He was knocked unconscious when his head struck the ice."

The Bruin required 11 stitches to close a stick cut in his forehead, four stitches to close the wound where his head hit the ice four more stitches inside his mouth where his lips were cut. He also lost a tooth and suffered a broken nose, not to mention two black eyes. Lindsay needed a single stitch to close a stick cut above his eye and required treatment for badly scarred and swollen knuckles on his right hand.

Each player was suspended for the next three games and fined $300 each by president Campbell. Lindsay played a total of 67 games and finished with 59 points (24-35) while Abel topped him by two (69-23-38-61) and remained a force on the Production Line.

The Rocket's icy glare.

If there was a downer about the 1950-51 regular season it was Metro Prystai's inability to play up to Jack Adams' expectations. Prystai was unable to smoothly move between Lindsay and Howe. Prystai played 62 games, collected 37 points (20-17) and proved effective but not in a starring role.

In the eyes of most analysts, the road to the Stanley Cup was virtually cleared of obstacles for the Motor City sextet. Their first-round opponents in the playoffs would be third-place Montreal, a club which finished 36 points behind them. Detroit had beaten the Habs eight times and tied twice out of 14 regular season games.

The series opener at Olympia hardly was a waltz for the Wings. Howe opened the scoring and twice the home squad had the lead, but Montreal came back and it was 2-2 going into the first overtime; 2-2 heading into the second overtime; and still 2-2 going into the third overtime.

Early in the fourth sudden death Richard demonstrated why he still was the clutch scorer of all-time. The Rocket filched a careless Red Wing pass and skirted the defense, giving himself a one-on-one with Sawchuk. His shot was to the corner and unstoppable at 1:09 of the fourth overtime. It was 1:10 a.m.

Game Two of the semifinals was no less exciting. After three scoreless periods the clubs battled through two scoreless overtimes. Just past the two-minute mark of the third overtime, Montreal defenseman Bud MacPherson seized the puck and sent a pass to Billy Reay. Instead of shooting, Reay faked a shot, lured Sawchuk to him and then skimmed a pass to Richard on the right. The Rocket wasted no time and the puck was in at 2:20 after 42:20 of extra play.

Despite the cloudy forecast, the Wings invaded Montreal and found sunshine. They won both games at The Forum and tied the series for Game Five in the Motor City. Montreal had 10 rookies in their lineup and despite Gerry McNeil's outstanding goaltending, the Wings were expected now to move ahead. They obliged by taking a 2-0 lead and gained another advantage when Richard was assessed a five-minute penalty for punching Lindsay to the ice late in the first period. Terrible Ted emerged with a cut cheek and black eye.

But Montreal successfully killed the penalty and then retaliated with three straight goals in the second period and two more in the third. The final score was 5-2 sending everyone in Detroit searching for answers.

"The Rocket threw one punch that flattened Lindsay," explained Dick Irvin, "and that big Detroit team just quit."

The Red Wings' chance for redemption came in Game Six in

Montreal and they failed. Having kept the score close — 2-1 Montreal in the third — Detroit discharged volley after volley at McNeil to no avail. Ivan tried every combination to get the tying goal. Down to the final minutes, the opportunistic Canadiens moved to the attack. Following a sharp McNeil save, Floyd Curry of the Habs broke free and slid a pass to a speeding Ken Mosdell who deposited the winner behind Sawchuk.

Still, the Wings didn't quit. With 45 seconds left in regulation time, Howe scored reducing the margin to one goal. But Detroit never could get that elusive tying counter and the Stanley Cup had to be relinquished after one year in Detroit.

"We just couldn't get the breaks when we needed them," explained Adams. "But no one can take anything away from McNeil. Or from the Canadiens for that matter. They did everything they were supposed to do. But I have to say this is the greatest disappointment of my hockey career."

A house cleaning of sorts was in order although Adams still had the nucleus of a great team. "We've got a lot of good young players coming up," he promised, "and we've got to make room for them."

On August 20, 1951, Adams made another blockbuster deal with Chicago. This time he sent George Gee, Jimmy McFadden, Max McNab, Jimmy Peters, Clare Martin and Rags Raglan

One of Jack Adams' best acquisitions was diminutive Tony Leswick who scored the Stanley Cup winner in 1954. Tough Tony is pursued here by Toronto's Joe Klukay.

Rudy Migay (left) and Eric Nesterenko of Toronto are foiled by Terry Sawchuk. Marcel Pronovost is the Detroiter in the rear.

to the Hawks for Hugh Coflin and $75,000. Coflin had been a promising young defenseman in the Chicago chain and played 31 games for the Blackhawks in 1950-51. Adams was impressed with his youth and promise.

Still to be found was a replacement for Abel who openly stated that he expected the 1951-52 season to be his last as a full-time performer. "I can't go like I used to," he allowed. "The schedule is too long and arduous. It's play tonight, travel and play tomorrow night. It wears me out."

Neither Howe nor Lindsay showed any signs of wear and tear. "Gordie will be the dominating right wing for a long time," Lindsay predicted, "Richard or no Richard."

Maple Leafs' assistant general

manager Hap Day agreed. "They should give two pucks every time that Detroit team plays," chuckled Day. "Give one to the other team and the second one to Howe. He's always got the puck anyway!"

The Abel dilemma would be solved in the manner Adams most enjoyed; through his farm system. Alex Delvecchio, a likeable center from Fort William, Ontario, had played one game for Detroit in 1950-51 and would be given a full opportunity to make the big club in 1951-52. The thinking was that Delvecchio had the right stuff.

Certainly, Terry Sawchuk did. He was so good and so durable that the Red Wings were able to unload Sugar Jim Henry without compunctions.

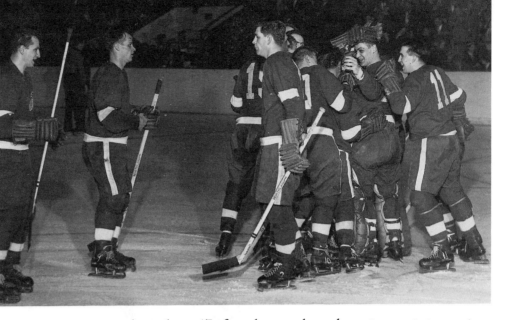

Another promising prospect was Marcel Pronovost, a Red Kelly-like defenseman who played half a season in 1950-51 and was ready for full-time duty.

With everything in place, it was now time for the Detroiters to make good on their vow to regain the Stanley Cup. Tommy Ivan had a few new faces up front — most importantly hard-nosed Vic Stasiuk and Fred (No Kid) Glover as well as Tough Tony Leswick who was obtained from the Rangers in June 1951 for Gaye Stewart. The latter would prove to be Adams' most under-rated move for a long time.

If there was any difference between the 1950-51 and 1951-52 squads it was in the grit department. The departures of Stewart, Gee, McFadden and Peters were more than complemented by Leswick, Stasiuk and Glover. Then again, Sawchuk was a year older, a year wiser and, arguably, the best goaltender in hockey.

Sawchuk dropped his average to 1.90 from 1.99, had 12 shutouts instead of 11 and played every single game as he had a year earlier. Once again, he won 44 games.

Remarkably, Howe again had a league-leading 86 points but upped his goal total to 47, four better than the previous season. If there was a key stat, it was in the area of total points. Virtually from the opening month, Detroit simply ran away from the opposition and remained in first place with a comfortable lead to the very end.

When the 70-game schedule had concluded, the Red Wings had 100 points, 22 more than runner-up Montreal. Of course, long-memoried Motor City fans were only partially gratified by the results. They still were smarting from the 1951 playoff loss and the fact that Toronto went on to win the Stanley Cup; the fourth time in five years! No less ominous was the Leafs' placing in the regular standings. A third-place finish meant that Toronto, the defending champions, would play Detroit in the first round.

If Detroiters had anything to fear about their foe, those concerns were

Congratulations are in order as the Wings skate over all opposition.

Metro Prystai releases a backhander.

Rocket Richard was held without a goal.

In Game Two it was Leswick again setting up the first goal while Lindsay got the winner in a 2-1 decision. Again, Richard was scoreless.

Game Three was no contest. Howe opened the scoring in the first period; Lindsay added one from Howe in the second and Howe closed matters with one more in the final period.

The fourth and final game was academic except for Sawchuk's quest for yet another shutout. And, sure enough, a goal in each period — Prystai, Skov, Prystai — gave Sawchuk the buffer and he repulsed every shot from the enemy.

Detroit had swept the playoffs in an astonishing eight straight games of which Sawchuk had four shutouts and a 0.62 goals against average. Some observers contend that it was the best exhibition of goaltending over eight playoff games that ever had been seen.

Lindsay led all playoff goal-scorers with five goals. Prystai and Howe, with five each, led in assists, and Lindsay was the playoff point leader at seven.

"This club," said Adams, "is the best-balanced Red Wing team I've had in my 25 years in the NHL. I'll let the figures speak for themselves and let any other club in the league try to match them."

Only one man in the hockey world seemed ready to deny the obvious — that this was one of the all-time great teams. An embittered Montreal coach

dispelled after the first two games at Olympia. Sawchuk was invincible, posting a pair of shutouts — 3-0 and 1-0. When the series moved to Toronto, the disparity in talent was even more evident. The Wings toyed with the Maple Leafs in a 6-2 Game Three decision and wiped them out 3-1 in the fourth and final game.

But coming up in the finals was virtually the same Montreal squad that had upset Detroit the previous spring. It was now that Jack Adams' trading genius became most evident. Tony Leswick scored the first two goals — including the game-winner — in a 3-1 decision over Gerry McNeil while

Dick Irvin snapped, "Why should I pretend something I do not feel? No Detroit executive or player congratulated us when we won last year. Let them celebrate their victory if they wish; I don't lose easily."

With Delvecchio now established as a first-rate center and Detroit solid at every other position, a run at a second consecutive Stanley Cup appeared not only in order but very likely in

1952-53. But, as Adams would learn, strange things can happen.

Despite the fact that he had been aging as a performer, Sid Abel still was a balance wheel on the Production Line. Granted, he was no longer the player who won the Hart Memorial Trophy as the league's most valuable player in 1948-49 and led the league with 28

One of the most valuable, yet least publicized Red Wings during their halcyon years of the 1950s was forward Glen Skov shown here lugging the puck out of his zone. Others are (left to right) Red Kelly, Terry Sawchuk, Harry Watson (white-jerseyed Maple Leaf) and captain Ted Lindsay.

goals, but he was important in several areas. One was in the dressing room where he reigned as team leader and another was between Lindsay and Howe with whom he had a special rapport. Abel, more than any center, had the ability to understand Howe.

"It was an instinctive thing," said Abel. "Gordie wasn't a positional player so you had to figure out where you were going to based on where he went. He made it easy for us. He'd just control the puck until one of us was open and he'd give it to us.

"One of my jobs was to get them going. Lindsay was so fiery. I had to get him to relax a little, to calm down and play. Gordie, every once in a while, you'd have to give him a little nudge. If he got riled up, they'd have to throw another puck on the ice for the rest of us to play with because Gordie wasn't going to let us have his puck."

When Abel had been at his peak with the Production Line, they played a razzle-dazzle game unlike anything seen in the NHL. Joe Falls, sports editor of the *Detroit News*, was one who observed the line in its halcyon years:

"They start the game and play shifts of two and three minutes," Falls wrote. "They control the puck, crossing and crisscrossing, until one of them lets a shot go on net. You watch them closely and marvel at their skills; Lindsay, with the perfectly combed hair, running into everyone, stick high, an assassin who looks like an alter boy;

Howe, with those sloping shoulders and thick neck, keeping the puck from everyone, even his teammates, making one amazing move after another; and Abel, the one with the shoulder pads weaving around the ice, taking the puck when it comes to him and looking for an opening to get it closer to the goal."

Starting with the Wings' elimination from the 1951 playoffs, there were questions about how long Abel could sustain the pace and keep up with his younger linemates. But to Lindsay and Howe, No. 12 was indispensable in a lot of ways.

"Sid taught us so much," said Howe. "We used to sit up in the trains for hours after the game, and he'd go over everything. He'd take us through the whole game, pointing out what we did right and what we did wrong. I think that I learned more on the trains than I did on the ice."

In an era when teams traveled exclusively by train, a special camaraderie developed which was especially evident in The Big Three.

"Boot [Abel] would take us into what they called the smoker end of the car," Lindsay recalled. "I guess you'd call it a bathroom these days, but they had only one john and about six sinks. They had benches against three of the walls, and we'd sit there and listen to him.

"He was also terrific with the guys on our days off or over the summer. He'd have Gordie and I over to his

house a couple of times a week for some of his wife's great Italian dinners, and in the summer he and Gloria would organize bowling leagues for all the players and their wives. No one was ever closer than those old Red Wings' teams. We did everything together."

The problem was that Abel was eight years older than Lindsay and 10 years older than Howe. That fact was not lost on Jack Adams even in the euphoria of the 1952 playoff sweep. With Alex Delvecchio ready to take a regular turn at center and with the other top pivots in place, Adams believed that the time was right to re-create the Production Line.

There were several reasons behind his move, more than the fact that Abel was approaching his career's end. At the time, the Norris family, which owned the Red Wings, also had a partial ownership interest in the Blackhawks. Perennial cellar-dwellers, the Hawks had fired Ebbie Goodfellow as coach after the 1951-52 season and was shopping for a replacement.

Adams solved their problem by selling Abel outright to Chicago on July 29, 1952. Abel would become the club's playing coach and finish his career in the Windy City.

Precisely how traumatic the loss of Abel was to the Red Wings' psyche

Bob Goldham (2) came from Toronto to Detroit and blossomed into a premier puck-blocking defenseman.

will never be known except for the arithmetic. Instead of finishing the regular season with 100 points as they had the previous season, Detroit only led the league with 90 points, still a full 15 more than runner-up Montreal.

Point-wise, neither Howe nor Lindsay were affected. Actually, Howe's 49 goals were just one short of Rocket Richard's record 50 in a season. Howe finished first in overall scoring with 95 points followed by Lindsay with 71. Sawchuk won another Vezina Trophy with a 1.90 goals against average, exactly the same as the previous year.

"We were in great shape for another run at the Cup," said Marty Pavelich. "Even though we had lost Sid, our centers were fine — Alex Delvecchio, Metro Prystai and Glen Skov."

Boston, which had finished under .500 and 21 points behind Detroit, would be the opening round foe. Coached by Lynn Patrick, who had taken the underdog Rangers to a seventh game final round against Detroit in 1950, the Bruins were without a superstar. Nevertheless, Boston boasted some elements of a threat. Goalie Sugar Jim Henry was a capable veteran and Boston forwards Ed Sandford, Fleming MacKell and John Peirson formed a solid front line.

None of this, however, was apparent when the series opened at Olympia on March 24, 1953. To the delight of the home throng, the Red Wings

poured seven shots past Jim Henry. Terry Sawchuk, looking very much like the four-shutout master of 1952, allowed nary a goal.

In a sense the rout was the worst thing that could have happened to Detroit because it raised the threat of overconfidence. Sure enough, in Game Two, the Bruins beat them 5-3 and Detroit suddenly was set back on its collective heels.

Sawchuk suddenly became eminently beatable and Howe virtually stoppable. Perhaps if Abel had been there to calm the shaky nerves and reinvigorate Howe, it might have been a different scenario. But Ole' Bootnose was not only steering Chicago into the playoffs but looking strong when he pressed himself into service at center.

Game Three at the Boston Garden would prove to be the most decisive of the series. With the teams tied at one game apiece, there was ample time for the Red Wings to regroup. However, Boston imposed a strategy that included containing Howe and nullifying Lindsay. Lynn Patrick assigned an old war horse left wing named Woody Dumart to guard Howe. Dumart performed his task with impeccable zeal. On top of that, Howe was playing with a debilitating injury that further cramped his style.

After regulation time in Game Three, the teams were tied 1-1. Play swung back and forth for more than a dozen minutes before Jack McIntyre,

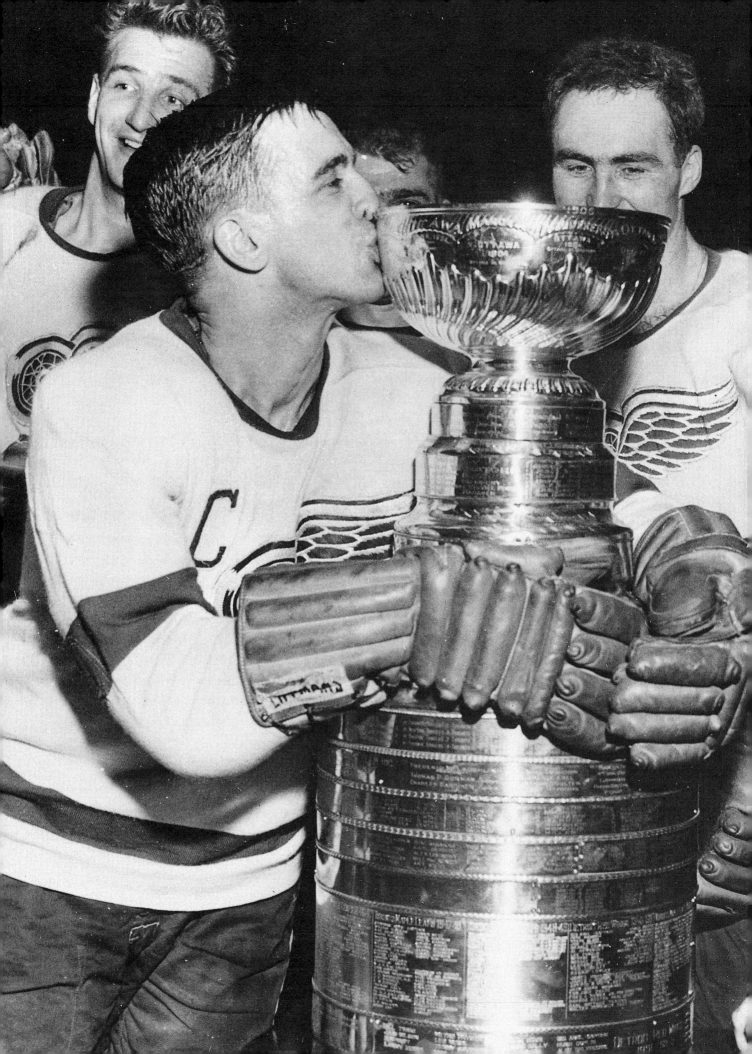

On St. Patrick's Day (March 17, 1955), a riot broke out at Montreal's Forum after a fan tossed a tear-gas bomb at ice level. The episode occurred shortly after NHL president Clarence Campbell announced the suspension of Maurice "Rocket" Richard for the remaining games of the season and the playoffs for belting linesman Cliff Thompson. The Rocket was leading the league in scoring at the time but lost the title to teammate Bernie (Boom Boom) Geoffrion.

who scored only seven goals all season, beat Sawchuk at 12:29. When the Bruins followed that with a 6-2 spanking of the defending champs, the Motor City was in panic. A 6-4 Red Wing victory in Game Five hardly was reassuring. Sawchuk, it seemed, had lost his touch and his teammates could not adequately compensate. When the Bruins put Detroit away 4-2 in the sixth game, it was almost with a sense of relief throughout Michigan that the series was over.

"Upsets happen," said Larry Zeidel, a defenseman on the 1952-53 Red Wings, who was traded to Chicago the following summer. "But there was no reason for Jack Adams to break up the club; not with the talent he had."

The boss hardly disturbed the line-up. He had a very promising center in the minors who was ready for the bigs. Earl (Dutch) Reibel was promoted along with right wing Bill Dineen. Each would make a significant contribution. In addition, Bob Goldham, who had come to Detroit in 1950, had evolved into one of the NHL's finest puck-blocking backliners.

Adam's confidence in his club — as well as coach Tommy Ivan — was well rewarded. Detroit won its sixth straight regular season title, tying them with the dynastic New York Yankees, and all hands seemed to be playing to their potential.

Reibel, almost overnight, emerged as a top-line NHL center who could play between Lindsay and Howe if Delvecchio was required for other duties. Howe led the league in assists and points while Lindsay was third on the point parade. Sawchuk's 35 wins was a league high.

If there was any disturbing footnote it was the margin of victory. Second place Montreal was seven points behind and was a distinct threat to Detroit. Future Hall of Famers such as Bernie Geoffrion, Dickie Moore, Jacques Plante and Tom Johnson were coming into their own along with standbys like Rocket Richard and Doug Harvey. When Montreal routed Boston four games to none in the opening playoff round, the Habs stock climbed even higher.

Having disposed of Toronto in five playoff games, the Red Wings were ready for the Montreal challenge. The teams split the first two contests at Olympia whereupon the Wings took the next two at The Forum. At this point Canadiens coach Dick Irvin dropped his starting goalie, Jacques Plante, and replaced him with Gerry McNeil. With 1-0 and 4-1 wins, McNeil had tied the series at three. The finale at Olympia was a classic. Floyd Curry beat Sawchuk in the first period and Red Kelly evened the count in the second. Nobody scored in the third period and the Red Wings found themselves playing for the Stanley Cup in the ultimate sudden death, as they had in 1950.

This time Detroit's hero was as unlikely as Pete Babando had been four years earlier. Tough Tony Leswick had come to the Red Wings in 1951 as a defensive forward who was assigned such dubious tasks as checking Rocket

Richard and other threatening scorers. But on the night of April 16, 1954, Tough Tony would momentarily grab the spotlight from Howe, Lindsay and Kelly.

Shortly after the four minute mark, Leswick took a pass from linemate Glen Skov and fired what amounted to a pop fly at Gerry McNeil. It would have been a routine save for the Montreal goalie except that defenseman Doug Harvey was in the way. An expert baseball player, Harvey thrust his glove in the air to bat the puck out of danger but only nicked a

piece of it. He did manage to alter its trajectory enough to send the rubber over the astonished McNeil and into the net at 4:29 of overtime. Detroit had regained the championship.

Nobody was more thrilled than Jack Adams. He had survived the death of his benefactor, James Norris Sr., who died in 1952 — replaced by Norris' daughter Marguerite Ann — and the departure of Abel. And Howe had remained the NHL's premier scorer despite Richard's threats.

"I'm a strong admirer of Richard," said Adams, "but for pure versatility, high purpose and team contribution, my guy is the greatest."

There was, however, one disturbing post-playoff note; Tommy Ivan, who had so successfully coached Detroit, accepted a management position with

the Blackhawks. Adams selected a Junior hockey coach, Jimmy Skinner, as Ivan's successor. In addition the manager added hard-nosed Marcel Bonin on the left wing and prepared Glenn Hall as a back-up for Sawchuk, should the latter tire in goal.

Otherwise the Wings were primed for another Stanley Cup. "There was a sign on the locker-room door," stated Johnny Wilson, "and it said, 'We supply everything but guts.'"

Courage was a surplus item in the Olympia room. Between Howe, Lindsay, Kelly and Goldham, the Red Wings had more of the right stuff than most other clubs put together. Then there were the checkers.

"Our checkers [Marty Pavelich, Tony Leswick, Glen Skov] weren't worried as much about scoring as players today," said Jimmy Skinner. "They would come back to our bench after a shift and say, 'Ha, those bastards didn't score on us this time.'"

By the 1953-54 season, when Johnny Bower was playing goal for the Rangers, Howe had already become a veritable legend in his own time. One night, Bower stopped a Detroit shot and Howe fell on top of him. Another Detroiter snared the rebound and shot again, but the puck bounced off Howe and rolled to the corner. While extricating himself from the goalie — an off-season fishing pal — Howe blurted, "You owe me one, John — I just made a leg save for you."

Howe had become the master stickhandler and sometimes seemed to have an invisible string that ran from his stickblade to the puck. A teammate once commented, "I don't mind this great stickhandling of yours, but why stickhandle around the same player three times?"

Ever since his near career-threatening injury, Howe never allowed any foe to take advantage of him without retaliation. Eddie Kullman, a nasty Rangers' forward, had a habit of spiking Howe in the back of his legs with his stick until Howe was bleeding. Finally, Howe warned him against doing it again, but Kullman only laughed.

"We went down the ice," said Howe, "and I flipped the puck over to Ted Lindsay. He was going in on the net all alone. Everybody's eyes were on him. Suddenly, I saw Kullman beside me and I turned around and I nailed him with my gloved hand. I broke his cheekbone. I was just keeping my promise."

Meanwhile, rapidly improving Montreal had become a powerhouse by the 1954-55 season. Rocket Richard was hellbent for his first scoring championship and Bernie Geoffrion became the originator of the first practical slapshot. Yet, Detroit continued on a first-place pace for most of the campaign.

"What really pulled us together is just that we wanted to win it so much," said Red Kelly. "In those days, if you scored three goals you could win 90 percent of your games."

After winning six straight Prince of Wales Trophies, Detroit earned the enmity — or call it jealousy — of non-Detroit fans. At one point during the 1954-55 season both Lindsay and Howe received threatening messages that they would be shot if they stepped on Maple Leaf Garden ice. Terrible Ted responded by gliding out onto the rink and pointing his stick, rifle fashion, toward the upper reaches of the arena as if to flush out the sniper.

On another occasion at The Forum, where NHL president Clarence Campbell frequented games, Vic Stasiuk of Detroit was berating the officials in purple language. Overhearing the diatribe, Campbell walked to the bench and demanded that Skinner calm his players. Instead the coach demanded that the president leave his bench area. A day later, Jack Adams congratulated Skinner.

"We used that stuff to our advantage," said Skinner. "I'd tell the guys, 'See, they don't want us to win.' Dick Irvin, who was coaching the Canadiens at the time, would tell the media that we were a bunch of half-assed players. That clipping would always find its way to our dressing-room board."

Entering the homestretch of the 1954-55 season, Montreal had opened up a substantial lead over Detroit in the run for first place. But with 10 games remaining, the Red Wings made up 10 games in the standings.

"Detroit's strength was that they

were so hard to score on," said Scott Bowman who would later coach the Red Wings in the 1990s. "Their offense was good enough, but they played in a lot of low-scoring games. It usually came down to Sawchuk. He was just unbelievable. Howe was the best all-around player, but The Rocket was a great goal-scorer, a more electrifying player. Howe was much more versatile."

Howe also could contain his temper, which, defiantly, was not the Rocket's forte and that, more than anything, would play a key part in the 1954-55 season's evolution.

During a game at Boston Garden with only a week remaining in the season, Richard slugged linesman Cliff Thompson and was suspended by Campbell for all the remaining games and the entire playoff run. It was a stunning decision which enraged not only Montrealers but the entire French-speaking province of Quebec. Richard was leading the league in scoring and the Habs still nursed a slim lead over Detroit for first place when the Red Wings came to The Forum for a match on March 17, 1955.

Well before the contest angry crowds circled The Forum and by game time it was apparent that the crowd might easily be ignited by an incident.

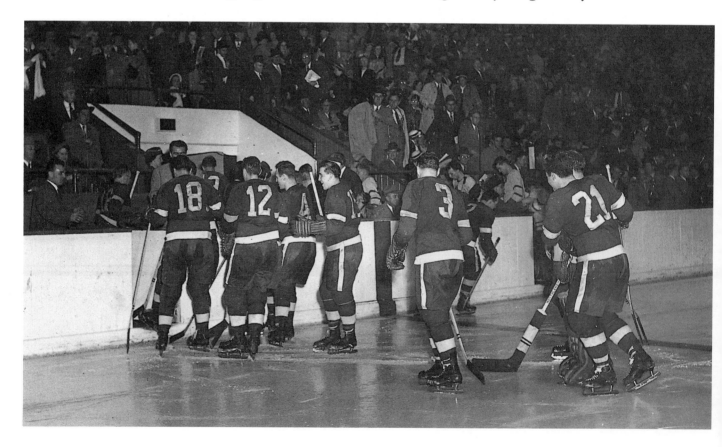

When the hated Campbell appeared midway in the first period, fans began to hoot him. One spectator ran up to the president and attempted to attack him. Soon a tear-gas bomb went off near rinkside, sending thousands of fans to the exit for relief.

The Red Wings, who were leading the game at the time, won the match on a forfeit while Jack Adams' skaters escaped the building without injury. On St. Catherine Street outside The Forum, a full-scale riot had erupted that ran well into the morning.

"After that incident," Marty Pavelich recalled, "we were able to take first place and hold on to it through the weekend when the season ended. It was the seventh straight time that we had finished in first place."

Riding the crest of their strong homestretch run, the Wings routed Toronto in four straight semifinal games while Montreal ousted Boston in five games. The stage was set for the grudge final in which Detroit opened with two wins at home. The Richard-less Canadiens rebounded for a pair of triumphs of their own as the series see-sawed down to a seventh game in Olympia.

Neither team scored in the first period, but at 7:12 of the second Alex Delvecchio beat Plante, followed by Howe and then Delvecchio again. A Canadiens' goal by Floyd Curry late in the match was academic; Detroit had successfully defended its Stanley Cup.

That meant four championships in six years.

Howe led all playoff scorers while Lindsay and Delvecchio were runners-up, respectively. Sawchuk finished with a respectable 2.36 goals against average and the defense remained intact. All the signs pointed to a third straight Cup in 1956.

But the third straight Stanley Cup was not in Detroit's cards and there were many reasons. In particular Red Wing veterans such as Johnny Wilson and Ted Lindsay grew to intensely dislike their manager, who had begun making questionable moves.

"Adams was a lousy hockey man," Lindsay told David Shoalts of the *Toronto Globe and Mail* during the 1995 playoffs. "He traded nine players from the 1955 team. I'm still mad at Adams because he cheated me out of five minimum and possibly seven or eight Stanley Cups."

If nothing else, Adams refused to stand pat. He had gifted young goalie Glenn Hall in the wings and knew that he was ready for the NHL; just as Terry Sawchuk had been when Harry Lumley ruled the crease. Once again, Adams dealt his first-string goalie in a huge exchange with Boston.

On June 3, 1955, Adams packaged Sawchuk, Vic Stasiuk, Marcel Bonin and Lorne Davis for Ed Sandford, Real Chevrefils, Norm Corcoran, Gilles Boisvert and Warren Godfrey. Then, there was the deal that Adams did not make; and one observer argued that Adams should have made that deal before any others.

Montreal's managing director Frank Selke Sr. was willing to trade defenseman Doug Harvey even up for Sawchuk, but Adams nixed the exchange. "If we had Harvey," said Lindsay, "we would have seven or eight Cups. Adams didn't want to make the deal because he didn't want to make Montreal stronger. Geez, they won the next five Cups, so how much stronger could you have made them?"

Wilson observed, "The players we got back in the trade were of equal ability, but Adams stripped away so many of the regulars that the chemistry that we had in winning the Cups was no longer there."

Adams had guaranteed Lindsay and Howe jobs in Detroit as long as they could lace on skates, but Lindsay began to grate his boss. "When Ted came to us he was a fine boy," said Adams. "But as he got older, it became a question of whether he was going to run the club or I was."

Lindsay remained with the Wings when the 1955-56 season began and the addition of Hall looked like a good one as he played 70 games and posted a 2.11 goals against average. But Skinner, who first came to Detroit from the Junior Hamilton Cubs, simply was not a Tommy Ivan behind the bench.

While Tommy Ivan was a strong enough personality to act as a buffer, cushioning Adams' wrath from the players, Skinner was less forceful. As a result, the manager was much more evident — and annoying.

"Skinner came in and there was Jack, sitting right behind the bench," said Kelly. "Jimmy would be trying to coach and Jack would be hollering at him. He'd turn around and respond and lose his concentration on the game."

Lindsay remarked, "Skinner was a door-opener, a yes-man for Adams. We changed the lines, we changed the penalty-killing and we changed the power play."

Yet, Skinner did orchestrate a stirring first-place finish in 1954-55 and also ably took his team to the Stanley Cup; no small accomplishment. What's more, he inherited a nucleus of players who were partial to Ivan and inevitably cool to a newcomer.

In an interview with Shoalts of the *Globe and Mail*, Skinner offered his view: "You always had players who bitched a little bit. They're never satisfied. When you are coaching, you have to handle that stuff. But with Jack Adams there was discipline and the players respected that."

They also respected their traded teammates. They were upset that the status quo was disturbed. "We had a great team, a great organization," said Wilson, "and we should have lasted a lot longer. I agree with Ted Lindsay.

We were so powerful we would have won the Stanley Cup for another five, six straight years beyond 1955.

"It wasn't only the Wings' varsity. We had farm teams on every level, the Windsor Spitfires, Omaha and Indianapolis all winning their league titles year after year. Things were so competitive that you would win the Stanley Cup one year and the next you were fighting for a job."

Wilson was traded to Chicago in June 1955 along with Tony Leswick, Glen Skov and Benny Woit for Dave Creighton, Gord Hollingworth, Jerry Toppazzini and John McCormack. "We could have gone on winning," complained Lindsay, "if Adams had let that team play on rather than breaking it apart."

There was no disputing the results; Detroit's seven-year run on first place abruptly ended in 1955-56. Montreal finished 24 points ahead of the defending Cup champions and, appropriately, met them in the finals.

It was no contest.

Apart from a third game win (3-1) at Olympia, the defending champions were knocked out of the box in five games. Jacques Plante snagged a 3-0 shutout in Game Four and had another 3-0 lead until Delvecchio scored in the third period of Game Five. The final score was 3-1, officially ending the Red Wings' reign; but only on one level.

Despite all the crabbing, there remained a solid group of players still dedicated to winning, and Howe was better than ever. "When Gordie was on the ice," said Wilson, "it was like Detroit had an extra player."

Howe played all 70 games in 1956-57. He led the league in scoring and goals while Lindsay paced the NHL in assists. Norm Ullman, a product of Adams' vast farm system, provided excellent center-ice power along with Delvecchio and Reibel. Kelly and Pronovost remained first-rate defenders and Hall was getting better in goal with a league-leading 38 victories. Better still, Detroit convincingly edged out Montreal for first place by eight points, despite the Habs loaded lineup.

But the playoffs were an utter disaster and painfully reminiscent of 1953. The third-place Bruins, who had finished eight points behind Detroit, dropped the Wings 3-1 in the opener at Olympia. It was déjà vu. The Wings managed a 7-2 victory in Game Two but then it was all Boston — 4-3, 2-0 and 4-3. The five-game ouster was shocking to Motor City followers, not to mention Adams, who was angry about a lot of things.

He believed that Glenn Hall had let him down and dispatched him to Chicago. He also was furious with Lindsay who was a major instigator of failed league-wide movement to establish a players' union. Adams soon forced the Red Wings to publicly disavow any connection with the union and then traded Lindsay to Chicago for Johnny Wilson, Forbes Kennedy, William Preston and Hank Bassen. He reclaimed Sawchuk from Boston for John Bucyk, thereby filling the goaltending gap.

If ever there were moves that proved to be the coup de grâce; these were the trades that led to the dynasty's demise. Detroit finished third in 1957-58 and were knocked out of the semifinals in four games by the Habs. A year later Adams' failure was utterly confirmed. The Red Wings finished last.

Throughout the whole mess, there remained one powerful, positive force — Gordie Howe. He was Mister Red Wing and it is important to place his value to the franchise in its proper perspective.

The Gordie Howe Effect

His given name is Gordon Howe and he was born March 31, 1928, in Floral, Saskatchewan, a town on the outskirts of Saskatoon, in the heart of Canada's wheat belt. Gordie Howe was the fourth of nine children and when he was three months old the Howe family moved from a farm in Floral to a two-story clapboard house on Avenue L North in Saskatoon. Today, Saskatoon has a population of approximately 200,000. When Gordie Howe was growing up there, the population was about one-fourth of what it is now. It has always been a friendly city and a quiet city. And, of course, it has always been a hockey city.

"I believe Gordie got his first pair of skates when he was about six," his mother, Catherine recalled. "A lady came to the door with a bag of clothes she was selling for 50 cents. I bought them, and Gordie jumped into the bag right away. He pulled out a pair of skates. They were much too big for him, but I remember he got four or five pairs of wool socks and got the skates on that way. From then on it seemed he was always wrapped up in hockey somehow. If he wasn't playing, he was collecting syrup labels so he could get hockey cards. He got hundreds of them.

Howe's father, Albert, remembered Gordie as a "big...awkward kid...always so much bigger than the others...and always very shy." And Catherine Howe added: "Yes, he was always clumsy as a boy. And he was a quiet boy. The kids, because he was so big and clumsy, used to call him 'doughhead.' Oh, how that used to make me angry. You know it means stupid, or someone who doesn't know anything. It used to bother him, but he'd never fight with the kids because he always seemed so conscious he was so much bigger than they were."

Howe's formal education ended after eight years of elementary school. "He failed two times in the third grade," his mother Catherine recalled with the clarity of a parent who remembered her son's setbacks as well as his triumphs. "He wasn't bad in school. He always tried. But the second time he failed, it took the heart right out of him. I remember seeing him coming down the street crying.

"I said, 'Sit down, Gordie, tell me what's wrong. Is the work too difficult? Don't you understand the teacher? Do you ask her questions about what you don't understand?' He said, 'No, ma, I don't want to bother her.' And then we both had a good, long cry."

For Gordie Howe, then, perhaps hockey was a way to escape the cruelties and harsh realities of life. Or perhaps he was just born to hockey greatness. At any rate, from the time he got hold of his first pair of skates, hockey became Gordie Howe's way of life.

He got his first hockey stick from Ab Welsh, who had been a forward on the old Saskatoon Quakers minor

league team. "I was nine years old when I got that first stick," Howe once said. "He never gave one to the other kids. He saved his broken sticks or the ones whose lie he didn't like for me. He used a No. 7 lie. That's probably why I used a No. 7 lie. I watched him and I studied his style. He was strictly a position player. I never heard an unkind word said about him."

Once he had a stick in his hands, Howe never let go.

"Any time of the year, any time of the day, you'd see him with a stick in his hands," Gordie's father recalled. "He'd walk along, swatting at clumps of dirt or stones. Once, one summer, I came home from work, and there's Gordie firing pucks at a barrel that was up against the side of the house. Shingles were all over the ground. I had to put my foot down on that."

His father Albert also remembered that Gordie was turned down the first time he tried to join one of Saskatoon's Midget teams. "And I told him never to take dirt from nobody. Because if you do, they'll keep throwing it on you."

Well, perhaps Howe took some dirt along the way to hockey greatness. But if so, it never robbed him of his determination to succeed. Mrs. Bert Hodges, who managed Howe when he was a member of the King George Athletic Club's Midget team, said of him: "Gordie Howe was always out there after dark. He knew what he

wanted and he got it. It could be the coldest night of the year, and Gordie would be out there practicing by himself."

He started out as a goalie, probably because he was deemed too big and awkward to skate as a forward or a defenseman. Playing between the pipes held no great attraction for Howe. Years later, he was to say: "I was a goalie for a couple of seasons as a kid and that was enough." Then, smiling, he added: "When I was playing in the National Hockey League there was a game against the Toronto Maple Leafs in which I made a heck of a save on Frank Mahovlich. It was the year he scored 36 goals [1962-63] and we were trailing by a goal so we pulled Roger Crozier [the Detroit goalie] in the final minute. Mahovlich got loose and I got back in the net just in time to catch his shot on my elbow. I'm still bragging about the save. But I told Crozier he didn't have to worry. I sure don't want his job."

Howe believed that his days as a kid goaltender — holding his stick with one hand — was one of the reasons he could switch hands and shoot from either side. He also remembered kicking out shots with "shin pads" that consisted of magazines and mail-order catalogues stuck in his socks. And he recalled vividly the icy winters in Saskatoon.

"I guess the coldest would be 50 degrees below zero. A lot of times it

Gordie Howe and retired star, turned broadcaster Syl Apps.

would be 25 degrees below. When I played goalie, I remember I used to skate a mile from my house to the rink, holding the pads up in front of me to cut the wind. At one rink they had a heated shack and a guy would ring a cowbell and the forward lines and defense for both teams would go off and sit in the shack by the potbellied stove and warm up while the alternates played."

Howe was a goalie for two years. Then, at the age of 11, he was shifted to right wing. Meanwhile, he kept growing. In the summers, Gordie worked for a construction company, lugging 85-pound bags of cement. He also worked on farms around Saskatoon, putting in 12-hour days, eating five big meals daily. At age 15, Howe weighed 200 pounds and was heavily muscled. Despite his bulk, he was no longer awkward — at least not while playing hockey. On the ice he was quick, graceful and assured. And so it was no surprise to the hockey buffs of Saskatoon when Fred McCorry, a

scout for the Rangers, chose Gordie for the Rangers' training camp at Winnipeg the summer that Howe was 15.

He arrived in the Rangers' camp carrying a small bag that contained a shirt, a set of underwear, a toothbrush and his skates. For a young man with an outgoing personality, a sudden introduction to the National Hockey League at the tender age of 15 would have been a frightening experience. But to a shy, introverted teenager such as Gordie Howe was at the time, the experience was close to shattering.

At the training table, for example, an older "pro" kept taking Gordie's plate. He was near the point of starvation when another veteran pro, forward Alf Pike, noticed what was going on. "Hey," he called to the plate swiper, "drop that and let the kid eat." Pike later became coach of the Rangers but eventually was fired because of his easy-going nature.

There were other embarrassments for Howe in the Rangers' camp as well. For one, he did not know how to put on his equipment.

"I just dropped the gear on the floor in front of me and watched the others," Gordie remembered. "I found out pretty early that the best way to learn was to keep my mouth shut and my eyes open."

But the others noticed Howe's equipment problem and teased him about it. Howe stuck it out, however, until his roommate was injured and sent home. Lonely and homesick himself, Howe fled back to Saskatoon a few days later.

That winter, a scout for the Red Wings, Fred Pinckney, spotted Howe. The following summer Gordie was introduced to the Detroit training camp at Windsor, Ontario. The Detroit boss at the time was Jack Adams, alias "Jolly Jawn," a tough hombre, as we've seen already, who could melt steel with a searing monologue but who had an unfailing eye for hockey talent.

"There was this day in Windsor and it was the first day I ever saw him,"

Adams said. "He was a big, rangy youngster who skated so easily and always seemed so perfectly balanced. It tickled me to watch him. So I called him over to the boards and said, 'What's your name, son?' A lot of kids that age choke up when they start talking to you. But he just looked me in the eye and said real easy like, 'My name's Howe.' I then remember saying, 'If you practice hard enough and try hard enough, maybe you'll make good someday.'"

Detroit signed Howe to a contract that called for a $4,000 bonus. About an hour or so after the signing Adams

found Howe standing in the hallway outside his office. He looked heartsick. "What's the matter?" Adams asked. "Well," Gordie replied, "you once promised me a Red Wing jacket when I signed, but I don't have it yet."

Howe got his jacket.

But then he ran into another problem, this one more serious. The Red Wings had assigned Howe to their Junior A amateur farm team in Galt, Ontario. Because Howe was from a western city, and because Galt was in the eastern part of Canada, his transfer to the Galt club was ruled illegal. And so, for his first year in organized hock-

ey, Howe was allowed on ice only for practice sessions and exhibition games.

Under those circumstances, Gordie's shyness again came to the surface and for a time it appeared that Detroit would lose its bright young prospect, just as the Rangers had. The Red Wings, however, acted where the Rangers had not. They enrolled Gordie in the Galt Collegiate Institute and Vocational School. Never much of a student, Gordie dropped out after a couple of classes. But at least the Wings had tried to help, and for that he was grateful.

The next year, which was 1945,

Howe was assigned by Detroit to its Omaha team in the U.S. Hockey League. Almost immediately, Gordie made it big, scoring 22 goals and adding 26 assists for the season. Ott Heller, who had played and starred with the Rangers before dropping down to the USHL, said of his first encounter with Howe: "I got the kid in the corner, but I didn't have him there for long. I thought I had a bag full of wildcats."

Within a few weeks of Howe's debut with Omaha, fans were lined up outside the dressing-room door, waiting for his autograph. Sometimes he went through what was for him the ordeal of meeting the fans face-to-face and affixing his signature to the pieces of paper which they held before him like so many offerings. Other times he just couldn't go through with it. On those occasions he would flee through the dressing-room window. Gordie remembered his fast exits. He also recalled Omaha's first road swing.

"We were in Minneapolis, and at about 4:30 I went downstairs in the hotel to eat. Some of the guys were already eating there, but I looked at that dining room and it looked so big and nice that I didn't want to go in. I went around the corner to a drugstore and had a milkshake." Then he smiled and added: "I got two goals on that milkshake and we beat them 3 to 1."

To help Gordie conquer his shyness, Red Wing officials assigned him a cocky and aggressive roommate named Ted Lindsay. Howe and Lindsay hit it off immediately. In years to come, they, along with Sid Abel, would form one of the most feared and productive lines in the history of the National Hockey League.

Often, the three of them would make it look terribly easy. But, of course, it was not. In their early years with Detroit, for example, Howe and Lindsay often practiced together when the regular workout was over. In the course of one of those extracurricular sessions, they discovered that the puck would bounce out in front of the goal if shot into the other team's corner at a certain angle. Naturally, they told Abel about the discovery, but it was essentially their play and the two of them worked on it for hours until it was perfected. The first time Howe and Lindsay used the play during a game it resulted in a goal. For the next two seasons, Lindsay scored on perhaps two dozen breakaways by skating straight at the goal while Howe shot the puck into that special corner. After two seasons, the other teams in the league figured out what Howe and Lindsay were doing. The Lindsay "breakaways" became less frequent, and eventually the other clubs copied the Howe-Lindsay specialty. Now, the play is a standard for NHL teams.

Lindsay ranked for years as one of the highest goal scorers in NHL history. An articulate, candid fellow, Lindsay helped Howe get over at least

some of his initial shyness. Gordie himself acquired a great deal of polish over the years.

"It took a while for the shyness to wear off," he admitted. "I think what helped was the way I improved on ice. As I became sure of myself as a player I felt better with the fans. I think the turning point came about 1954. Some of the other players and myself did public relations work for a brewery. I had to go out and meet people. After the first few times I got more at ease. Soon I realized that I had an obligation to the fans."

Once Howe opened up, he ducked no one. Not only would he stand around, sign autographs and banter with the fans, but he went so far as to say: "The only thing that bothers me now is when somebody won't come up to me. They'll stand sorta far away and say, 'Look, there goes the big shot.' Heck, I'm no big shot."

When Gordie Howe joined the Red Wings for the 1946-47 season, having been promoted from Omaha, the dominant teams in the National Hockey League were the Montreal Canadiens and the Toronto Maple Leafs. The dominant player was Montreal's "Rocket" Richard. The 1940s, in fact, were the "Richard Era," just as the 1950s were the "Howe Era." Richard, incidentally, wore No. 9 on his jersey. Except for his first season with the Wings, Howe also wore No. 9. During that first season with Detroit,

Howe wore No. 17, but he grabbed No. 9 when it became available because in those days hockey teams traveled by train and lower berths were assigned to the players with low numbers. Bobby Hull also wore No. 9 on his jersey, although he sported No. 16 during his first six seasons with the Chicago Blackhawks. There was undoubtedly more than coincidence involved in Hull's switch of numbers.

At any rate, Hull is on record as having called Howe the greatest of all hockey players, and he added, "I always looked up to Gordie as one I'd like to

be half as good as." Howe, of course, has always had a great deal of respect for Hull's talents, although he once pointed out: "Hull showed too much admiration for the established stars when he first came up. He shied away from hitting them, not because he was afraid, but because of respect."

That was not one of Howe's shortcomings. On Detroit's first road trip during his rookie season, Howe collided with Richard during a game at the Montreal Forum. Richard took a swing. Howe ducked, then swung at Richard and caught him flush on the jaw. The Rocket toppled to the ice but arose within a few seconds, more embarrassed than hurt. But as he got up, Richard heard Abel shout at him, "That'll teach you not to fool with our rookies, you phony Frenchman." Richard promptly skated over to Abel, threw a punch and broke Abel's nose in three places.

It would be nice — but inaccurate — to say that Howe achieved instant stardom. He did not. True, Howe did score a goal in his first NHL game, beating Turk Broda of the Maple Leafs. The date was October 16, 1946. "The puck was lying loose 10 feet from the net," Howe said of his first goal. "I just slapped it in." He retrieved the puck, took it home and gave it to his family. "But I have no idea what happened to it," Howe related. "The trouble with those things is that they lose their importance." But he notched only six more goals that season and added 15 assists for a total of 22 points.

And yet, even as an unseasoned rookie of 18, Howe betrayed flashes of brilliance that marked him for future greatness. There was, for example, the game against Boston in which Howe outfoxed the veteran, All-Star defenseman Dit Clapper, whose NHL longevity record was later broken by Howe. As Clapper went to check him, Howe changed hands on his stick and, with his body between Clapper and the puck, got off a clean shot on net. "I think," Ted Lindsay remarked, "that that's when Dit decided he'd quit hockey."

"What helps you on stickhandling," Howe said, "is that when you're a kid, you play with a tennis ball. There was a family in Saskatoon that had a rink with sideboards between the house and the barn. We'd go all day there with a tennis ball, 15 guys to a side, and when the ball got frozen we'd throw the frozen ball inside and my friend's mom would throw out the other one. That way," Howe continued, "you learn to stickhandle and pass without looking at the puck or where you're going to pass it. If you kept your eyes on the puck you'd end up in the rafters. You take glances at it, but you know it's there by the feel."

Detroit finished fourth during Howe's rookie season and lost in five games to Toronto in the first round of the Stanley Cup playoffs. Against the Maple Leafs, Howe failed to pick up either a goal or an assist, but he did accumulate 18 minutes in penalties, battling continually with Toronto rookie Howie Meeker and assorted other Leafs.

Gordie showed a marked improvement during his second season with the Wings. He netted 16 goals and added 28 assists for a total of 44 points in 60 games. The Red Wings wound up in second place but bowed to the Maple Leafs in the finals of the Stanley Cup competition.

The following year, Howe missed 20 games because of a torn cartilage in his right knee. The fact that the torn cartilage was one of the few major injuries he sustained is also part of the amazing Gordie Howe story.

Hockey, like football, is basically a contact sport. Of the two, hockey is probably the more dangerous, simply because NHL players skate at speeds up to 25 miles an hour. When two players collide on ice, chances are that one, and sometimes both, will suffer an injury ranging anywhere from a minor cut to a fractured skull.

The hard rubber puck also poses a danger, particularly when it comes off a stick at 100 miles an hour. Skates, too, can cause injuries, especially during pileups in front of the net, when seven or eight players may be fighting for the disk. And sticks, of course, can become lethal weapons, sometimes intentionally and sometimes not.

In 1966, for example, Detroit's All-Star defenseman, Doug Barkley, lost an eye after being hit by the sharp edge of a stick blade. In that instance, Barkley was the victim of an unfortunate accident. In the 1950 Stanley Cup playoffs, Howe was to suffer an unfortunate and near-fatal accident. But aside from

Howe the All-Star is tripped up in front of Turk Broda.

This bout at Madison Square Garden during the 1958 season effectively ended Fontinato's career as a tough guy. Howe, shown here in a white jersey behind the net, broke Fontinato's nose and otherwise humbled him. Fontinato is hunched over – on the receiving end of a flurry of Howe uppercuts – in front of referee Art Skov.

that, he was relatively free of any disabling injury. There were reasons: his brute strength, his magnificent reflexes and his special instinct for avoiding dangerous situations before they developed. Another – and perhaps more important – reason was Howe's habit of keeping himself in top condition during the off-season as well as in the hockey season. He did not smoke, for instance, and never has.

"Early in my career," Howe explained, "my coach told me it wouldn't do me any good to smoke cigarettes, so I never tried them. All I know is that when I see a boy smoking I know he's either a little shot trying to be a big shot, or he's gone over to the social side and doesn't want to be a hockey player."

Of all the injuries suffered by Howe, the most bizarre occurred at the Montreal Forum in 1961. There was a face-off in the Detroit end and Howe

was the Red Wing involved in it. Just before the puck was dropped, defenseman Marcel Pronovost skated over to Howe and asked him to step aside when the puck went down on the ice. Pronovost wanted a clear shot at a Montreal player who had dealt him a stiff check a few minutes earlier. Howe did as he was asked, but the play got fouled up and Gordie shifted himself right into the line of fire. Pronovost missed his target and slammed full tilt into Howe. Gordie ended up with a broken shoulder and missed six games.

"Naturally, I felt pretty bad about it," Pronovost said in relating the incident. "But all Gordie said in the first-aid room was, 'Marcel, you're a rotten body checker. You better get your eyes tested.'"

Following surgery to repair the damaged cartilage in his right knee, Howe appeared in 40 games during the 1948-49 campaign. He netted 12 goals, added 25 assists and was selected for the second team of All-Stars. It was a creditable performance for a third-year man, especially when the man in question was only 21 and coming back after knee surgery.

Yet, there was a nagging suspicion among some Detroit fans, and some players around the league for that matter, that perhaps Howe had been over-rated, that perhaps he had matured too early and had reached his peak as a teenager. After all, 35 goals in three seasons was hardly anything to write home about. Certainly he continued to show those flashes of brilliance, but at the same time he had failed to correct two major faults which had marked his formative years in the National Hockey League.

One was his irritating tendency to misuse his talents for the sake of show-manship. Sid Abel recalled that "Gordie would come in and stickhan-dle around a defenseman...then he'd swing back and stickhandle around the same defenseman again, beating him a different way. I guess he just wanted to show that the first time was no fluke."

His second major fault was a ten-dency to draw too many needless penalties. It is one thing not to be intimidated by opponents. It is another

By 1957 Gordie Howe had established himself as the NHL's most domi-nant forward. He is shown here breaking through the Boston defense to beat goalie Don Simmons during the 1957 playoffs. Teammate Norm Ullman is behind Howe. The other Bruins are defenseman Leo Boivin (20) and Fern Flaman in the rear.

to go looking for fights, which is exactly what Howe was doing during his first three seasons in the league. Finally, Jack Adams took Howe aside and snapped at him, "What do you think you have to do, Howe, beat up the whole league player by player? Now settle down and play some hockey."

Howe got the message, just in time for the Stanley Cup playoffs. Detroit had finished atop the league and had little trouble beating the Canadiens in the opening round. But in the finals against Toronto, the Wings came out second best. The Detroit setback was no fault of Howe's. Gordie, in fact, emerged as the star of the Stanley Cup competition by scoring eight goals and adding three assists in 11 games, which was tops in goals and points. Recalling that performance, Howe said with a

grin: "I still wasn't so sure I was a star, because one day, back home in Saskatoon, a kid came up and asked for my autograph. While I signed it he said, 'Mr. Howe, what do you do in the winter?'"

But, of course, he was a star. His overall performance against Montreal and Toronto in the playoffs had pushed Howe over the thin line that divides the good players from the great players.

The following season, 1949-50, Howe scored 35 goals — matching his total for the three previous years — and added 33 assists for a point total of 68. For the second consecutive season he was voted to the second team of All-Stars, again finishing behind Rocket Richard in the voting for the right-wing position. More importantly, Howe was the league's third highest scorer. Only his linemates, Lindsay and Abel, compiled higher point totals.

The Howe-Lindsay-Abel "Production Line" had become one of the best in the history of professional hockey, and Howe, more mature and confident, blended in perfectly. For hockey fans of that era, there were few greater thrills than

watching Howe, Lindsay and Abel on a rush into enemy ice. The Production Line helped Detroit to a first-place finish that year and the Wings were favored to win the Stanley Cup. No one realized it at the time, but the Red Wings were embarking on a period of success all but unmatched in National Hockey League history.

It was at that point — at the start of the semifinal round — that Gordie Howe was struck down, nearly for life.

The Howe injury caused thunderous controversy amid charges that he was deliberately fouled. But Ted Kennedy was ultimately exonerated by NHL president Clarence Campbell and Howe returned to the ice as a spectator amid thunderous cheers when the Red Wings won the Stanley Cup at Olympia over the New York Rangers.

Less than three months after his near-fatal injury, Howe was well enough to start playing baseball in the Northern Saskatchewan League. By the time he reported to the Red Wings' training camp he was in near-perfect condition, and, as the 1950-51 season opened, Howe pronounced himself ready to go.

Still, his teammates and opponents wondered if he would play as aggressively as he had before the accident. Had he left a little bit of heart back in that hospital room? Would he be gun-shy? Would he occasionally take his eye off the puck and glance about for a defender when he was near the boards?

Would he slow himself down just a bit at the blue line and perhaps lose that valuable half step? Would he pass up the opportunity to throw a hard check at an enemy forward?

Howe answered those doubts — and perhaps his own subconscious fears as well — in the best of all possible ways. He went out and scored 43 goals and added 43 assists — good enough to lead the league in both goals and total points.

The Wings again finished first, only to be upset by Montreal in the first round of the Stanley Cup playoffs. The loss of the Cup, by the way, was no fault of Howe's. He had four goals and three assists in the six-game series.

During the 1950-51 campaign, Howe also reached a personal milestone — the first of many. He scored his 100th NHL goal on the night of February 17, 1951. The goalie was Montreal's Gerry McNeil. The game was played at the Montreal Forum, and Howe's goal proved to be the winning score. But most embarrassing of all, it came on "Rocket Richard Night."

Howe's rise to the "superstar" class coincided with the start of a four-year period during which the Red Wings overshadowed the Canadiens, who, until then, had been regarded as the premier players of professional hockey. Beginning with the 1951-52 campaign and continuing through the 1954-55 season, Detroit finished atop the league, while Montreal placed second.

During that same period, the Wings won three Stanley Cup championships, and the Canadiens took the Cup but once.

Howe regarded the 1951-52 team as the best Detroit club he has played on. And with good reason. That season Detroit compiled 100 points in 70 games — while second-place Montreal picked up 78 points. In the first round of the Stanley Cup playoffs, the Wings beat Toronto four straight. In the final round against the Canadiens, the Wings again won four straight.

"The way we were playing," Howe said in talking about the Stanley Cup sweep, "I think we could have won 35 straight."

Certainly, Howe appeared so omnipotent on the ice one suspected he could score at his pleasure. I recall seeing him demoralize the Maple Leafs in the third game of the Stanley Cup semifinal round in Toronto on March 29, 1952, shooting with bombsight accuracy and brushing past enemy defenses as if they were made of cardboard.

When Gordie was at the top of his game, as he was that night, he skittered effortlessly from one end of the rink to another, like a water bug on a pond. His shot had a deceptive quality about it. Instead of being heralded first with a flamboyant windup, Howe's blast was unobtrusive, like a gunshot felling a beast without any warning because of a silencer over its muzzle. So it was with Howe's release — quiet, true, but packing enormous velocity until it hit the twine behind the net.

Unlike Rocket Richard, Howe occasionally would return to his boyhood traits and just plain fool around with his ability — and his opponents. In that memorable Toronto game — which, incidentally, Detroit won 6-2 — I recall Howe breaking away from the entire Leaf team at center ice and cruising in on rotund Turk Broda, helplessly alone in front of the Leaf net.

Almost dreamily, Gordie loped along the left side, nonchalantly executed a couple of feints that lured Broda several feet out of the net and left him flopping on the ice. Then, with nothing but the six feet of yawning cage in front of him, Howe playfully shot for the far right post, trying for a billiard carom shot. This was the only challenge left for him. The puck nicked the right post and slipped harmlessly into the corner.

Howe worry? Why should he? Next time he wouldn't fool around, and the puck would go in.

That year, Howe scored 47 goals in regular season play and added 39 assists to lead the league in total points and goals. He also was awarded the first of his six Hart Memorial trophies as the league's Most Valuable Player.

The 1951-52 season marked the end of the Production Line. Sid Abel, as we saw, was traded to the Chicago

Blackhawks at his own request. The Hawks had offered him the dual job of player-coach. So, at the start of the 1952-53 campaign, Howe and Lindsay had a new center — the affable, easy-going, but talented Alex Delvecchio. It would be inaccurate to say that Abel was not missed. Players of his caliber are few and far between. But it also would be inaccurate to say that Delvecchio was not an adequate replacement. He was all of that — and then some.

Centering for Howe and Lindsay, Delvecchio scored 16 goals and added 43 assists. He was named to the second team of All-Stars. Howe and Lindsay, of course, were named to the first team. For Howe, in fact, the 1952-53 cam-

paign was the best of all his many great seasons.

He led the league in scoring with 95 points and in goals scored with 49. His 49 goals were just one short of the single-season record then held by Rocket Richard at the time. Both Bobby Hull and Bernie Geoffrion later tied Richard's mark. Hull, of course, shattered the record with his 54 goals in the 1966-67 season. Howe's 1952-53 performance also earned him his second consecutive Hart Memorial Trophy. He thereby matched a feat of two hockey immortals of the 1930s — Boston's Eddie Shore and Montreal's Howie Morenz. Oh, yes. Howe played 15 games of the 1952-53 season with a broken right wrist. He broke the wrist

Gordie Howe (left) and Alex Delvecchio storm the Toronto goal, but Harry Lumley, an ex-Wing, makes the save. Ron Stewart of Toronto is on the far left. The referee is Bill Chadwick.

Gordie Howe bisects the Leaf defense for a shot at goalie Harry Lumley.

in a Christmas night game, had the wrist placed in a cast and played out the full 70-game schedule as if he was in A-1 condition.

Gordie repeated as scoring leader the following season, this time with 33 goals and 48 assists for a total of 81 points. Again he was named to the first team of All-Stars. But he missed out on the Hart Memorial Trophy. That award went to Al Rollins of the Chicago Blackhawks, whose team had

finished in last place with a total of 12 wins in 70 games played.

The Wings did regain the Stanley Cup, however, as Howe scored four goals and added five assists in the play-off competition. He also chalked up 31 minutes in penalties.

As a team, the Wings maintained their championship touch during the 1954-55 campaign. Again they finished atop the league and did so even though Howe had, what was for him, a sub-par

season. Missing six games because of a leg injury, Howe managed but 29 goals and 33 assists for a total of 62 points. As a result, he failed for the first time in six years to make either the first team or second team of All-Stars.

But being Gordie Howe, the type of player who always managed to rise to the occasion, he proceeded to lead the Wings to their second consecutive Stanley Cup by notching nine goals and adding 11 assists in 11 playoff games. That still ranks as one of the top performances by an individual player in the history of the Cup competition.

The following season Detroit failed to finish in first place for the first time in eight years. The Wings were second, behind Montreal. Howe had 38 goals and 41 assists for a total of 79 points. And he was selected for the second team of All-Stars behind Richard, who enjoyed his last truly great season. Montreal went on to defeat the Wings in the finals of the Stanley Cup. In 10 playoff games, Howe had only three goals, but did chip in with nine assists.

Detroit bounced back during the 1956-57 campaign, finishing in first place. Howe captured the scoring title with a total of 89 points on 44 goals and 45 assists. Again the Wings went into the Stanley Cup playoffs favored to win. Again the Boston Bruins turned the tables, ousting the Wings in five games during the opening round.

To most hockey observers, the years between 1952 and 1957 marked the second phase of Gordie Howe's career.

Following Sid Abel's departure from Detroit, Howe and Lindsay formed the most productive and fearsome one-two punch in the history of professional hockey. Yet, they did not take their success for granted. Despite their pre-eminence in the world of hockey, Howe and Lindsay continued their habit of practicing together after the regular practice sessions. They learned each other's moves and perfected their timing to the point where they could hit one another with passes more by instinct than by sight.

On one of their favorite plays Howe would carry the puck across the opposing team's blue line, then would skate down the left side and cut sharply toward the goalmouth. Without looking, Howe would whip a cross-ice pass to a point just to the left of the net. Lindsay and the puck would arrive at the same time. And more often than not, Terrible Ted would snap the disk past the helpless goalie.

During this second phase, however, Howe's critics noted a tendency on his part to let some of the other players on the team perform the rigorous chores of hockey — the fore-checking and back-checking. Not that Howe didn't do well in these areas. It's just that he might have done even better if he had applied himself more diligently to the tasks at hand.

But as the fortunes of the Wings began to fall following the 1956-57 season, Howe took on more responsibility. In so doing he reached full maturity as both a hockey player and a person and entered the third and final phase of his fabulous career.

When the Wings were locked in a tight game, for example, Howe would skate with his own line, then fill in for a full turn on one of the other lines. He became the balance wheel of the Detroit power play, sometimes working from the point position and at other times muscling his way in front of the enemy cage for a tip-in or rebound shot. When the Wings were a man short, Howe went out as a penalty killer. His very presence on the ice often forced the opposing team to play more conservatively. For even though the other club was playing with five skaters to Detroit's four, the enemy forces still had to guard against the type of miscue that would give Howe a breakaway opportunity.

Between 1957 and 1964, Howe averaged 40 to 45 minutes per game on ice — twice the ice time put in by most NHL forwards. (Current NHL observers marvel when Chris Chelios, Jeremy Roenik or Doug Gilmour average over 30 minutes.)

"Howe has rewritten the entire game," said one NHL official. That he did, especially in one vital area: It was Howe who first used the wrist slap shot with any degree of regularity. In his book, *Hockey — Here's Howe*, Gordie described the wrist slap shot this way: "The blade of the stick should come back waist high or higher on the backswing and should hit the puck cleanly off the heal. Tighten your grip too much and your stick will turn and the puck will wind up in the corner. Snap your wrists as you hit the puck. Keep your eye on the puck because you can 'fan' on it all too easily, which can be a little embarrassing."

Howe, needless to say, was seldom embarrassed.

The Players Speak

What was it like to be a Detroit Red Wing during the 1950s era of Motor City Muscle?

The answer to that can only come from the players themselves. And with that in mind, we tape-recorded a cross section of players; a second-line forward who made significant contributions, a superstar defenseman and a potential ace who almost became the permanent center for Gordie Howe and Ted Lindsay.

The second-liner was Johnny Wilson, a left wing who joined the club in the 1949-50 season and played eight playoff games in the Wings' successful run for the Stanley Cup.

The superstar was Leonard (Red) Kelly, a Hall of Fame defenseman who became the first of the post-World War II backliners to regularly carry the puck.

The promising Red Wing whose career was aborted by injury was Max McNab, who made the big club in 1947-48, and also skated for the 1950 championship team.

In separate tape-recorded interviews, each of the representative Red Wings offers us this rich oral history of NHL life during hockey's golden era.

JOHNNY WILSON

Born in Kincardine, Ontario, on June 14, 1929, Johnny Wilson made his National Hockey League debut with Detroit in 1949-50. At five feet 10 inches, 175 pounds, he had the perfect physique for a hockey player in that epoch and Wilson had the wheels to go with it. Speed, intelligence and an accurate shot made him a valuable member of the Detroiters. Wilson also became renowned for his durability. Beginning in the 1952-53 campaign, when he played all 70 games of the regular schedule, Wilson then proceeded to play eight straight seasons of 70 games without missing a single contest. He truly earned the "Iron Man" label. During an interview with Detroit hockey reporter Jim Ramsey, Wilson recalled life under manager Jack Adams and what made the Red Wings such a powerful organization.

Right: Johnny Wilson (left) was one of the most unheralded but valuable forwards on the dynastic Red Wings.

The best way to understand the Red Wings is to know about the man who made them tick. That would be Jack Adams, who managed our club and had been the coach for many years before Tommy Ivan took over in 1947-48.

One reason why our team was so successful was because of Adams' personality. Jack was a perfectionist and, because of that, a tough man to play for. You had to give him a maximum effort every game or you heard about it. By the same token, if you played well he would be the first one to acknowledge your efforts.

Jack's moods were easy to read. One day I walked out of the dressing room after a practice and Adams was walking in the other direction. Normally, he would wish me "Good morning!" but this time there was not a word. He walked past me as if I didn't exist and that was the message for me; Jack didn't like the way Johnny Wilson was playing.

That was okay with me because I knew that Adams was fair. He didn't favor one player over another. On any night he would walk into the dressing room and pick on the stars as much as the scrubs. Gordie Howe, Ted Lindsay, Alex Delvecchio and Terry Sawchuk — our best players — would be picked on by Jack as much as anyone.

If Adams had a favorite, it was Terry Sawchuk because he always had a tender spot for goaltenders. When somebody scored on Sawchuk, Adams said that the goal developed in the offensive zone. If I missed my check or a defenseman like Marcel Pronovost missed his check or didn't grab the rebound, that would be the problem, not the goaltending.

The greatest player in the game was Gordie Howe, but Adams — as much as he loved the big guy — was unsparing in his criticism. One night Jack was in his favorite spot, sitting in the back of the dressing room when he suddenly got to his feet and walked over to Gordie. "You know, Gordie," Adams said, "you were terrible out there tonight. You were so bad, you should have paid to get in the rink."

After that, Adams walked out, but the guys were feeling bad for Gordie. One of us said, "Don't worry, Gordie, a bad game for you is a great game for everyone else." That's how much better he was than the rest of us.

After Adams retired as coach, he still kept his nose in the coaching side of the business. He would sit right behind our coach Tommy Ivan and when we did something wrong, we would hear a big clang behind the bench, like the clash of metal. That was Jack's gate and when you heard that around the building, you knew Adams was unhappy.

On this particular night, I was playing on a line with Alex Delvecchio, who would go on to be one of the best centers in history, and Metro Prystai, a pretty darn good forward. Our problem was getting out of our own end; it seemed like we were going one way and the puck was going another. Sure enough, we heard Adams' clang which meant trouble for us.

After the period ended, he came into the dressing room. The three of us were sitting next to each other with our heads bent over, which was a customary stance when you know you're going to get hell from your manager or coach. I could see Jack's big feet right under my nose. His fists were clenched as he started screaming, "I don't know what kind of game you guys are playing out there tonight, but it sure isn't hockey!" In case we hadn't gotten the message, Jack warned us that unless we shaped up, we'd be shipping out to either Indianapolis or Omaha.

Needless to say, the minute the sec-

ond period began, we played as if we had been shot out of a cannon. I mean we never stopped because of the fear Adams had instilled in us.

Johnny Wilson (left) was one of the most unheralded but valuable forwards on the dynastic Red Wings.

Not that I'm complaining; far from it. I believe that today's hockey players should have a little more fear. Now they have three-year contracts and can't be sent to the minors; not even to overcome an injury to get back in shape. If we made a mistake or got hurt, we could be sent to the minors in a second — and never come back.

Another thing about Adams which was important to the Red Wings' philosophy was his refusal to let complacency grow in the dressing room. We would win Stanley Cups, but to Adams that meant nothing. For example, we beat New York [Rangers] for the Cup in 1950, but when we came to camp that fall every single player on the Detroit roster had to fight for his job all over again. That was the way Adams handled his players. Nobody was secure with the possible exception of Gordie Howe and Ted Lindsay, our best players. The rest had to fight all over again and, of course, the veterans lived in fear that a rookie would come along and take his spot. I mean it was a constant war and a player like myself had to give himself a pep talk or he might not be around the next season.

That's why we were so tickled to be in the NHL and why it was relatively easy for Jack to trick us into signing contracts. Adams had what we called "Three-way Contracts."

He would get a player in the room

with him and then say, "Son, where do you want to play — Detroit, Indianapolis (AHL) or Omaha (USHL)?" Now everyone knew that there was about a three to four thousand dollar difference between Detroit and Indianapolis and another difference between Indianapolis and Omaha. As a result, the natural reaction of just about everybody was, "Mister Adams, where's the pen?"

One notable exception was Billy Dineen who came to the big club in 1953 and wanted a raise the next year. Jack was sitting there waiting and made his offer which Billy rejected. Adams said to Dineen, "You know, son, you were so bad last year, people around here are accusing me of being a relative of yours!" P.S. Billy wound up signing on Jack's terms.

Adams' contract ritual began after a week of training camp, once everyone had worked the kinks out of his body. Then, the word would go out that Jack was starting to sign players. Mind you, he had about 110 players in the entire organization to deal with but he'd wipe them out in a week's time.

What Jack would do is take 10 to 15 a day. He would sit each fellow down and say, "Did you have a nice summer? You look like you're having a pretty good camp and we're looking for a great year from you." Then, he would pull out the contract and say, "Son, this is what you're getting; this is for Detroit."

Then, he'd throw a few bonuses in, hand you the pencil and wait for you to sign. If you said, "Yeah, but..." he'd shoot back, "But, what? Son, where do you want to play — Omaha or Detroit?" That did it; you'd say, "Detroit, Mister Adams," and sign right up. Then, you'd send in another guy and, before he went in, you'd tell him, "Boy, I got a big raise — I scored 20 goals and Jack gave me a $250 raise." Today that's postage stamp money.

Mind you, I'm not knocking Jack Adams. He was a tough son of a gun, but he was also a great guy and a great coach and manager.

Of course, he had some pretty good talent on his clubs and that made life a little easier for him. I mean, how many managers can boast that they have a Gordie Howe in his lineup?

I've watched a lot of hockey players over the years — and I'm talking about a half-century — and I've seen them all. Rocket Richard was my idol when I was a kid. I watched Bobby Orr, Jean Beliveau, Phil Esposito, Wayne Gretzky and Steve Yzerman; the best.

And if an NHL club owner came up to me and said, "Johnny, of all the great players you've seen, which one would you pick to start a team?" I'd say Gordie Howe.

The reason why I pick Gordie over the rest of them is that he could do anything. He could stickhandle; he could shoot; he could get into the toughest battles and he would fight. He would do anything asked of him and, brother, could he back-check. When Gordie Howe was on the ice, it was like having a third defenseman playing for your team.

In any battle, nine times out of 10 Howe would come up with the puck, open up the play and move it up the ice. He was always around the puck and the opposition had an expression, "Howe plays 'the funny kind of game,' he doesn't let anyone else touch the puck."

He could score more goals than anyone during an era when it was a lot tougher to score than it is nowadays. He could throw the most vicious checks that you would ever see and always come out on top. In today's hockey you couldn't find a coach who could tell a Wayne Gretzky or a Sergei Fedorov or a Steve Yzerman or other great players, "Listen, to win tonight's game, we've got to go out and slap this guy around." But you could with Gordie because he'd be the first guy there. The others that I mentioned would back off because they're finesse players.

Gordie Howe was the most well-rounded player there was. For a while, his competitor was Rocket Richard who was great in his own right. But The Rocket was only great from the blue line in or on the perimeter of the crease. And Bobby Orr, Gretzky and Bobby Hull all had their specific tal-

ents, but Gordie was the most complete.

He also was incredibly team oriented. Gordie would do whatever was necessary for the Red Wings to win even if he was injured. One year in particular comes to mind. This was the semifinal playoff round in 1953 after we had swept the 1952 playoffs in eight straight games. We had Boston in the opening round in '53 and beat them 7-0 at Olympia in Game One. Then they came back and surprised us 5-3 in the second game at Detroit and went on to win the series four games to two. That was quite an upset; them beating us at that time and a lot of people were wondering how it happened. Well, the Bruins had a big, smart veteran left-winger named Woody Dumart who was assigned to check Gordie and Dumart got a lot of credit for stopping our big guy. But it wasn't so much that he contained Gordie, it was that Howe was playing the entire series with cracked ribs and an injured wrist.

The thing was, Gordie never complained; he went out there and played and because of the injuries, he was missing chances that he ordinarily might have put away. They got a couple of fluke goals and beat us. Meanwhile, Gordie accepted all the blame; put it all on his shoulders and had tears in his eyes after the series was over. He was saying, more or less, "I let you guys down." That was the type of player he was.

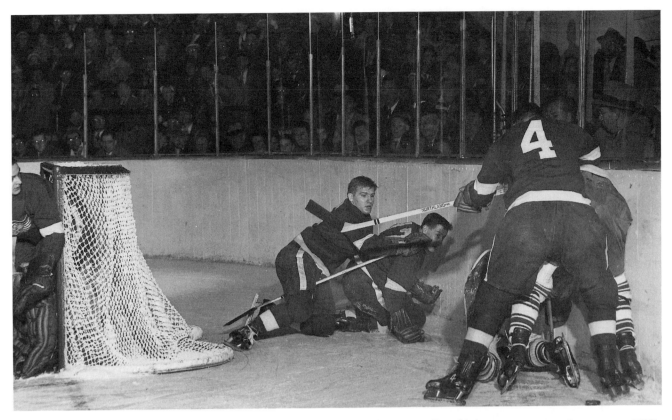

A perfect cover-up. While Terry Sawchuk peers from his goal crease, teammates Johnny Wilson (center) and Red Kelly (4) ensure that no Maple Leaf escapes in 1954 playoff action.

His sidekick was Ted Lindsay, one of the best left-wingers of all time and, after Sid Abel left Detroit, a great captain. I enjoyed playing alongside Teddy because he could get you up for a game better than most. He hated the opposition more than just about anybody I ever knew, but he hated the Canadiens more than any team.

As a leader, there were none better. When a rookie broke into the lineup, he would take the kid aside and spend time giving him an education about life in the NHL. And he always made a point of telling the kid that he, Ted Lindsay, would be there to back him up. "Just go out there and play your game," he would tell the kid, "and we'll support you."

The thing about Teddy is that he not only motivated the kids, but he could do it for the older players as well — including Gordie Howe. He was

constantly inflating Gordie's ego, telling Howe that he was the toughest, the best and that he could outskate anyone. Another thing about Lindsay was his size. He wasn't very big, but pound for pound he was about the meanest I've ever encountered.

Here's a good example. I had been traded to Chicago for the 1955-56 season and we had a game against Detroit. Now I'm skating on a line with a brash kid named Hector Lalonde against Lindsay. Before we took the ice, I warned Lalonde, "When you go into the corner with Lindsay, get your stick up because he'll rub your nose in it if you're not alert."

So, Hector said, "Don't worry about me, Johnny, I'll straighten out that little guy."

No sooner are we on the ice when there's an altercation in the corner between Lindsay and Lalonde. They've

Terry Sawchuk, who registered 103 career regular season shutouts.

goaltending; which is where Terry Sawchuk comes into the picture. In plain English, Sawchuk was the greatest goaltender I have ever seen; that includes old timers to the present. He finished his career with a total of 103 shutouts in his career over regular season games. One hundred and three; think about that. And a dozen more shutouts in the playoffs. How many goaltenders can make that statement?

Sawchuk was a moody guy and people would complain about that aspect of his personality, but I would be moody, too, if I had guys taking potshots at me in the morning during practice and then again at night during the games.

The bottom line is that Sawchuk did his thing and did it well. As good a team that we had, it also was necessary to get the big save at the right time to turn a game around.

Here's a good example of how Sawchuk made a difference. In the 1953-54 Stanley Cup finals we played against a terrific Montreal Canadiens' team with Rocket Richard, Boom Boom Geoffrion, Dickie Moore and Jean Beliveau. They had Gerry McNeil in goal and we had Sawchuk and the series came down to the seventh game at Olympia. Floyd Curry scored for them in the first period and Red Kelly tied it for us in the second. It was 1-1 late in the third period when Kenny Mosdell, one of Montreal's best forwards, somehow worked his way

got their sticks up and it was getting worse. Being as I had been a pal and teammate of Lindsay for several years, I skated in between them in an attempt to separate the pair. I turned to Lindsay and said, "Teddy, leave the kid alone!"

Lindsay looked up at me as if I was some foreigner and said, "Get that head of yours out of the way before I cut it off!" Obviously, there were no friends on the ice with Ted Lindsay.

As good and tough as our scorers were, we wouldn't have nearly been the great team we were without special through our defense. If he scores it's all over, but Terry came up with the big save and we went into the dressing room still tied.

Early in the first overtime Tony Leswick fired a blooper for us that hit off their defenseman Doug Harvey's glove and bounced over McNeil and that's how we won the Cup. But if Sawchuk hadn't come up with that save, we wouldn't have won anything.

He made the spectacular save when it counted.

When Terry came into the league his style was different from the others. He didn't stray too far from the net, basically staying around the crease. But this was a time when screened shots had become more prevalent and to stop them, Sawchuk developed this crouch which enabled him to peer through the legs and see the puck. He would go

Below: Terry Sawchuk was a master of the pads-stacking art and demonstrates it here as Tod Sloan of the Maple Leafs breaks through the Detroit defenses. Bob Goldham is on the left.

down, look through his defensemen or the opposition and see the shot coming.

As great players go, Terry was unusually modest and tried to evade stardom. He was like a blue-collar guy who preferred the background. He also was one of the last goaltenders to use the face mask. He played most of his career without one and got hit in the face more than a few times. With the blood dripping down his head, he would go into the dressing room for 10 minutes or so, get sewn up and then come right back to the net. He was a gamer.

One thing I learned when I joined the Detroit organization was that this was a team of rich tradition. It had won two straight Stanley Cups in the 1930s and already had a long list of great players in the alumni. When I came to Detroit in 1949-50 one of their top defensemen, Black Jack Stewart, was finishing his career with the Red Wings, but he still was a big help to a kid like me.

I recall one incident when I wound up with the puck at training camp behind the net and tried one of those spectacular end-to-end rushes. Anyhow, I picked up the puck and took about four strides when I found myself skating right at this big hulk, Jack Stewart. He looked me right in the eyes and said, "Son, you'd better keep your head up or the next time it will be curtains."

I learned something valuable right then and there from Black Jack.

Not that I didn't already know about him. One of the old time Red Wings, Carl Liscombe, played on the 1943 Cup winners when they beat Boston in four straight and he said that Stewart and Jimmy Orlando would team up to be one of the toughest defense combinations in NHL history. He told me, "They would chew up the opposition and spit them out in little pieces." After watching Black Jack in action, I knew what he meant.

But my most memorable moment with Black Jack happened during the 1950 finals against New York. The series was tied at three games apiece with the last game at Olympia. During the series, Jack Adams had us staying at a place in Toledo, Ohio, so that players could be shielded from the media and their families. It was then that Stewart announced that we were going to have a team meeting in his room; no manager, no coach. Just the players gathering in Black Jack's room.

Sure enough, he got us all together — I'm talking about our captain Sid Abel, Ted Lindsay and the rest — and Black Jack stood up before all of them. "You guys are a bunch of patsies. You're letting the Rangers skate all over you. I'll tell you one thing; you'd better get your asses in gear for the next game. If you've got to hit every damn guy on the ice, hit him!"

Black Jack turned the whole team around and we went out and won the game and the Stanley Cup. The thing

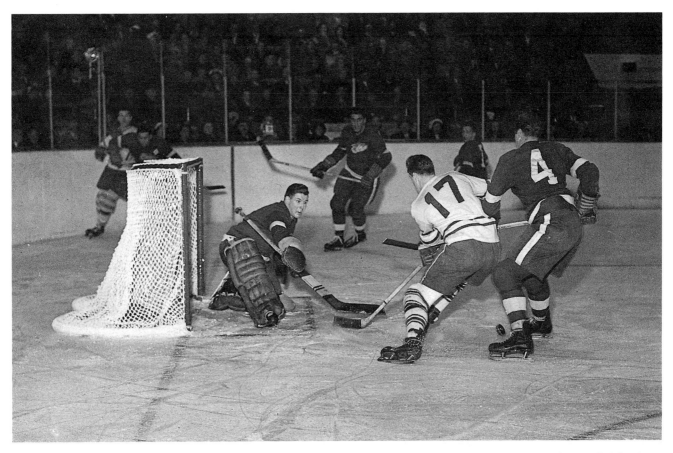

Leaf center Cal Gardner is checked by Red Kelly (4) as Harry Lumley pushes the puck away.

was, you never wanted to disappoint Jack because he would look you in the eye and scare you to death. You either did what he said or you didn't belong on the team. When I saw a guy like Stewart, almost ready to kill to win, I said to myself, "Hey, I'd better do something about this to help the guy along."

After Stewart left the club Red Kelly soon became the best defenseman on the team although he had a totally different style and disposition than Black Jack. Red was tough, to be sure, but he didn't display his toughness as obviously as Stewart. Even though he was a defenseman, Kelly liked to rush the puck and he was a splendid enough skater to be able to do that.

One of Kelly's assets was his use of the skates to move the puck. He was one of the few players ever to be able to use his feet as well as his hands. This technique was particularly effective along the boards. While most guys were trying hard to get their stick on the ice to get the puck, Red wouldn't even worry about that. He would just drag his foot and kick the puck up to his skate and get it out of our zone.

Red was a great skater who could shoot as well as make the pass. In one 70-game season he scored 19 goals, which was amazing for the team. Another time he got 50 points in 70 games.

To top it all, he was a very nice guy and always in first-class shape. During the off-season he worked on a tobacco farm that his family operated in Ontario and would always ask Jack

Adams for permission to miss the first four or five days of training camp so that he could harvest the tobacco. Jack, who normally wasn't into granting such special favors, did so with Red because he knew that the first day Kelly jumped on the ice, he would be flying.

Since Kelly was one of those Ontario boys, he could very well have been playing for the Maple Leafs, but he was with us along with another Ontario boy named Ted Lindsay, not to mention myself. The fact that any one of us could have been a Leaf probably helped make our rivalry a bit stronger; not that it wasn't strong enough.

In those days of the early 1950s, when the NHL was only a six-team league, the intensity of play in each game was unbelievably high and part of it had to do with the fact that you

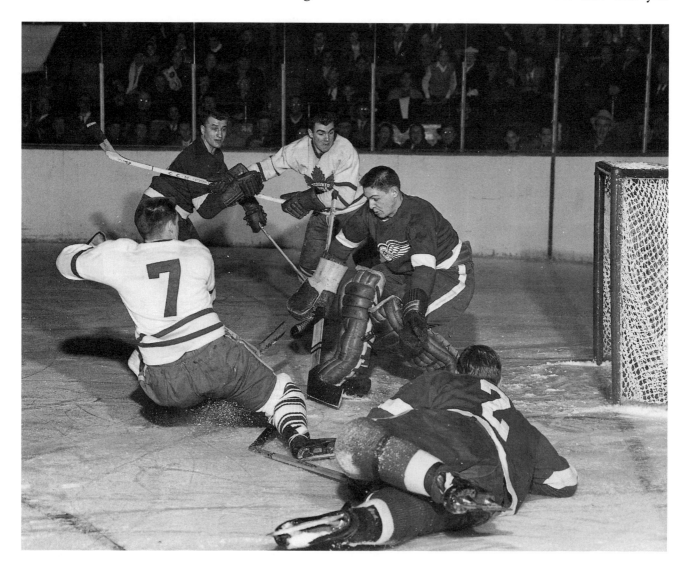

played each other so many times. It was not unusual for us to play a club like the Rangers on a Saturday night at Olympia and then return to Madison Square Garden for a Sunday night game in New York. When you have back-to-back games so often as we did then, the games reach a fever pitch.

Every team had its share of tough guys. Toronto had Bill Barilko, Gus Mortson, Jim Thomson and Bill Ezinicki. Montreal had Butch Bouchard and Doug Harvey and so on. But the rivalry between Detroit and Toronto seemed to be the most intense of all because of an incident that took place during the 1950 playoffs. This was in the first game of the semifinals between the Wings and Toronto. Howe tried to check their captain Ted Kennedy and wound up hitting the boards. A lot of people in Detroit thought that Kennedy had tried to injure Gordie, but I know Ted Kennedy personally and I can assure you he was not the type of player who would try to injure Gordie Howe.

Nevertheless, there was a lot of bad blood as a result of Gordie getting seriously hurt and it stimulated an intense battle between the Wings and Leafs. It was a natural reaction.

Naturally, I'm very proud to have been a part of those championship clubs in Detroit, especially the 1952 winner when we swept Toronto in four and then Montreal in four. I finished the series with four goals — tied with

Rocket Richard and Floyd Curry of Montreal — only one less than Ted Lindsay who led everybody.

I got all four of my goals in the opening round against Toronto. We won the first game 3-0, but Toronto played strong in Game Two. Old Turk Broda was in goal for them and he played the game of his life, but I managed to get one past him and we took the game 1-0, which put us in great shape to take the next two games at Maple Leaf Gardens, which we did.

My only assist in the series was a big one, too, because it was on the Stanley Cup-winning goal in Game Four of the finals. Alex Delvecchio and myself helped set up Metro Prystai who beat Gerry McNeil at 6:50 of the first period. We got two more goals later, but ours was the winner. I finished the playoffs with four goals and an assist. My five points left me only two behind Howe, Lindsay and Prystai, who led our team with seven each.

Prystai was an important name on our championship club because he represented the second-liners behind the stars. And we had plenty of solid, back-up players. They included Glen Skov, Marty Pavelich, Tony Leswick who all were hard-working guys but were overshadowed by the greatness of Howe and the others. But I'll tell you one thing; if it hadn't been for the contributions of these guys, I don't know if we would have ever won a Stanley Cup.

I played on championship teams in

1950, 1952, 1954 and 1955, but the first one is always the most memorable. This was 1949-50, the year that Gordie suffered that serious injury in the collision with Ted Kennedy. Howe was lost to us for the remainder of the playoffs so when we went up against New York in the finals, we had to play without our best player.

As things developed, the Rangers had their problems as well. In those days, the Ringling Brothers' Circus took over Madison Square Garden, their home ice, in the spring and there was no provision for the circus and hockey to coexist. So, what happened was that when the Rangers got to the 1950 finals against us, they were allowed to play two "home" games at Maple Leaf Gardens in Toronto.

New York played a terrific series and it came down to three wins apiece with the seventh game on our ice. Remember, that was the time that Black Jack Stewart got us together for the big meeting in his room before Game Seven. Believe me, we needed all the inspiration we could get because we fell behind 2-0 before the seventh game was eight minutes old.

But we never quit and had the game tied 3-3 by the time the second period was over. We went a full sudden-death period without a goal and then in the second overtime, Pete Babando beat Chuck Rayner in their goal and we had the Cup.

The weird thing was that a year later the Rangers didn't even make the playoffs and we went out in the first round. That was the spring when Rocket Richard was hotter than a pistol. We went up against him and the Canadiens in the first round and lost the first two games in sudden death to them at Olympia. Then, we beat them twice at The Forum, but then they came back and won the next two and the series.

Rocket was one of the fiercest hockey players I have ever faced. I would try to check him in our zone and he'd shoot the puck right through me. He'd play against an opponent like me as if he didn't even see me; like I was a shadow. I mean his eyes were glued on that puck. It was unbelievable. And he was powerful. The interesting thing about Richard was that his backhand shot was as good as his forehand; it didn't make any difference, the shot was always on goal.

Richard wasn't much at handling the puck coming out of his own end, but his centerman would set him up and from the blue line in, if you so much as blinked your eyes or turned your head, he was gone. He also had a knack of sticking out his left leg as he cut left toward the net. He would sort of slip that leg out and spin in toward the net. He would lock in with the puck on his backhand. To stop him, you had to stay to the inside of him because if he got to the inside, he had you beat.

My first Stanley Cup win in 1950 was terrific because it was the first and because we won it with Gordie Howe on the sidelines. But the second championship in 1952 was the greatest thrill as far as I'm concerned because we won it in eight straight games and had a shutout in every one of the four games we played at home. That was when Terry Sawchuk was at his absolute best; every game was up and down and the intensity was fierce. You just didn't want to make a mistake for fear that it would cost the team and, of course, I wanted to be a hero just like the next guy on the bench. Once we started putting the wins together people in the press began to talk about an eight-game sweep, but all we would think about in the dressing room was winning that night's game; that's how focused we were.

That year we worked hard, created our own breaks and won, but, as I said, Sawchuk was phenomenal; four shutouts and a 0.62 goals against average. To this day I maintain that that was the greatest Detroit team, ever.

I say that for several reasons. First of all, we had tremendous confidence in our ability. We always seemed to know — or feel — that we were going to win, no matter who we played.

In the 1952 playoffs Jack Adams had us holed up in Toledo as he had in other years and then we would take a bus to Detroit for the games. When we got on that bus in Toledo you could

hear a pin drop all the way to our destination. We'd get out, walk into the dressing room and you still could hear the pin drop! Coach Tommy Ivan would come into the room and Teddy Lindsay would say his little speech and we all went out on the ice knowing we would win. It became routine.

While all of this was going on, Adams would be playing his little games with us. He always knew when to pull some psychological ploy on an individual or the entire team.

Once, before the playoffs began, he got us in the room and said, "I got a very disturbing phone call." Naturally, everybody in the room started looking around at each other trying to figure out what this was all about. Adams never identified anyone, but then he went on, "A good friend of mine called me and said he saw several of you guys walking out of a bar and you'd had more than one drink."

Meantime, we were thinking, "Jack, let us know which bar," but he would never say. So, after he left the room all the guys would get together and say, "What the heck was that...what bar...who went?"

Of course, we would find out later there was no such thing. Jack had invented the whole story just to make sure we didn't go into bars during the playoffs.

Because of Adams' powerful personality, our coach Tommy Ivan was in the shadows so to speak. Yet, Tommy was a great coach for our team. He knew he had the talent and he never interfered. He knew how to change lines and he would go with whoever his best players were on any given night. Those were the days when teams only used three forward lines and Ivan saw to it that everybody played a lot.

Tommy didn't say much, but then again, he didn't have to because we had such a great team. We didn't need reprimanding because, in a sense, we coached ourselves and disciplined ourselves. Ivan just guided us along.

When things were going a little bad, Adams would be sure to stir things up because he didn't believe in sitting back and letting the coach run the team. Jack wanted to be a part of it. Despite that, Ivan and Adams got along, but eventually Tommy jumped to Chicago where he became manager of the Blackhawks. Jack was disappointed in that Tommy didn't tell him about it; he found out by reading it in the newspaper.

Adams wasn't alone when it came to managerial interference. In those days the managers were very powerful; Adams in Detroit, Conn Smythe in Toronto, so it wasn't unusual for them to get involved in the operation of the club.

I remember one time when Metro Prystai was in a slump and we were having a practice. Adams came down to the sideboards and called Metro over right in front of the entire team.

"Let me see your stick," Adams said. Prystai liked to doctor his stick with more and more tape so it wouldn't break.

Jack alluded to Aurel Joliat, a little guy who had starred for the Canadiens during the late 1920s and early 1930s. "That looks like one of Aurel Joliat's sticks that's been out in the rain all summer," said Jack. With that, he took the stick and threw it right across the rink. "Go in there and get yourself a new stick."

He did something like that to Gordie Howe who used a short stick even though Adams wanted him to use a longer one. One year we had a rookie named Billy McNeill who also was using a short stick. Jack called Billy over because he wasn't scoring any goals and said, "Let me see that stick. I want you to use a long stick like Gordie's." So, Billy went over and got one of Gordie's sticks and it was even shorter than his!

My last Stanley Cup win was in 1954-55, a season that had one of the wildest endings in NHL history. That was the year that we were neck and neck with the Canadiens for first place, but they were leading down the stretch and Rocket Richard was sitting on top of the scoring race.

As we hit the last week of the season, it looked like Rocket was going to win the Art Ross Trophy and that Montreal would sew up first place. But Richard had an incredible temper and had been in hot water with the league over problems he had had with referees all season. On the next to last Sunday night of the season, he got into a battle in Boston and floored a linesman named Cliff Thompson. The league president Clarence Campbell ordered a hearing on the following Tuesday and then stunned everyone by suspending Richard not only for the remaining games of the season but for the entire playoffs as well!

It so happened that the schedule called for us to play a game at The Forum on St. Patrick's Day night, March 17, 1955, which was right after Campbell had announced his suspension of Richard. You can imagine that Montreal was in an uproar. The Rocket was the biggest hero in the entire city, if not the entire Province of Quebec, and the fans — especially the French Canadians — were furious about the decision.

We knew all about this by the time we got into our dressing room for the start of the game. Richard was sitting in the stands near the ice, and later, Campbell would come to his seat — up higher — with his secretary.

The game started and when Campbell arrived, late, a fan ran up and attacked him. Then somebody threw a tear-gas bomb and the smoke went all over the arena. Adams got us all together and said we had better get dressed and get out of the arena as fast as we could. He said the people outside on St. Catherine Street were rioting. Suddenly, a couple of policemen came down and we followed them out of the building. The riot went on into the night, but we escaped unscathed.

As a result, the game was forfeited to us and we went on to win the regular season championship again. That was our seventh first place in a row. Rocket Richard lost the scoring title to his teammate Bernie Geoffrion and we wound up playing Montreal in the finals. They didn't have The Rocket but they took us to seven games before we beat them at Olympia. That was the last time Detroit won the Stanley Cup.

RED KELLY

Leonard Kelly ranks among the greatest players of all time. He became a Red Wing in the 1947-48 season at the age of 20 and wasted no time earning a regular berth despite intense competition and his relative youthfulness.

The redhead had a fluid skating style, an accurate shot and an intelligence that surpassed most of his peers. At six feet, 190 pounds, he was perfectly configured for the defenseman's role. Yet, he displayed such a knack for the attack, his bosses — Jack Adams and Tommy Ivan — had no compunctions about allowing Kelly to orchestrate assaults against the enemy territory. Their reasoning was that Red was uniquely capable of quickly returning to his defensive position before any damage had been done by a counterattack from the opponents.

Born in Simcoe, Ontario, on July 9, 1927, Kelly grew up on a tobacco-raising farm and learned the values of hard work from his father. When he moved to Toronto for his Junior hockey training at St. Michael's College, the Maple Leafs had this jewel of a prospect right under their collective noses. And yet, somehow, Toronto managed not to sign him to a contract.

Toronto's loss was Detroit's gain; in spades! Once Kelly reached the National Hockey League, he never looked back; not for 20 years, of which the first 13 were spent in the Motor City.

He became the cornerstone of a defense that included Black Jack Stewart, Bob Goldham, Marcel Pronovost and Leo Reise Jr. This solid bloc of backliners enabled Detroit to win Stanley Cups in 1950, 1952, 1954 and 1955. With Kelly starring at the blue line, the Red Wings peeled off a remarkable seven consecutive first-place finishes starting with the 1948-49 campaign and ending with the 1954-55 season when the men from the Motor City won their last Stanley Cup.

Kelly might have been a Red Wing for life had he not clashed with Jack Adams. But in February 1960, the Redhead was dealt to Toronto for defenseman Marc Reaume. It was one of the worst deals ever made in big-league hockey. Reaume was no factor at all for Detroit, whereas Kelly went on to star at center for the Maple Leafs. He also was a major asset in no less than four Stanley Cup championships for his new club.

Kelly, now an Ontario-based businessman, recounted his Detroit experiences with Toronto hockey reporter R. Wayne Geen.

Life takes some funny turns. My first meaningful hockey experience was at St. Michael's College in Toronto which was more or less of a training school for the Toronto Maple Leafs. Yet I wound up playing the first half of my National Hockey League career with the Detroit Red Wings.

How did I wind up at St. Mike's? Well, my dad sent me there because he was an alumnus of the school and my grandfather had gone there as well.

I had been working on the family farm when a gentleman, bird-dogging for the Maple Leafs, thought he could get me in the training camp, but he couldn't. The Leafs were training in St. Catherines and I got all enthused about the possibilities of seeing the

Leafs, but I went to St. Mike's and tried out for the A team. I lasted one practice and then got cut, so I tried out for the B team, lasted one practice and got cut again. Finally, I tried out for the Midget-level club and they cut me too — after one practice.

By that time, I didn't think I'd be playing at all, so after classes I simply went to the open-air rink they had and I played there just for the fun of it. As luck would have it, one of the seminarians who was going through to the priesthood — Bill Conway — was playing there too and saw me. Conway went over to Father Flanagan of St. Mike's and said, "You'd better take another look at this guy, Kelly."

Father Flanagan took the advice and invited me to try out with the Midget club again and this time I stayed. My first year with the Midget club we won the championship so I was promoted to the B team and we won the championship and then I got promoted to the A team which, of course, was the best they had. We went all the way to the Memorial Cup finals and lost out to the Winnipeg Monarchs in seven games. But the next year we went to the Memorial Cup finals again and this time we beat Moose Jaw in four straight. This was quite an accomplishment and, as a result, the city of Toronto gave us a ticker-tape parade right up to City Hall.

If you're wondering why I wound up playing for Detroit instead of

Toronto, it happened while I was with the B team at St. Mike's. The Leaf scouts apparently didn't notice me, but a fellow named Carson Cooper, who was connected with the Red Wings, did and he put me on the Detroit list. Things were different back in the 1940s than they are now in the sense that there was no draft. If a scout like Cooper liked a kid, all he had to do was put his name on a list — lots of times

Red Kelly

the players didn't even know about it — and that made him property of the NHL team. Myself, I didn't know I belonged to the Red Wings until quite a while after Cooper had listed me.

I wasn't the only player Cooper found right in the shadow of Maple Leaf Gardens. A couple of years earlier he scouted Ted Lindsay and signed him for Detroit, even though Lindsay was playing in Toronto for St. Mike's. Ted was three years ahead of me.

Normally, when a youngster finished with his Junior A team in those days, he would wind up apprenticing for the NHL on a farm club either in the United States League or the American League where the Red Wings had teams in Omaha and Indianapolis, respectively. But I got lucky and went straight to the Red Wings.

In the fall of 1947, the Red Wings were training in Waterloo, Ontario, and this, of course, was my first ever pro camp. It wasn't an easy one because a lot of the people I was competing with had played for the Red Wings' Junior team in Galt, Ontario. They had been the enemy to me during my years at St. Mike's and now we were fighting for jobs in the Detroit organization.

At first it looked like I'd wind up in Indianapolis, but when training camp ended, I had survived all the cuts and, lo and behold, they took me with them to Detroit. In the 1947-48 season most NHL clubs only carried five defensemen; two pair of regulars and one reserve. I was their fifth defenseman.

When the season started, I sat on the bench most of the time although I did get some ice. But just before Christmas, Doug McCaig, one of our big, hitting defensemen, broke his leg and I was moved into his slot, playing regular for the first time. I must have made an impression because when McCaig recovered, Jack Adams traded him to Chicago.

Now I was one of the starting four defensemen, playing alongside Bill Quackenbush who had been in the league for four or five years. Bill was a rock-steady kind of player who played hard but clean. Of course, there were times when it wasn't all that easy for anyone to play a clean game when the rivalries got super hot. The best example of that was the playoff round we had against Toronto in 1949-50. We had faced the Maple Leafs in the 1948 finals and they beat us in four straight. The next season, 1948-49, we finished first and then knocked off Montreal in a tough seven-game series. That was a humdinger in that the first game went three overtimes — and we beat them — and the second game went into sudden death as well; and we won that game, too. Still, we took them in seven and then played Toronto and they beat us again in four straight.

By the time we met again in late March 1950, the intensity between Toronto and Detroit was very high. So the series opened at Olympia Stadium, our home rink, and on this one particular play, the Toronto captain and center, Ted Kennedy, was carrying the puck along the boards coming into our end of the rink. Meanwhile, Gordie Howe, who had become our top right-winger and one of the best young players in the league, was back-checking on the play and began overtaking Kennedy. Simultaneously, our big defenseman, Jack Stewart, was also steaming for Kennedy.

Something had happened earlier between Kennedy and Stewart and Black Jack thought this was the golden opportunity to even things up a bit. Jack saw Kennedy between the boards and Howe, and Kennedy realized that Howe was coming up on him and Stewart was there so he couldn't go that way and he couldn't go this way. The result was a three-way collision that became one of the most controversial collisions in a long time.

Kennedy pulled back at the last split second as Howe was going for him. Also I think there was a broken stick involved. In any event, Howe hit the boards headfirst and was seriously injured. His eyeball was scratched and there was internal damage to his head; later the doctors had to drill a hole and let the blood out. So, Gordie was on the operating table until about four in the morning.

Right after everyone realized how seriously Gordie was hurt, everybody was really up in the air. Toronto beat us five-nothing that game but that just made us so much more gung-ho to win the second game which ended up in a huge free-for-all.

How did it start?

The referee missed a call. Ted

Lindsay was carrying the puck for us and their defenseman, Gus Mortson, stuck his hand out and caught Lindsay taking his feet right out from under him. Everybody in the rink saw it, except the referee. There was no call but a few seconds later our defenseman, Lee Fogolin, hit somebody on the Leafs and he got two minutes. Before you knew it, everybody was fighting. Vic Lynn, a big Toronto left wing, and I ended up fighting down in the corner of the rink. One of my defense partners, Leo Reise, had been nicked with a stick and started bleeding. Reise went a little berserk. He came around with his stick and caught Jimmy Thomson of Toronto on the shoulder. He was fortunate he didn't get it in the head. Soon, the two goaltenders, our Harry Lumley and Turk Broda of Toronto, met at center ice and with all their equipment on went at it, rolling around on the ice. By now everyone was on the ice and people were throwing chairs from the stands at Olympia. It was almost a riot.

When the tempers finally cooled out, we went on to win the game 3-1, and that set the stage for a terrific series even though we didn't have Gordie for the rest of the playoff. We were down three games to two with the sixth game at Maple Leaf Gardens. Lumley pitched a 4-0 shutout that night to send us home for the final game which was another doozie; nothing-nothing into overtime.

I remember it well because the game was on Easter Sunday and the goal-scorer was a fellow who hardly ever scored goals. Leo Reise, who oddly enough scored the sudden-death goal in double-overtime of Game Four, was the hero again. I can still see the puck going in. Leo backhanded it at Broda and it bounced once and it bounced twice and at the second bounce, Broda kicked it and it went over the top and into the net, eight and a half minutes into the first sudden death.

That set us up for the finals against the Rangers and that also went the full seven games. Only this time the last game went into double-overtime and I can see the winner on that one, too. George Gee took the face-off for us and got the puck to Pete Babando. He fired and it went right in and that was my first Stanley Cup.

We did it with a lot of ingredients including some excellent goaltending from Harry Lumley. Applecheeks they used to call him. If someone scored a goal against him, his cheeks would turn beet red. There would be two goal lights; the regular one behind the net and Harry's cheeks. By 1950 I had played a few years in front of Harry and let me tell you it wasn't fun for a defenseman if he was on the ice when a goal got past Lumley. He would give us a searing look that could burn through iron. But it was just a look; no words. In all the years I played in front of Harry not once did he ever call me

Coach Tommy Ivan congratulates goalie Harry Lumley after a 1950 win in the finals with New York.

down. He was a great guy to have on your club.

When Gordie came back to us the following training camp, people figured that we could win at least two Stanley Cups in a row, maybe even three the way Toronto had done in the late 1940s. But the Canadiens took us in six games even though we had finished first.

A year later we got our revenge after coming out on top again. We beat Toronto four straight in the first round. The series opened at Olympia and we won 3-0 behind Terry Sawchuk. Then Sid Abel, our captain and top center, got hurt so they moved me up to center between Lindsay and Howe. In the fourth game, we were leading near the end, but Toronto was coming on strong. I went into their end for the puck with Howe coming in behind me. I tried to get the puck and pull it back to Gordie, but Jimmy Thomson hit me with his stick along my glove and broke the bone in my hand.

Now we're playing Montreal in the finals and even though my hand was broken, they dressed me without telling anyone about my injury. For protection, the trainer put padding over my hand but that didn't help my mobility. You see, the injured hand was the one I held high on my stick; which meant it was the one that I normally used for control of the puck. I was able to skate all right but there wasn't a lot I could do with the puck.

Would you believe it, we wound up with two men in the penalty box and my coach, Tommy Ivan, sends me out to kill the penalties. Well, I couldn't do anything with my injured hand because if I applied any pressure it was useless. Which meant that, basically, I was playing with one hand and could use that for holding out the stick for poke checks. The next problem was what do I do after I poke-check the puck free; how do I get it down the ice?

There was only one way for me to get any power on the puck and that was to let it get at the middle of my stick blade and then kick the stick like a whip and that's how I got the puck out.

We won the first two games of the 1952 finals at Montreal, but they didn't dress me for the third or fourth games — we won them both on shutouts — and that was my second Stanley Cup.

Just the way Harry Lumley helped us win my first championship in 1950, Terry Sawchuk did it for us two years later. We called him Ukie and he was as special in his way as Lumley was; maybe even better. I had played against Sawchuk in Junior hockey when he was with the Galt team and I played for St. Mike's.

Terry had an unusual body structure; he was wide in the body and rather chunky as a kid, although that changed a lot later. In his early playing days, they kept saying that he weighed too much, but he used to fill up that

goal and had a crouching style that was unusual for its time. When he was right, he was one of the top goaltenders but a real loner among the guys. Then again, goaltenders as a group were different and when you stop to think about it, anyone who plays in a lonely position like that is apt to be a loner.

But all Jack Adams was concerned about was Ukie stopping pucks and he was doing that for us awfully well. Jack's theory was that if we scored three goals in a game, we should win 99 percent of them. Jack wasn't so much interested in big scorers as he was in stopping the other guy from scoring. He taught us to play the game two ways; offensively and defensively. That's why we worked closely with our goaltenders, steering off forwards so that the shots they got were not wide open. Our goaltender usually didn't have to make more than three or four big saves a night.

When you played for the Red Wings, you listened to Jack, or else! In a way, though, he was like a Santa Claus with his big, round, reddish face. But when he had to be, he was as tough as they come. And he was very mule-headed. Stubborn. Of course, in his job you couldn't be wishy-washy.

Our coach, Tommy Ivan, was a perfect gentleman and reminded me of my Junior coach, Joe Primeau. Tommy never used foul language and didn't berate us very much, although he could lay down the law when necessary. With a personality like Jack Adams behind him, Ivan had to have tremendous patience and he always toned down Jack when he began to erupt. Jack might blow up over the team, but lots of times Ivan would act as the buffer and keep it from us.

Adams had tremendous power in Detroit when I was there and part of that was his control over the newspapermen covering hockey. The writers wrote what he wanted them to write; at least most of them did. But Jack's biggest problem was self-control. He would bust referee's doors down going after a fellow like Red Storey if he felt he called a bad game against us, and if they had the door locked, he would go right through the door to prove his point.

No winning team ever stands pat in the off-season and we were no different in that respect. But one move that really hurt was Jack Adams selling our captain Sid Abel to the Chicago Blackhawks in July 1952. Ole Bootnose, which is what we called him, was a terrific center who was getting up in years and had an opportunity to be player-coach in Chicago, so Jack let him go.

Abel had been a good captain with a terrific sense of humor so he always managed to keep things light; plus he knew how to handle Gordie and Ted. He'd give them blue blazes if they didn't pass him the puck when he was in the hole. They wouldn't take it from

Right: By the 1953-54 season Red Kelly (center with "A" on his jersey) ranked among the best NHL defensemen. Here he is poised to snare a rebound from a Terry Sawchuk save.

anybody else, but Ted and Gordie would take it from Sid. He was the veteran and he commanded our respect but especially Gordie's and Ted's. You see those two were always looking out for one another when it came to passing the puck back and forth. Lindsay would look for Howe and Gordie would look for Ted, and in the process they might forget about their center. But Ole Bootnose made sure they never forgot about him. Other centers who followed — Alex Delvecchio, Norm Ullman and Dutch Reibel — found that out; they would be standing wide open and wouldn't get the puck. It was frustrating to some of those guys.

But Teddy and Gordie were two of a kind. Lindsay was a lot like Rocket Richard; a fiery competitor — mean — and you weren't going to get to him without going through his stick. He wasn't the biggest guy in the world, but he wouldn't hesitate to cut you. He was solid and took care of himself. Yet off the ice, Teddy was very quiet; just the opposite of when he played.

By this time we had finished on top four consecutive years and we had swept the 1952 playoffs in eight straight, so it was only natural that we would repeat again in 1953. Sure enough, we won the regular season championship and played Boston in the first playoff round. We beat the Bruins badly, 7-2, in the first game, but then they tried a new strategy; they put Woody Dumart against Gordie and

they beat us, 5-3, in the second game and they went on to beat us in six games. In that series, Terry Sawchuk, who had four shutouts in eight games the previous year, was having a tough time. He was fighting the puck — which happens sometimes to goalies — and they wouldn't pull him. Ukie was a great goaltender and management's feeling was that if the club was going to go down, they would go down with their top guy in the net. But I could see the difference in him in one year. In 1953 if they had thrown a football at him it would have gone in. We got so desperate that we would be trying to stop the shots from the blue line from even getting near that goal of his. Mind you, it wasn't that Sawchuk wasn't trying or anything, but rather that he was fighting the puck.

The turning point was the third game after we had tied them at one apiece. Game Three was tied 1-1 after regulation and then it went into sudden death. Their goalie, Sugar Jim Henry, was stopping everything and you could tell just by looking at the ice; all the skate marks were inside the Boston blue line.

Finally, with more than 12 minutes left in the first overtime, they broke out and a third-stringer named Jack McIntyre backhanded one from way deep in the corner and it went into the net. They beat us 6-2 in the next game and went on to win the series.

Nothing worked right for us in that

playoff; Sid Abel had moved on to become playing-coach for the Blackhawks and Jack Adams thought he had the perfect replacement in Guyle Fielder, a center who had a terrific record in the minors. He played four playoff games for us and didn't get a single point.

The next year Alex Delvecchio was put on the line with Lindsay and Howe and we finished first again! This time

nobody had done in any major professional sport. The Yankees had won six so we were well-motivated to win a seventh and stand alone. The difficulty was in our opposition. Montreal had a terrific team that year and was ahead of us in the standings toward the end. But then Rocket Richard got suspended for hitting a linesman and we had to play in Montreal in the game after that.

Montreal was one very angry city

we didn't make any mistakes in the playoff. We beat Toronto in five and then took Montreal in seven although we had to go into overtime of the seventh game.

Now we were going for our seventh straight first-place finish which

when we arrived. The fans were upset with NHL president Clarence Campbell because he not only suspended Richard for the rest of the season — which was about a week — but also for both Stanley Cup rounds.

So, here we are arriving at The

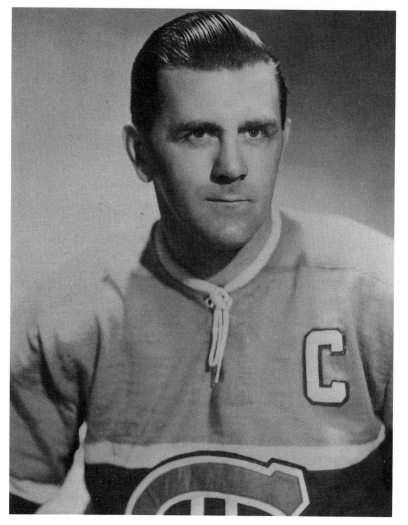

Forum for the big game and still a chance for us to finish first. As we arrived at the arena we could smell trouble. The lobby was jammed about an hour and a half before the game and there were a lot of people wearing leather jackets. We had to squeeze our way through just to reach the dressing room. Meanwhile, outside the rink fans were carrying picket signs calling Clarence Campbell every kind of name.

We managed to get through the crowd without incident and suited up for the game as if it was any other big one. We knew we had to win this one if we were going to make it seven straight first-place finishes and we played like it. Likewise, we expected the Canadiens to play hard because they wanted to compensate for the loss of Richard.

Once the game started the only thing we had on our minds was winning; we couldn't afford to lose if we wanted to win that seventh straight championship. That's what we were after. Never mind Richard's suspension and all the fuss that was going on around us. So, we went out and jumped into a big lead. At the end of the first period it was 4-1 for us.

Meanwhile, some strange things were happening. Halfway through the first period — while the action was going on — we heard a rumble reverberate through the building. Clarence Campbell had arrived about 10 minutes after the opening face-off with his girlfriend [Phyllis King, his secretary] and they climbed to a seat. I happened to be on the ice when the president arrived and I heard this strange noise that had nothing to do with the game itself. I said to myself, "What the hey is going on?"

The noise was the crowd reacting to Campbell coming into the arena and going to his seat. Spectators were angry at the sight of him and they weren't too happy about us leading either. As I was leaving the ice, I remember looking up and seeing the president trying to protect his girlfriend's hat. There was stuff flying and fans were throwing cabbages, tomatoes, whatever and there was rumbling right in front of his seat.

That was the last that I could see because I disappeared into our dressing room with the rest of the team.

Once we got into the locker room we tried to settle down. We knew we had two periods to go and didn't want to blow the lead. So far, so good; the Canadiens had come flying out of the chute; we held them in check, took the lead and now we were in good shape.

Just as we were getting ready to go back out onto the ice our club doctor came running into the room and he seemed to be crying; which was very strange. He was yelling that some fan had thrown a tear-gas bomb in the arena. On hearing that, we grabbed a bunch of wet towels and put them around the cracks in the doors so that gas wouldn't seep through into the dressing room.

We didn't really know what was happening on the outside except for bits of information that people would deliver from minute to minute. One fellow came into the room and reported that people were running up and down St. Catherine Street breaking windows and then someone told us that they had to clear the building because of the tear-gas bomb. Meanwhile, we were just waiting there trying to keep our minds on the game and the second period that was coming up.

Unfortunately, they couldn't clear the fumes from inside The Forum and they had to evacuate the entire building and, naturally, canceled the game.

Meanwhile, we were just sitting there waiting for instructions until somebody said, "Get dressed, quick, and stay together in one single line and move out to the back door and into the team bus." Which is exactly what we did. It was odd because usually after a game at The Forum a lot of the guys would hang around and chat with relatives and friends but not on this night. It was straight to the bus and out of there.

When we got to the bus, we could see the mobs of people on the street. Normally we would just go out the back of The Forum and then drive up St. Catherine Street to Westmount where they held the train for us. This time we went out to the corner and there was this mass of humans, so we turned and went another way and managed to get to Westmount. In the meantime there was chaos in downtown Montreal as people looted stores and set fire to newsstands and turned over police cars and threw rocks and hunks of ice and snow through the streetcar windows. I imagine if there had been a leader among that mob, they would have hanged somebody.

In any event we escaped successfully to Westmount, caught the train to Detroit and felt pretty darn lucky to get out of there alive. Because of the rioting, the game was forfeited to us and now we're on the train heading west and I was sitting with Jack Adams. Suddenly, a thought came to

me, "What would happen if somebody threw a tear-gas bomb in our building? Would we have to forfeit the game to Montreal?"

Jack said he had never thought about that, but we no doubt would lose the game. That gave Adams an idea so he made sure that when we played our next game at Olympia, everybody who came in to the arena got checked for things like tear-gas bombs. We were lucky; there was no incident; we won 6-0 and Ted Lindsay, who had just finished a suspension, scored four goals. So, we won our seventh championship which really was something!

During that championship period,

I was averaging 15-16 goals a season playing defense and reached 19 in 1952-53. I liked carrying the puck up the ice, but I couldn't fool around and make mistakes. We were winning the Vezina Trophy in those days and Jack Adams didn't necessarily believe in that kind of style. Nevertheless, I managed to wind up among the top 10 in scoring for quite a few years. What I would do was carry the puck out of our end and then join the rush. I would make one foray and try to keep the puck ahead of me, but I wouldn't hang around in their zone; I'd just go down, make the play and then get back to my defensive position. Otherwise, Jack

Adams and Tommy Ivan would have shot me.

I've been asked why I got into the puck-rushing mode when it was pretty much taboo. Actually, I began that style when I was a kid playing hockey in Port Dover and Simcoe. I'd get the puck and would take it down through everybody; that's just the way I was brought up, I guess. My dad told me how to score goals and when I got the chance and got in there to look the goaltender in the eye, he'd never know when I was going to shoot; he'd have no warning. And that was because of what my dad had told me: "Look him in the eye and he has no idea of when you're going to pull the trigger. Don't put your head down or anything; just keep the puck out in front of you." And I listened to his advice.

Not that I became a Rocket Richard. Far from it. The Rocket, among my opponents, was in a class by himself. In fact I would rate him the toughest guy I ever had to stop, one-on-one. The reason for that was the way he would drive for the net. He was a right wing with a lefthand shot. Playing the off-wing, he would carry the puck 'way out here and his body and arm would be between you and him and if he had a half a step on the defenseman, it was good-bye!

When most other players would get a half step on me, I could catch up, get my stick in — and the arm — and just dislodge the puck. But with the Rocket, it would be different. He just grabbed my stick and pushed it over. He used to be able to cut at right angles full tilt and then go full tilt crashing the net.

After he did it the first time, I thought I had figured a way to stop him. The next time he came down on me, I just dropped my stick right to the ice. All I had gripping the stick was two fingers at the tape wound around the end. So, I put the stick flat and Rocket has his hands down to block me, but when he brought his hand up for the shot, I used his knee as a lever and lifted his stick just as he shot.

Before Gordie Howe established himself, Richard was considered the Babe Ruth of hockey, and even after Gordie became the NHL's top scorer there were lots of debates about who was the better player, Howe or Richard. Gordie was a better all-round player and a better checking forward, but the one thing Richard had in more abundance than Howe was fire. The Rocket had dynamite in him, but Gordie wasn't quite the same. I don't know whether it was Richard's French background, his personality or what it was, but the Rocket had it. Yet night in and night out Howe was the better all-round performer.

While I had to watch out for the Rocket as a scoring threat, I also had to keep an eye out for others who might hurt us — or me, for that matter — in other ways. I'm talking specifically about players who could hurt physically. One of the most dangerous was Bill Ezinicki, a muscular right wing with the Maple Leafs.

His nickname was Wild Bill and he delivered some of the hardest body checks you would ever see. One of his special techniques was to come skating in from behind the defenseman. One of our players might be tangled up with a Toronto defenseman and all of a sudden — BOOM! — Ezzie leveled him with a tremendous hit.

Hits came in various shapes and forms, but there was a different style of hockey played then compared to the modern game. For example, today running into the boards is commonplace, but when I was playing you couldn't check a guy three feet from the boards. If you were going to hit a guy, you couldn't take more than three steps.

I remember once when we played against Chicago and Doug Bentley was one of their best scorers. One of our checking forwards, Marty Pavelich, ran Bentley into the boards. He hit him so hard that even Marty bounced off. Doug got up and said, "Kid, don't ever do that again!" Naturally, when Marty got the chance, he ran at Bentley, but Doug was true to his word. As Pavelich came at him, Bentley lifted his stick and Marty was almost impaled on it; the stick almost went right through him. P.S. Pavelich never did that again!

After that, we entered the playoffs and advanced to the finals against Montreal, again. The series went back and forth, but the last game was at Olympia and we beat them, 3-1, for the Cup. Detroit looked to be in terrific shape at the time. We now had seven straight titles, won our second straight Stanley Cup and had plenty of good players.

But this is where Adams' temper proved our undoing. He had brought in Jimmy Skinner as our coach in 1954-55 after Tommy Ivan moved over to Chicago to become general manager. Skinner couldn't handle Adams the way Tommy could. Jimmy would be like walking barefoot on spikes when Adams was around. When Jack would holler, it would befuddle Skinner and he would lose control.

It didn't hurt us in Skinner's first year behind the bench, but Jack's quick temper began to tell with the players. After the Cup win, Jack traded Terry Sawchuk to Boston and brought Glenn Hall in to be our goalie. Then, something happened between Jack and Glenn. One night Jack criticized the goalie and Hall told him to bleep off. That was it; Hall was gone. That's what I think happened with him and Ted Lindsay.

Adams got mad at Lindsay and Montreal beat us out for first place in 1955-56. The next year we finished first again, but the trouble between Adams and Lindsay really had gotten hot. Teddy was our captain after Sid Abel left and had been one of Jack's favorites. In fact he is the only player I know who ever got a rest in the middle of the season. Management actually sent him to Florida. But then Lindsay got involved with forming the first players' association and that did it. Adams decided to take the captaincy away from him, saying that the club now was going to rotate the captaincy. He approached me about being captain, but I turned him down. First of all, if they took it away from Ted, it would hurt him and if it hurts him, it will hurt his play and that will hurt the team. It didn't mean beans to me being captain. They came back and told me that Ted was not going to be the captain and if I didn't take it, somebody else would; so I became captain.

After the 1956-57 season Lindsay was traded to Chicago along with Glenn Hall. We got Johnny Wilson, Hank Bassen, Forbes Kennedy and Bill Preston in return. Meanwhile, we were changing coaches rapidly. Jimmy Skinner had taken over as head coach in 1954-55 when we won our last Cup and he remained behind the bench until the 1957-58 season when he was replaced in the middle of the year by Sid Abel.

In 1958-59, Sid's first full year behind the bench, the roof fell in on us. I had broken my foot part way through the year and we were struggling. It was touch and go whether we would make the playoffs or not, and we wound up getting knocked out in the last two games of the season against Toronto and New York.

Back to the broken foot; it happened during a practice; they put a cast on it and didn't say anything to anybody. They didn't announce what it was and passed the word around that nobody should know about it. Then, the team went on the road and lost three straight games. By that time, Adams came to me and asked if I thought I could play because the club had gotten pretty desperate by now.

He had a doctor with him and when he explained the situation, I said I would give it a try, but frankly, I didn't know if I could hack it. They took off the cast and taped up the leg up to my knee. I could skate and I could get by, but I couldn't turn to the outside; I could turn one way but not the other. That meant that when I was playing defense, I had to leave room for the guy coming down against me because I knew that I couldn't make a proper turn and that's the way I had to play the rest of the season.

After each game the trainer would remove the tape and put it back on before the next game. From time to time it would get sort of bloody, but I kept on playing. Meanwhile the club didn't say anything to anybody so nobody really knew about it. In any event, we finished in last place, missing the final playoff berth by seven points.

I returned home for the summer and then, all of a sudden, I began reading stories about how I had a bad year! Nevertheless, I was determined to come to camp in top shape and I spent all summer running on a sandy beach until I got that ankle back into shape.

By the time training camp began, I felt real good and the team got off to a much better start than the year before. We looked like a playoff team again when we went into Toronto for a game with the Leafs. The club stayed at the

Royal York Hotel downtown and while we were there one of the local columnists, Trent Frayne, asked if he could interview me and I agreed to sit down with him.

He started off by saying, "The team is doing better, isn't it?" And I said, "Yeah, we're doing a little better."

Then, he added, "And you're play-

ing pretty good. How come? They said last year that your legs were gone."

I was taken aback momentarily and then said, "They say lots of things. I don't know. Things are just going better, I guess."

But Frayne was persistent. "Aw, c'mon, now," he went on, "there's got to be something more than that."

I knew there was but I didn't know whether I wanted to tell him or not. For a few seconds, I thought about it and then I decided that it wouldn't hurt. After all, the reason why we didn't mention my broken foot was because the management was afraid that the opposition would take whacks at it; if they knew I was hurt, they'd slash me and then I'd be lost to the team. But that was last season and I figured it didn't matter now, so I told Frayne what had happened and he wrote the story.

Once the interview was over, I completely forgot about it and it remained forgotten until the club returned to Detroit. The morning after we arrived home, Ted Lindsay's wife, Pat, phoned my wife, Andra.

"Have you got your bags packed?" Pat said.

"What do you mean?" Andra asked.

"Haven't you seen today's paper?"

Andra had not gotten the newspaper and didn't have a clue as to what she was talking about. "You'd better get the paper," said Pat, "and you'd better get your bags packed because you'll be going!"

When Andra told me about the phone call, I headed downtown to pick up the papers. Sure enough, Marshall Dann of the *Detroit Free Press* had a story with a big headline: WAS RED KELLY FORCED TO PLAY ON A BROKEN FOOT?

Then, I read the piece but it didn't

Although Terry Sawchuk was primarily a stand-up goalie, he occasionally would stack the pads to make a save. Red Kelly is on hand to clear the rebound.

say anything like that in the story. The headline was misleading and, frankly, I didn't worry too much about it. I had already played 50 games for Detroit that season and was on a better point-per-game average than I had the previous year. That night we were playing the Rangers at Olympia and everything seemed honky-dory until the second period when somebody must have mentioned to my wife that I had been traded to New York.

I still had no idea about any deal and finished the game as I would have finished any other game. Only after the game I was given word that Jack Adams wanted to see me in his office; Jack and Bruce Norris, the Red Wings' owner.

As soon as I got up to the office, they gave me the news: "We just traded you to the New York Rangers. Report to Muzz Patrick [Rangers' general manager] at 8:30 tomorrow morning at the Leland Hotel."

The Rangers. They already had gone through a coaching change — Phil Watson to Alfie Pike — and were dead last in the league with absolutely no chance of making the playoffs. The deal was supposed to be myself and a young forward named Billy McNeill for defenseman Bill Gadsby and forward Eddie Shack.

I imagine that Adams and Norris expected me to obligingly accept the trade since that was the way things were done in those days. Instead, I said, "I'll think about it."

That took Jack by surprise. "What do you mean, you'll 'think about it.' You be at the Leland at 8:30 in the morning."

"I said," I replied even more firmly, "I'll think about it and I'll let Mister Patrick know!"

I walked out and went home, stayed up all night and thought about it. Then, I went to church early in the morning, then phoned Muzz Patrick and told him that I was not reporting to the Rangers. "I'm retiring," I said.

A lot has been written and said about my decision, but the plain and simple reason for the decision had nothing to do with New York, or Muzz Patrick or the Rangers' team. It had to do with the implication that they had put on me that my "legs were gone" and that was supposedly the reason why Detroit had missed the playoffs the previous year. So, I didn't owe the Red Wings anything. They had paid me up through that Rangers game and now I was retired. So, I phoned the guy I had worked for during the summer and asked him if I could start work first thing in the morning. He was kind of shocked but said, "Sure."

No sooner had I announced my retirement when I got a call from the president's office. Clarence Campbell was on the phone and he said that the deal had been killed and Gadsby and Shack had to go back to New York. Meanwhile, Billy McNeill had quit hockey. (He had just lost his wife not too long before that.) Meanwhile, Campbell wanted me to know that Adams was going to suspend me.

"If he suspends you," warned Campbell, "it will be for life. You won't be able to have anything to do with hockey in any capacity whatsoever — coaching, refereeing, playing, anything! I'm holding him off to give you time to think about it."

I said, "Thank you very much, Mister Campbell, but I've thought about it and made up my mind. I've given everything I had since I was knee-high to a grasshopper. If that is what you want to do, suspend me for life, but I'm not reporting!"

With that, I returned to my non-hockey job, but it was tough. Wherever I went, whatever I did, people I encountered all wanted to talk hockey. Meanwhile, I had just been married and with a new wife I wanted to make a living.

All of a sudden, the phone rang one day and Andra picked up. It was King Clancy who then worked closely with Punch Imlach who was general manager and coach of the Maple Leafs. Clancy asked Andra whether I would consider playing for Toronto. Clancy and Imlach were in Boston at the time, but Andra managed to get word to me and I called him. I said I didn't want to discuss this on the phone but rather I felt it would be better if we met in person.

This was very touchy business and the last thing I wanted was for any newspaper people to know about this. The meeting between me and Clancy would be in Toronto so I decided to wear a disguise — I put on a homburg hat — and flew out of Windsor under

an assumed name. When I arrived in Toronto, I was still in disguise. Clancy was awaiting me at the airport but had no idea that I was incognito. As I walked down the ramp, I could see people waiting for the passengers. Clancy was behind the pane of glass, trying to find me, but it was obvious that my disguise even had him fooled. I walked right past him and then behind him and he still was looking for me. Now everybody was off the plane and poor King thought he had missed me or that I wasn't even on the plane. Finally, I gave him a tap on the shoulder and surprised him. "I didn't even think you were coming," he said. We then went downtown where I checked into the Westbury Hotel under the name of Stan Obodiac who was the Maple Leafs' press agent.

We met and talked until dinnertime and then decided to go to Winston's for dinner to continue our discussions. The moment we got to Winston's I noticed the Montreal Canadiens sitting there for the team dinner so we quickly hustled out of there and headed down the street in their car. Imlach and Clancy were sitting in the front while I was in the back. As they started driving, Imlach shouted, "Duck!"

I didn't know what that was all about until Punch pointed to a man crossing the street. It was Jim Vipond of the *Toronto Globe and Mail*. Punch had to stop the car to avoid hitting him. "Wait til Vipond realizes he was this far from the big story," chuckled Imlach.

After dinner we returned to the hotel and continued talking until one in the morning when we finally agreed to a deal. Imlach was so anxious to have me play, he said he even wanted me to dress the next night against Montreal.

"I don't have my skates," I said.

"No problem," snapped Punch, "we'll fly them in."

"I haven't skated in 10 days," I told them. "I'd hate to go out there and make mistakes and cost the club a goal or two."

"That's all right," said Imlach, "we're going to play you at center against Jean Beliveau. What do you think?"

What could I think? They wanted me so badly and Toronto was an up-and-coming team which had made the playoffs the previous season, beating out the Rangers. Now they were even better.

"It's great," I said. "If I make a mistake at center, there's going to be a defenseman behind me."

Before I left the room, Imlach had one other message for me: "In order for us to win the Stanley Cup, we're going to have to beat Montreal. You're the last piece; we need somebody to check Jean Beliveau."

I was glad to oblige and the results were satisfactory. Toronto finished second that season and Detroit fourth. As luck would have it the Leafs and Wings met in the opening playoff round and my new club beat my old club four games to two. Even though Toronto got swept in four straight by Montreal in the finals, I did okay for myself; I finished third overall in assists with eight and third overall in points with 11.

If the Red Wings thought my legs were gone they had another thing coming. I became a full-time center with the Leafs and played six more full seasons with them, retiring in 1967. During my stint in Toronto we won four Stanley Cups while the Red Wings didn't win another.

MAX McNAB

Like Red Kelly and Johnny Wilson, Max McNab also owns a Detroit Red Wings' Stanley Cup ring. The tall, likeable center from Watson, Saskatchewan, earned his championship jewelry playing for the 1950 Stanley Cup team.

At the time the 6 foot two inch, 170 pounder was considered the natural successor to Sid Abel as center on the Production Line with Gordie Howe and Ted Lindsay.

Until then, McNab had done everything the right way; at least according to Detroit's hockey boss, Jack Adams. Max had climbed the ladder from Junior hockey into the minor professional ranks with the Red Wings' United States League club in Omaha. He made his professional debut in the Motor City during the 1947-48 season, a year after Howe had made his NHL debut.

However, injuries got in the way of what appeared to be a promising major-league career for McNab, and after a playoff appearance in 1951, he finished the remainder of his career in the minors where he was eminently successful.

McNab later became a beloved executive, completing his hockey stint with the New Jersey Devils with whom he was both general manager and vice-president before retiring in 1994.

Max reminisced about the Detroit days during an interview at his Secaucus, New Jersey home with reporter Keith Fernbach.

I came to Detroit by way of Saskatoon. My birthplace was Watson, Saskat-chewan, but Saskatoon was the big city in the province and when I was a teenager they had an excellent Junior-level team called the Quakers. Fortunately, I made the team and that was quite an experience for a fellow my age because I was playing alongside some awfully good young players. One of them was Keith Allen who later had an excellent and long career as an American League defenseman and eventually wound up as coach and then general manager of the Philadelphia Flyers.

Strangely enough, the stick boy on that Saskatoon Junior team in 1942-43 was a lad named Gordie Howe. He was always hanging around the rink, but our coach knew he was going to be a great player and kept an eye on him, figuring he'd be with us in a year or two. We finally had Gordie practicing with us, but one day our captain, Bob Dawes, went up to the coach and said, "I don't think you should let the stick boy practice with us anymore; he's going to hurt somebody!" Gordie was all of 13 years old at the time.

World War II already was under-way and I joined the Royal Canadian Air Force where I served for two years. Once the war ended in 1945, I enrolled at the University of Saskatchewan and played hockey for them while on the side I also played for the Saskatoon Senior hockey club.

At the time, Detroit had a scout named Fred Pinckney — he's the bird

dog who discovered Gordie Howe — and he spotted me during a game. Pinckney must have liked what he saw because he asked me if I wanted to attend the Red Wings' training camp.

That was a very attractive offer, but I also wanted to finish school so I told him, "No, I'm going to continue at the university."

But Pinckney wanted me badly and he figured out how I could squeeze in a visit to the Detroit camp right after Labor Day and still not miss any classes. So, I went to the camp and, like everyone else there — big stars and

small ones — I signed a one-year deal. In those days there was no such thing as a five-year or even a three-year contract. Everybody was signed for a one-year deal and it was all accomplished in a couple of days. When the manager, Jack Adams, made up his mind, he signed the whole team.

Since the university didn't begin its semester until October 1st, I had a couple of weeks to see how I'd do against the pros. I figured, what the heck, I'd enjoy the experience and then come back to Saskatoon.

But a new fellow like myself was not easily welcomed. The players were very clannish and stuck together; so it was not easy to crack a team. Practices were tough. There were at least three or four guys on the team who had lost a friend from a roster cut and they didn't want any rookie to think he could just waltz into a regular spot on the lineup.

But I must have done something right because one day Adams asked me to come to his office. To my surprise, he wanted to talk contract with me. He was offering me $2,000 to sign and a first-year contract of $4,000 to play in the minors. Wow! That was more than a lot of the players were getting, but since I was regarded as a "college player" they seemed to want me more; possibly because they knew that I wasn't dependent on them.

The kind of money they were offering me was more than I had expected, so I phoned home and told my mother that I wasn't going to continue college and that I was about to turn pro. She wasn't exactly delighted with that; not a bit.

She said, "Maybe you should look into getting into something with more security."

You have to remember that my mother had lived through the Great Depression and people like that were very security conscious. She didn't think a professional hockey career had any longevity, but in retrospect, I got 48 years out of it.

Even though my mother was against it, I signed the contract and was assigned to the Omaha Knights in the United States League. It was my first professional experience and I daresay it was fun. Adams had a lot of good prospects down there and, of course, the best of all was our goalie, Terry Sawchuk, who was out of Winnipeg. He was only 17 years old at the time, but even then you could tell that he was incredible. Even in practice it was almost impossible to score on him.

Terry and I roomed together in Omaha. In those days, long before the big salaries, it was customary to put young, single players in rooming houses. The club knew a bunch of families in the community who would put up the players in a sort of bed-and-breakfast. Before we went to the rink we'd have breakfast with the family and then take off for our hockey business. It was a nice atmosphere and worked out quite well.

We had a good team in Omaha and a good part of the reason for that was Sawchuk, although for a brief time, we thought his career would be drastically abbreviated by an eye injury. We were in Houston at the time and during the game a screened shot got through a maze of players and hit Terry right on the eyeball.

It was very serious stuff; so serious that Jack Adams chartered a plane from Detroit the minute he heard about it and flew down. Believe me, when someone chartered a plane at that time, it was major stuff. But as I said, Sawchuk was Detroit's prize young goalie and even then was considered a million-dollar prospect.

They put four stitches in the eye-

ball and then everyone held his breath, hoping that the surgery would work. Meanwhile, Sawchuk was just the picture of courage while we were all worrying whether he'd ever play goal again. When the stitches came out Terry was all right and that was quite a relief for us.

In those days of the late 1940s, Sawchuk weighed 195 pounds and was a great, big, happy-go-lucky, chubby kind of guy and, already, very successful on the level he was playing. But later on someone advised him that he would be even quicker in the net if he went on a crash diet and he went down to 172 pounds. After that, he never could put the weight back on and played the rest of his career as a sort of skinny kind of fellow.

I played the 1946-47 season in Omaha and when our playoffs were over, I was called up to the big club just to watch them in action; not to play. Detroit got beat by Toronto, four games to one, in the first round so I went home for the summer wondering where I would be once the 1947-48 season began.

Well, the next season I went to camp and impressed them enough to have them ask me to join the big club once the regular season began. I started in Detroit, played a dozen games, had two goals and two assists and two penalty minutes and then we played the Rangers. One of New York's defensemen was a fellow named Pat

Egan; nicknamed Boxcar. He really earned that one because he was built like one; not that tall but filled with muscle on a fireplug frame. When he hit you, it hurt!

And, brother, did he ever hit me. It was a body check that first made contact at my elbow and drove it back until I separated my shoulder. I was out two or three weeks and I remember Jack Adams driving me to the Detroit airport after I recovered so that I could get back into condition with Omaha.

"We'll pick you up here in two weeks," said Adams.

So, I returned to Omaha and two things happened; the Red Wings started winning and the Knights started winning. Detroit didn't need me and Omaha was tickled to have a player who finished with 44 goals in 44 games.

Once again, the Red Wings called me up to Detroit after the U.S. League playoffs were over and Adams picked me up at the airport. "Hiya, kid!" he laughed, remembering his early promise, "that was a long two weeks." Jack hadn't forgotten what he had said, but he just had forgotten to call.

Anyhow, I played in three playoff games for Detroit and that earned me an invite to training camp for the 1948-49 season. This time I stayed in "the show," but it wasn't easy. Even though they hadn't won the Stanley Cup in a while the Red Wings were building a very strong team. They had an excellent goalie in Harry Lumley, a fine defense with fellows like Black Jack Stewart, Red Kelly and Bob Goldham and terrific forwards — Ted Lindsay, Gordie Howe and Sid Abel, as well as second-liners such as Jimmy McFadden, who had won the Calder (rookie-of-the-year) Trophy in 1947-48.

Of all the group, Lumley was one of the more interesting because he joined the club during the World War II years, and he was just a boy when he broke in and the youngest goalie ever to become a regular in the NHL. Harry was a big, robust guy who would whack you if you happened to be around his net. He was also very superstitious and funny about his use of time.

In those days the games used to start at eight in the evening so we would be on the ice at 7:45, warm up and then the game would start. So, everybody would be in the dressing room at half-past six to get ready. But Harry would come in at 7:30 — zip, zip, put on his pads, stand up, the trainer would put a puck in his hand and he would be ready to go. As soon as Tommy Ivan said, "Let's go!" Harry would stand up, put on a glove and the trainer would smack a puck into it — they only warmed up with one puck in those days — and off he went.

Another fascinating character was our left-wing ace, Ted Lindsay. The first time I had been at the Red Wings' training camp, I had heard stories about Teddy. He was a little guy and when he had first come to Detroit, the betting was that he wouldn't last a full season; he'd be out of hockey. They figured that he was such a troublemaker somebody was surely going to get him. But he was a tough, cocky guy and, for his size, he could fight.

At first everybody ran at Teddy and he ran right back at them. Hit for hit, he was right there because he was one of the gutsiest players you'd ever want to see. But the thing I admired most about Lindsay was the fact that he was in better shape than anybody. After only 48 hours of training camp he was ready for the whole season.

Once Howe came to the team and won a spot, he and Lindsay became teammates and linemates and, after a while, they became inseparable both on and off the ice. They went everywhere together and did everything together. If there was a fight, Gordie would move in to finish the guy off if Ted needed any help. They had a special bond.

According to Jack Adams' plan I was supposed to center for Lindsay and Howe while Sid Abel would kill penalties. But after I got hurt, Abel was moved in there and the Production Line was formed and became the best line for the next several years. Sid was reborn because he had the two great, young kids doing all the work. That's not to take anything away from Sid; he was excellent in front of the net, a terrific playmaker and a good face-off man. He could do all the things and, besides that, he was the team captain. He was the guy who got everyone together for the team meetings. I might add, Abel also was an awfully nice guy.

Even though Sid was thriving with Howe and Lindsay he was up in years and he'd get tired when they had long shifts. So what Ivan did was have Abel go for 40 or 50 seconds and then send me in to mop up for the remainder of their shift. My job was to do defensive work and let them take care of the offense.

Since I quickly understood that our club had oceans of talent, I knew that I had to find a role for myself if I was going to stick in the NHL. What I

realized most of all was that I had to learn how to check; and I worked hard at that and, after a while, I got better and better as a checking center.

It didn't hurt me that we had an All-Star defense. There was Black Jack Stewart, a genuine hard hitter, Red Kelly, a fantastic puck-carrier and Bill Quackenbush, who was just a solid all-round defenseman. Also, Leo Reise who was very solid and later Marcel Pronovost and Bob Goldham.

My favorite of all time was Black Jack. He had unbelievable strength and would take on anybody and never lost. Naturally, he was not a favorite among out-of-town fans. When we would go play in Toronto, Montreal, New York, Boston or Chicago, Jack would be the last one to step on the ice for us. At the very last minute this unbelievable booing would start. I would look up into the stands and be thinking, "What the hell is that all about?" Then, I'd realize that the booing was because Black Jack had just stepped on the ice. He just skated around like a prince but that booing from the enemy fans actually was the greatest form of respect that a visiting player could get.

Unfortunately, Black Jack, as good as he was for our team, had been living on borrowed time with us because a few years earlier he had gone over Jack Adams' head to get a new contract. Our owner, Jim Norris, gave it to him and Adams never talked contract with him again. After we won the Cup in 1950, Adams traded him to Chicago.

In contrast to Stewart there was Bill Quackenbush who actually won the Lady Byng Trophy which was really unusual for a defenseman. I'll never forget the first scrimmage I had with Bill. He put three passes on my stick that were so perfect, I couldn't believe them. In fact, I missed every one of them because I never thought Quackenbush could find the space to put them through such a maze of players. I had never seen anybody who could pass the puck like that. Bill also was a great poke checker and also was magnificent on the power play alongside Red Kelly.

In 51 games I scored 10 goals and 13 assists for 23 points, but the important thing was that I did what I was supposed to do for the club and that was really all that mattered to management.

When the 1949-50 season began I was put on a defensive line with Marty Pavelich and Gerry (Doc) Couture. Marty was a terrific little hockey player who usually was given the unpleasant assignment of checking the great Rocket Richard; which, by the way, he did pretty well.

Detroit had finished in first place a year earlier and now we were on top again. This was when the NHL had only six teams so when the playoffs started, the first place team played the third place club and second played fourth. Our first assignment was the

Maple Leafs who had wound up third but already had won three consecutive Stanley Cups starting in 1947.

It really rankled Jack Adams that we couldn't beat Toronto in the play-offs; I mean it really bothered him. Plus, Jack had such a terrible temper. If we were losing a game, he would come into the locker room and, all of a sudden, every single player would lean down and pretend to tighten his skate laces. Jack would walk up and down by the training table where we had oranges cut up in quarters for the players to eat between periods. If he didn't like the way you were playing, he'd throw the oranges at you to get your attention. But it was only because he wanted to win so badly.

We opened the 1950 playoffs at Olympia and that first game has since become quite famous — or maybe infamous is the better word — because of what happened to Gordie Howe. After Rocket Richard, Gordie was the best right wing in the league and he was fast becoming the best player. Period!

Gordie could do everything; and I mean everything; he had a terrific physique with sloped shoulders and a powerful skating stride. He could shoot from either side — which was very unusual — he could fight and, well, he could do just about everything but play goal. And I'm sure that had he put his mind to it, he would do that well, too.

So, now it's the big first game;

Toronto had beaten Detroit in eight straight playoff games and we had something to prove, right.

Well, before the game is over we've lost Gordie Howe and we also lost the game by a big score. Naturally, everyone was talking about Howe because he was pretty near death.

Gordie was trying to hit Teeder Kennedy of Toronto and wound up sliding into the boards where he hit his head against the dasher. Everybody in Detroit said that Kennedy had illegally used the butt end of his stick on Gordie, but I was sitting at the end of the bench watching the action take place and what I saw made Kennedy innocent.

What happened was that as Kennedy saw Howe coming at him he jumped out of the road and just then Howe lost his balance and went into the boards. Of course in those days there was no such thing as television replay to check it out so everybody had his own version and, naturally, the Detroit people had it in for Kennedy. To hear some of them talk, Kennedy had given our guy a vicious backhander.

In any event the injury to Howe dominated the newspapers for several days and we, the players, were more worried about Gordie surviving than anything else. That was our main concern. I can't begin to tell you how devastated Jack Adams was. Here was a guy who I had only seen with one emotion; "Go get 'em, gang!" But after Gordie's injury, Adams came in the room and I saw him cry.

This episode taught me a lesson and that was that I never thought there was a weakness in anyone who shed a tear.

We were absolutely devastated, especially since we had lost 5-0 in a blowout at our home rink. It was like somebody opening and exposing your heart. Here we had lost the guy who had finished his first big year with 35 goals. He was the power; the one player who got things going. He was the policeman; he was everything.

Personally, I didn't have any vindictive feelings toward Kennedy, but some of my teammates who had been in the NHL a lot longer than me and had played against Teeder had an axe to grind with him. Obviously, they saw things differently and when we played Toronto in Game Two, all hell broke loose with fights all over the place.

Me, I was a skinny kid and not one

of the heavyweight champions of the NHL. But we had a lot of tough guys so I didn't feel that I had to get involved in a big way. But after a while it got to the point where everybody was on the ice and each player was taking a man from the other team.

One the most surprising aspects of the brawl was the role of our defenseman Red Kelly. Normally, Red was one of the most peaceful guys you'll ever meet; a true gentleman who never cursed or screamed. But on this night he was right in the midst of it and that didn't help the Leafs because among other things, Kelly was as physically strong a player as you'll ever meet in the league.

More importantly, we bounced back to win Game Two and that set the stage for one fantastically exciting series which we finally won in overtime of the seventh game. The winning goal

came in sudden-death overtime and what was strange about that was the Cup-winning score came off the stick of one of our lowest-scoring defensemen. Leo Reise was a big, tough defensive defenseman who scored only four goals in 70 games that season, but he already had one sudden-death goal in the Toronto series and now he got his second one. I can still see the face-off in the Leaf end. The puck swung around and came back to Leo and he banged one that went past Turk Broda. That we did it without Howe in the lineup was quite a feather in the cap of our management team, manager Jack Adams and our coach Tommy Ivan.

While we were beating Toronto, the Rangers had taken the Canadiens which put them into the finals against us. New York had a good team with Lynn Patrick behind the bench. Charlie Rayner was their goalie – one of the best; and they had some nifty forwards like Bones Raleigh, Pentti Lund and Edgar Laprade. What we had to do was figure a way of compensating for Gordie Howe's loss. We had managed against the Leafs, but the Rangers were a whole other story and here's where good management came into the picture. Adams and Ivan made sure that we all were in the proper frame of mind and when I say all, I mean all of us.

Especially Ivan. He had the knack of making a fourth-line guy thinking that he was as important to the team as

Lindsay, Abel and Howe. What Tommy did was take Joe Carveth, a veteran right wing who was at the tail end of his career, and put him in Gordie's spot with Sid and Ted. It was the most difficult transition anyone could ask of a player, but Joe came through like the trooper that he was.

One reason why Carveth was able to do so was because of Ivan's coaching. Tommy had made Joe feel that his contribution was as significant as anyone else's, so when he went alongside Abel and Lindsay, he did so with a lot of pride. Tommy knew how fragile the confidence factor was and how players were scared that this might be their last year, especially with the strength of our farm teams.

Anyhow Joe came off the bench and by the time we came up against New York, he was a regular fixture on the first line. Still, we missed Howe and we were still far from the Cup. Before the finals started, Black Jack called a team meeting in my room and he said to the younger guys like myself, "You fellows are going to be around for another 10 or 12 years. Me and Sid have to win it this year so I don't want to see you guys screwing around. And if anybody has a bad night because he isn't ready or isn't working, just remember one thing; when the game is over and you come into the dressing room, I'll be the first guy you'll meet. And I don't care what Mister Adams says tomorrow or what Mister Ivan says

tomorrow; that doesn't mean anything. Just listen to what I'm saying or you'll meet me after the game."

That was the strongest pep talk I ever heard in all my years in hockey. And, let me tell you something; Black Jack Stewart was the last guy in the world you would want to mess around with; the last!

Nevertheless, as hard as we tried, we missed Gordie, big-time, and the Rangers had us down three games to two and actually had us down 3-1 in Game Six. But that's when Joe Carveth came through and set up our second goal and then set up Abel for the game winner midway through the third period. That tied the series, but we still had our work cut out for us.

In Game Seven, we were down 3-1 but tied it up on two power-play goals and the game went into double-overtime before we finally got the winner.

Talk about planning a big play, this was a classic. The face-off was deep in the Rangers' zone and we had a fellow named George Gee out there to take the face-off. His linemate was Pete Babando. They were lining up to the right of Chuck Rayner and just before the linesman dropped the puck, Gee yelled, "Wait a minute!"

He skated back to Babando and moved him about 18 inches from the original spot where he had been lining up for the face-off. This was like right out of a Hollywood script — like in a big football game where the quarter-back designs the play — when everything works just picture-perfectly. I mean it had everything, including Gordie Howe being there, watching from the stands. So, George, God bless him, seemed to know who he was going up against and exactly what he had to do. Then George went back for the draw and on the face-off, he won it perfectly and slipped it right back to Babando. Pete slapped at it one time and, fortunately, had a little bit of a screen in front of Rayner and he fired it right past the goalie.

Every once in a while I stop and wonder what would have happened if Babando had stayed where he had been originally; the puck would have been won by Gee but it would have come right back to Pete's skates and he wouldn't have been able to get the shot off and we might have lost the game and the chance to win the Cup.

How does it feel to win your first Stanley Cup?

Good question. Start with one word — euphoria. Or another — unbelievable. I mean without Howe, we were really underdogs when you think about it; which is why winning was so terribly sweet. It was a dreamy sort of experience and never in a million years did I think I was going to get a chance to be on a Cup winner.

So, there we were all out on the ice celebrating and then the topper came when Gordie was escorted out to cen-ter and Lindsay met him and they had a hug. Gordie was wearing a fedora at the time so Teddy took Howe's hat off his head and threw it up in the air. There was Gordie standing with an absolutely bald head. You see they had done the surgery on his skull and, to do so, they had to shave his whole head. Nobody had seen Howe before the game so when they realized he now was bald it was sort of a shocking sight for the fans.

The only downer out of the whole thing came after the game at a party thrown for the team at the Book-Cadillac Hotel. You see the guys really were beer drinkers, completely unaccustomed to champagne. And don't forget, they had just finished a seven-game series and double-overtime of the seventh game so we were all dehydrated. Now here we are at the hotel and, instead of beer, there were bottles and bottles and more bottles of champagne. We all started taking swigs of the stuff, but our systems were not receptive and, as a result, quite a few guys got a little crazy. But that was all right.

Our team was on top of the hockey world and the sky was the limit for us. As long as Gordie could return in good shape, the team figured to be a winner for years. He was the player who made the Red Wings great and it would be proven in the years to come. Granted, he was surrounded by a lot of All-Stars and it was a great organization; a great, great organization partly because Jack

Adams had built such a terrific farm system while demanding loyalty from all hands.

In fact, Nelson Hubbard's song, "Loyalty," hung in the Detroit dressing room for years and that meant a lot to Adams. If you were loyal to Jack, he would reciprocate. He may have had disagreements with a lot of players and a lot of players hated him because of the trades, but as a person, he had a good heart.

Likewise, Tommy Ivan was also good to me. When I played for him I was just a hard-working defensive kind of player. Sure, I had scored big in the minors but Tommy had enough goal-scorers so I knew my place. And when Alex Delvecchio made the big club at center it didn't surprise me that I was traded to Chicago.

Then, I hurt my back in the Blackhawks' training camp and they put me in a Chicago hospital for two months. The doctors there couldn't find the problem so I came back to Detroit to pick up a car and drive out to Vancouver where we were living. I happened to bump into Jack Adams at a hockey game and he said, "Jesus Christ, kid, what's the matter?"

I said, "I've got a bad back and I'm going back to Vancouver because the Chicago doctors can't find the problem."

He said, "Why don't you come and see our doctors?"

So, I saw the Red Wings' doctors even though I was now with Chicago and they checked me all over and suggested I return the next day. Sure enough, they sent me to an orthopedic hospital where the doctors ran some tests and said I needed back surgery.

The operation was done, but the amazing thing was that during my stay in the hospital my Chicago boss, Bill Tobin, never once came to see me. But Tommy Ivan and Jack Adams visited me three or four times a week.

As I said, I was around for only the 1950 Stanley Cup. Detroit missed it the next year, then won it in 1952, missed in 1953 and won two in a row in 1954 and 1955. Some people have wondered why they didn't win more Stanley Cups, considering the talent they had. The answer is simple; the competition in the NHL was so close in those days that any team had a good chance in any given year.

Me, I only wish I could have played longer in Detroit because they had a terrific bunch of guys. We used to travel by train all the time in those days and we didn't have such electronic magic as video replay, but we knew how to compensate. After a road game, we'd be sitting in the parlor car of the train, discussing the game. Somebody would fetch a bar of soap and draw a picture of the rink, with the red and blue lines and goals. They then would diagram the goals that were scored and the mistakes that led to them. Then, everybody would sit and argue.

But when I look back at those years with the Red Wings, I consider it a great run. And to think, my mother thought I should get into something with more security!

Aftermath

On the night of April 14, 1955, approximately five minutes after the Detroit Red Wings had beaten Montreal for the Stanley Cup, NHL President Clarence Campbell walked out on the ice and presented the silver mug to Captain Ted Lindsay.

Dripping with sarcasm — a fact that went virtually unnoticed to the capacity crowd — Lindsay delivered a short speech that had significant overtones for the years to come: "Thank you, Mr. Campbell. We couldn't have won without the great managerial help of Jack Adams and that great little coach, Jimmy Skinner. Earlier in the season, we were a bunch of bums, so I guess it takes a bunch of bums to win the Stanley Cup."

Of course, what Lindsay meant was that the Wings could have done very well without Adams and probably could have won the Cup with Howdy Doody behind the bench. Lindsay, Marty Pavelich and other Red Wings had become disenchanted with Adams' leadership and totally unimpressed with Skinner's coaching. When Lindsay attempted to help organize a players' union, a full-scale rift developed between the captain and the commander.

"So I shipped him to Chicago," said Adams.

Actually, Adams had unloaded several players before bumping Lindsay. Glen Skov, Tony Leswick, Johnny Wilson, Benny Woit, Vic Stasuik, Marcel Bonin and Lorne Davis all were part of the championship combine. Without them, the Red Wings simply weren't the same.

"They should have won the Stanley Cup three or four more times," said St. Louis Blues' vice-president Ron Caron, who was in his mid-20s when Adams was breaking up the Red Wings.

Not that Adams dismissed all of his stars. Red Kelly was in his 13th season when Adams traded him after the 1960 season. By this time the Norris family had begun restructuring the high command. Tall, handsome Bruce Norris took control of the team and following the 1961-62 season he fired Jack Adams and put Sid Abel in complete command. The club improved under Abel and reached the Stanley Cup finals in 1963 and 1964. They lost the former to Toronto four games to one, but in April 1964 they appeared to have another Cup within their grasp. Detroit led three games to two and 3-2 in what would have been the clinching game at Olympia. But with only 2:12 to go the Leafs tied the score and won in overtime. In the finale Detroit lost 4-0. They reached the finals again in 1966 and once more looked like winners. They beat the Habs in the first two games in Montreal but then proceeded to lose the next four straight.

After that, Mediocrity became the Red Wings' middle name. Gordie

Howe retired after the 1970-71 season, in which Detroit finished last in the Eastern Division. It wasn't until the construction of Joe Louis Arena and the advent of the Mike Ilitch ownership that the franchise took a significant upturn. The renaissance began with the stewardship of Jacques Demers behind the bench and later Scotty Bowman.

During the lockout-abbreviated 1994-95 season, the Red Wings finished with the best overall point total and appeared to be favorites to win their first Stanley Cup in 40 years. But an upstart New Jersey Devils team spanked them in four straight games and the "wait 'til next year" chant was heard throughout Michigan once again.

Epilogue

part VI

I had the good fortune of watching a Stanley Cup final at Olympia Stadium on April 16, 1961. At the time, I was writing a profile of Chicago Blackhawk's star Stan Mikita, but I also had a keen interest in the Red Wings. Detroit had tied the series at two games apiece, then lost Game Five 6-3 in Chicago. The feeling at the time was that Detroit still could take the title, and they opened Game Six with a goal by Parker MacDonald on passes from Gordie Howe and Alex Delvecchio. It looked good for Detroit until the second period when Chicago scored twice and then put the game away with three more goals in the third period. I returned to Detroit a couple of years later and watched them lose to Toronto this time, as Gordie Howe began aging and Terry Sawchuk slipped from outstanding to merely very good.

Frankly, I had a soft spot in my heart for the Red Wings at this time and sadly observed the team's demise after that.

It was a long wait for another shot at the Cup, but in the spring of 1995 I thought I might be there to see it happen. By now I was covering New Jersey Devils' telecasts for SportsChannel and was in the Motor City for the Devils-Wings finale. Everyone and his Uncle Dudley had Detroit pegged for the Cup. I sensed the impatience in the crowd when the public address announcer began introducing the Devils one by one before the opening face-off. As each Devil's name was broadcast the crowd chanted, "Who cares! Who cares!"

It was one of the last occasions when the partisans had anything to cheer about. The Devils smote the Wings in both games at Joe Louis Arena and ended their misery two games later at Brendan Byrne Arena.

The alibis were plentiful when it was all over, but the bottom line was that the drought was now into its 41st year and counting.

The Players: An Anecdotal Listing

Sidney Gerald Abel

Born: Melville, Saskatchewan, February 22, 1918

Position: Center, Detroit Red Wings, 1938-43, 1945-52; Blackhawks, 1952-53; Coach, Chicago Blackhawks, 1952-54; Detroit Red Wings, 1958-68; St. Louis Blues, 1971-72; General Manager, Detroit Red Wings, 1962-71; St. Louis Blues, 1971-73; Kansas City Scouts, 1973-?

Awards: Hart Trophy, 1948-49; All-Star (First Team), 1948-49, 1949-50; All-Star (Second Team), 1950-51; Hockey Hall of Fame, 1969

There may have been better centers in the National Hockey League than Sid Abel (alias "Ole Bootnose" because of his prominent proboscis), but few were more productive in the vital areas. He was a dogged and creative playmaker, the balance wheel between Gordie Howe and Ted Lindsay on Detroit's Production Line. He could score as well as develop goal-making plays for others.

Reared in the wheat fields of Melville, Saskatchewan, Abel became a member of the Red Wings in 1938-39, remaining in the Motor City until 1952 when he was released to become player-coach of the Chicago Blackhawks in 1952-53.

Abel is best remembered for his exploits in Detroit. "Sid," said hockey historian Ed Fitkin, "will go down in the Red Wings' history as the greatest competitor and inspirational force the Red Wings ever had." Few would have bet on that when he arrived in Detroit as a 19-year-old in the fall of 1937.

A six-footer who weighed in at only 155 pounds, Abel was greeted by manager-coach Jack Adams. "You got a future, kid," Adams told him, "but you have to build yourself up."

Abel was named alternate All-Star left wing for 1941-42, but he was a thoroughly distraught young man in April 1942. His Red Wings took on the Toronto Maple Leafs in the Stanley Cup finals. The Red Wings were a distinct underdog, yet Detroit won the first three games of the best of seven series and seemed certain to win the Cup. When it appeared that the Red Wings would wrap up the series at Olympia Stadium, Toronto rallied for a victory and then won the next three games and the championship. "To Abel," said a friend, "it was the greatest disappointment in his life."

The balm was administered the following autumn when manager-coach Adams named Abel captain of the Red Wings. Detroit finished first and won the Stanley Cup. Significantly, the

Wings defeated Boston 6-2 in the opening game of the finals, and Abel enjoyed the most productive night of his career to that point with a goal and three assists. He finished the playoffs with five goals and eight assists for 13 points in 10 games.

Prior to the 1943-44 campaign, Abel enlisted in the Royal Canadian Air Force, but not before marrying Red Wings' secretary Gloria Morandy. He was away from hockey for almost three years, serving as a physical training instructor for the Royal Canadian Air Force both in Canada and overseas.

Abel returned to the Red Wings in February of 1946. He was 28 years old and there were suspicions that he, like many returning war veterans, was too old and had been away too long. Still, he stayed with the Red Wings and survived training-camp cuts in 1946-47, scoring 19 goals that season.

At the start of the 1947-48 race, Abel was installed as the center between galloping youngsters Gordie Howe (right wing) and Ted Lindsay (left wing), a pair he had worked with occasionally in previous years.

"I don't know where I would be without Sid," said Howe. "He just has to whack me with his stick when I'm not playing well and say 'Get going' and that's all I ever needed."

Lindsay, who developed into one of hockey's best left-wingers under Abel's guidance, swore by his veteran center. "Sid is the greatest of them all," said

Lindsay. "He seems to know more about what I'm doing than I do myself, and he's always in the right spot."

It wasn't until the 1948-49 season, at age 31, that Abel realized his dream of a 20-goal season. He scored 28 that year, with a little help from his friends, Lindsay and Howe. "It just seemed," said Abel, "that every time I shot I scored. I kept telling my wife to pinch me. I felt sure that one day I'd wake up and find out that I was just dreaming."

The Lindsay-Abel-Howe combine developed into the dreadnoughts of the ice lanes. Abel had the savvy, and both Howe and Lindsay percolated along with a mixture of style, explosiveness and aggression that terrorized opposing teams. With the Production Line orchestrating wins, Detroit captured the first of seven consecutive Prince of Wales (first place) Trophies in 1948-49. The Red Wings won the Stanley Cup in 1949-50 and again in 1951-52 whereupon Abel decided to try coaching — and playing — with the Blackhawks.

Joseph Gordon Carveth

Born: Regina, Saskatchewan, March 21, 1918
Position: Forward, Detroit Red Wings, 1940-46, 1950-51; Boston Bruins, 1946-48; Montreal Canadiens, 1948-50

The advent of World War II spelled the end of several big-league careers as stickhandlers joined the Armed Forces and returned with their skills dimmed beyond redemption. On the other hand, the war provided opportunities to lesser-skilled skaters who blossomed in the diluted brand of wartime hockey. One such player was Detroit Red Wings' right wing Joe Carveth, a native of Regina, Saskatchewan, who, after several trials, played his first full season with the Red Wings in 1942-43 and remained in the Motor City through the 1945-46 season. His best year was 1943-44 when he scored 21 goals and had 35 assists for 56 points. A year later he compiled 54 points. He was traded to Boston in 1946-48 for Roy Conacher and in 1948-50 dealt to Montreal for Jim Peters. He finished his NHL career back in Detroit, after being traded back to the Wings in the 1950-51 season for Calum MacKay. Carveth helped the Detroiters to a Stanley Cup championship in his swan song.

Alex Peter (Fats) Delvecchio

Born: Fort William, Ontario, December 4, 1931

Position: Center, Detroit Red Wings, 1950-73; Coach, Detroit Red Wings, 1973-75; General Manager, Detroit Red Wings, 1974-77

Awards: Lady Byng Trophy, 1958-59, 1965-66, 1968-69; Lester Patrick Trophy, 1974; All-Star (Second Team), 1952-53; Hockey Hall of Fame, 1977

"He's not the brawniest hockey player I ever saw — but he is one of the brainiest." Those were veteran Red Wings' trainer Ross (Lefty) Wilson's words in describing his longtime teammate and friend as he presented Alex Peter Delvecchio the Lester Patrick Trophy in New York on March 18, 1974.

No one was better qualified to assess the talents of the former Red Wing than the irrepressible Wilson who watched Delvecchio through 22 seasons as a player with the red and white machine.

Then, in the 1973-74 season, Wilson and all of hockey watched as the likeable and well-respected Delvecchio moved from the role of team captain and highest scoring active player (Detroit and NHL totals: 1,549 games played; 456 goals; 825 assists; 1,281 points; and 383 penalty minutes) to coach and general manager of the team he skated with for so long and so well.

Taking over as coach on November 7, 1973, Delvecchio quietly replaced turmoil and uncertainty with harmony and new spirit. The change was so evident that owner Bruce A. Norris tapped the former number 10 to be number 1 in shaping the future of the Red Wings. On May 21, 1974, Delvecchio became general manager and coach with full authority in every phase of the club's operation. In June 1975, he gave up the coaching reins to Doug

Barkley and concentrated on managing, which he continued to do until 1977.

William Patrick Dineen

Born: Arvida, Quebec, September 18, 1932
Position: Forward, Detroit Red Wings, 1953-57; Chicago Blackhawks, 1957-58; Coach, Houston Aeros (WHA), 1972-78; General Manager, Houston Aeros (WHA), 1975-78; New England Whalers (WHA), 1978-79

A solid journeyman forward, Bill Dineen became coach of the WHA's Houston Aeros and led them to the Avco World Trophy in 1974 and 1975. During an NHL career that spanned 1953-58, Dineen played for Detroit and then Chicago. In his rookie season, 1953-54, Dineen scored an impressive 17 goals in 70 games. His manager, Jack (Jolly Jawn) Adams promised Dineen a bonus in his contract from $6,000 to $6,500 for the 1954-55 season. "I thought I was getting a raise of $500," Dineen recalled. "What I didn't know at the time was that the NHL had raised its minimum salary from $6,000 to $6,500. So all Adams did was give me the minimum once again!"

George Gee

Born: Stratford, Ontario, June 28, 1922
Position: Center, Chicago Blackhawks, 1945-48, 1951-54; Detroit Red Wings, 1949-51

If, as many critics have argued, the winning goal of the seventh game of the 1950 Stanley Cup finals between the Red Wings and Rangers was one of the biggest scores of all time, then the man who delivered the key pass on Pete Babando's shot deserves credit. That man was George Gee.

A native of Stratford, Ontario (birthplace of legendary Howie Morenz), Gee played three and a half seasons for Chicago before being dealt to Detroit. Always reliable, Gee centered a line with Babando and Gerry (Doc) Couture against the Rangers until just past the eight-minute mark of the second sudden-death period of the seventh game in April 1950 at Detroit's Olympia Stadium. Opposing Gee at the face-off was the Rangers' center Buddy O'Connor. Gee made one vital move. He turned to Babando before the face-off. "Move over behind me," Gee instructed, "you're too far to the left." Gee then won the face-off and delivered the puck to Babando whose shot beat Rangers' goalie Chuck Rayner to win the Stanley Cup for Detroit. Gee returned to the Blackhawks in 1951-52 and ended his career in Chicago after the 1953-54 season.

Robert (Bob) Goldham

Born: Georgetown, Ontario, May 12, 1922
Position: Defenseman, Toronto Maple Leafs, 1941-42, 1945-47; Chicago Blackhawks, 1947-50; Detroit Red Wings, 1950-56

Bob Goldham turned hero immediately in his rookie NHL season (1941-42), playing defense for the Toronto Maple Leafs in the Stanley Cup finals against the Detroit Red Wings. Goldham, who had been elevated from the American League's Hershey Bears, was among several green, young players inserted into the Maple Leafs' lineup to replace such aging veterans as Bucko McDonald and Bingo Kampman as the Leafs fell behind three games to none. The Toronto team, sparked by the youthful Goldham, Ernie Dickens, Don Metz and Wally Stanowski, rallied to win the next four games and the Cup. In time Goldham matured into an effective defenseman who was especially good at dropping to the ice to block enemy shots. During the 1947-48 season he was part of a package — including teammates Gus Bodnar, Bud Poile, Gaye Stewart and Ernie Dickens — which the Leafs sent to Chicago for ace center Max Bentley and utility forward Cy Thomas. Goldham was dealt to Detroit in

1950-51 and finished his career with the Red Wings in 1955-56.

Glenn Henry (Mr. Goalie) Hall

Born: Humboldt, Saskatchewan, October 3, 1931
Position: Goalie, Detroit Red Wings, 1952-57; Chicago Blackhawks, 1957-67; St. Louis Blues, 1967-71
Awards: Calder Trophy, 1955-56; Vezina Trophy, 1962-63, 1966-67 (with Denis DeJordy), 1968-69 (with Jacques Plante); Conn Smythe Trophy, 1967-68; All-Star (First Team), 1956-57, 1957-58, 1959-60, 1962-63, 1963-64, 1965-66, 1968-69; Hockey Hall of Fame, 1975

Glenn Hall, one of the greatest professional netminders of all time, managed to appear in an amazing 502 consecutive contests without missing a single game. Yet Hall was so fearful of his hazardous occupation, he would often get violently ill before games.

Over his 18-year big-league career, Hall labored for three NHL clubs — the Detroit Red Wings, Chicago Blackhawks and St. Louis Blues. He was named the first team All-Star goalie seven times and had his name inscribed on the Vezina Trophy three times as the league's top goaltender.

Despite receiving scores of painful stitches in his face, Hall did not don a goalie mask until the twilight of his career, claiming it restricted his vision when the puck was at his feet. One night, during the 1957 Stanley Cup playoffs, a screened shot suddenly flashed out of a tangle of bodies and smashed into Hall's maskless face. The game was delayed for a half hour while Hall took 23 stitches in his mouth before returning to finish the game.

Hall was named to the Hockey Hall of Fame in June 1975.

Gordon (Gordie) Howe

Born: Floral, Saskatchewan, March 31, 1928

Position: Right Wing, Detroit Red Wings, 1946-71; Houston Aeros (WHA), 1973-77; New England Whalers (WHA), 1977-79; Hartford Whalers (NHL), 1979-80

Awards: Hart Trophy, 1951-52, 1952-53, 1956-57, 1957-58, 1959-60, 1962-63; Art Ross Trophy, 1950-51, 1951-52, 1952-53, 1953-54, 1956-57, 1962-63; Lester Patrick Trophy, 1967; Gary L. Davidson Trophy, 1974; All-Star (First Team), 1950-51, 1951-52, 1952-53, 1953-54, 1956-57, 1957-58, 1959-60, 1962-63, 1965-66, 1967-68, 1968-69, 1969-70; All-Star (Second Team), 1948-49, 1949-50, 1955-56, 1958-59, 1960-61, 1961-62, 1963-64, 1964-65, 1966-67; Hockey Hall of Fame, 1972

It was a measure of Gordie Howe's dominant position in hockey that when he finally retired from the NHL prior to the 1971-72 season, he had played in 1,687 regular season games, scored 786 goals, 1,023 assists, 1,809 points and received 1,643 minutes in penalties.

Between the years of 1946 and 1971, Howe won the Hart Trophy as the most valuable player six times and the Art Ross Trophy as leading scorer six times. His artistry, versatility and durability, and the fact that he successfully spanned three distinct hockey eras, marked him unique in sports and at the apex of hockey achievements.

"He was not only the greatest hockey player I've ever seen," said former teammate and Hall of Famer Bill Gadsby, "but also the greatest athlete."

Howe was born on March 31, 1928, in Floral, Saskatchewan, a town on the outskirts of Saskatoon in Canada's wheat belt. It was in Saskatoon where Howe learned to play hockey.

When he was 15, Howe packed a shirt, a set of underwear and a toothbrush into a little bag and took an overnight train to Winnipeg, where the New York Rangers were holding their training camp. He was a big, shy kid, and the thought of being away from home among big-league hockey players frightened him. He almost starved because of it.

He was young and homesick. Finally, when his roommate left for home, Howe sulked for two days and then he, too, departed. The next year he was invited to the Wings' camp in Windsor, Ontario. He was signed to a contract by Jack Adams and assigned to the Wings' Junior team in Galt, Ontario. Because of the Canadian Amateur Hockey Association ruling, he was unable to play for a year. Instead he worked out with the team and played in exhibition games.

The next year found him playing with Omaha, and in 1946 he joined the Red Wings. In his first three years he scored seven, 16 and 12 goals. His genius finally surfaced during the playoffs in 1949, when he was the high scorer with eight goals and 11 points.

"I still wasn't so sure that I was a star," he said. "When I went home to Saskatoon that summer, I started playing baseball again. One day, a kid came up to me for an autograph and while I signed it, he said, 'Mr. Howe, what do you do in the winter?'"

The goals began to come in bunches, and Howe mesmerized both enemy and teammate alike.

Tommy Ivan, who had taken over for Adams as the coach of the Red Wings, likened Howe to Charlie Gehringer, one of the finest baseball players to wear a Detroit Tigers' uniform. "Like Gehringer," Ivan explained, "Howe has the ability and the knack for making the difficult play look easy, routine. You can't miss the skill of a player like Maurice Richard; it's so dramatic! Gordie — you have to know your hockey or you can't appreciate him."

As a hockey player, Howe reached the top in 1950-51 when he led the NHL in scoring with 86 points (43 goals, 43 assists); in 1951-52 with 86 points (47 goals, 39 assists); in 1952-53 with a record 95 points (49 goals, 46 assists); and in 1953-54 with 81 points (33 goals, 48 assists). No other player before then had ever led the league in scoring for more than two years in a row. Howe again was at the top of the scoring list in 1956-57 with 89 points (44 goals, 45 assists) and continued to dominate the game through the late '50s and early '60s.

Dave Keon, who became captain of the Toronto Maple Leafs, once observed, "There are two weak teams in the league and four strong ones. The weak ones are New York and Boston, and the strong ones are Toronto, Montreal, Chicago and Gordie Howe!" Howe remained a factor in the NHL until his first retirement. Then, to everyone's amazement, he resurfaced again, this time in 1973 in the World Hockey Association.

Miracles occur in big-league hockey about once a half-century. In 1973-74 there were three: Gordie Howe returned to the ice at age 45, and his sons, Marty and Mark, signed to skate alongside their father with the Houston Aeros. Those add up to a lot of miracles. Then the three Howes led Houston to the Avco World Trophy and the WHA title. And Gordie Howe starred for Team Canada in 1974 against the young Russians, before orchestrating a second Avco Trophy win in 1975. He would later go on to play for the New England Whalers before taking one last stab in the NHL with the Hartford Whalers.

Thomas N. Ivan

Born: Toronto, Ontario, January 31, 1911
Position: Coach, Detroit Red Wings, 1947-54; Chicago Blackhawks, 1956-58; General Manager, Chicago Blackhawks, 1954-77
Awards: Hockey Hall of Fame, 1974

When a severe facial injury ended Tommy Ivan's playing career in Junior hockey, his love for the game kept him around as a referee and then as coach of a Junior team in Brantford, Ontario.

After serving as a gunnery instructor in the Canadian army during World War II, Ivan began his pro career as a scout in the Detroit Red Wings' organization. In 1945-46 he coached the Omaha Knights of the now defunct United States Hockey League, and the following year he was promoted to the Indianapolis Capitals of the American Hockey League.

In 1947-48 Ivan made his National Hockey League debut as a coach with the Detroit Red Wings when Jack Adams relinquished the position to become the Wings' general manager. His teams won six straight NHL championships and three Stanley Cups (1949-50, 1951-52, 1953-54) in six years.

While with the Red Wings, Ivan coached in four All-Star games, leading the All-Stars to successive wins over Toronto in 1948 and 1949 with identical 3-1 scores. He then piloted the Wings the next year to a 7-1 win over the All-Stars, and finally, coached the first team All-Stars to a 1-1 tie with the second team.

In 1954-55 Ivan left the winning Detroit team and took the general manager's job with the Chicago Blackhawks.

From 1959 on, the Blackhawks, with Ivan again solely as general manager, qualified for the playoffs every year but one and won the Stanley Cup for the first time in 23 years in 1960-61. In 1966-67, the Hawks captured their first division title in their 40-year history, added another one three years later and then won three successive division championships when they moved over to the West Division in 1970-71.

Building an excellent farm system, Ivan transformed the floundering and financially troubled Blackhawks into one of the most powerful organizations of the NHL. Retiring in 1977, Ivan remained with the team as assistant to the president, devoting time to amateur hockey in the United States.

Leonard Patrick (Red) Kelly

Born: Simcoe, Ontario, July 9, 1927

Position: Defenseman, Detroit Red Wings, 1947-60; Toronto Maple Leafs, 1960-67; Coach, Los Angeles Kings, 1967-69; Pittsburgh Penguins, 1969-73; Toronto Maple Leafs, 1973-77

Awards: Norris Trophy, 1953-54; Lady Byng Trophy, 1950-51, 1952-53, 1953-54, 1960-61; All-Star (First Team), 1950-51, 1951-52, 1952-53, 1953-54, 1954-55, 1956-57; All-Star (Second Team), 1949-50, 1955-56; Hockey Hall of Fame, 1969

One of the most versatile and talented players of his time, Red Kelly broke into the NHL in the mid-'40s with the Detroit Red Wings after a distinguished playing career with St. Michael's College Junior team. The big defenseman became somewhat of an institution in the Motor City where he became a member of eight championship squads and four Stanley Cup winners as well as being named to eight All-Star teams. Among the many honors bestowed on the artful Kelly were four Lady Byng Memorial Trophies and the Norris Trophy as the league's top defender.

Kelly was reborn in 1960 when he was traded to the Toronto Maple Leafs. At the age where most players consider retirement, Kelly switched to forward-line duty where he helped guide the Leafs to one championship and four Stanley Cup wins. While manning a full-time pivot position in Toronto, Kelly somehow found time to serve a term as a member of Canada's Parliament. The redhead bowed out of the political arena when he found his dual career too strenuous.

Kelly finally retired as a player after the Maple Leafs' stunning 1967 Stanley Cup win and accepted the coaching post for the fledgling Los Angeles Kings. After two seasons in Los Angeles, he moved on to serve as coach and general manager of the Pittsburgh Penguins.

In 1973 John McLellan was forced out as coach of the Toronto Maple Leafs and Kelly stepped in, leading the young team to a playoff berth.

Crusty Leaf owner Harold Ballard complained at length and also in public that Kelly was too nice a guy, and in 1977 Roger Neilson replaced Kelly behind the bench.

Anthony Joseph (Tony) Leswick

Born: Humboldt, Saskatchewan, March 17, 1923
Position: Left Wing, New York Rangers, 1945-51; Detroit Red Wings, 1951-55, 1957-58; Chicago Blackhawks, 1955-56
Awards: All-Star (Second Team), 1949-50

In 1946 it was clear to Frank Boucher, who had taken over the helm of the Rangers, that new blood was needed to replace the prewar heroes who had lost their spark and their style. One of the first "finds" was a small, bulldog-type forward named Tony Leswick. Within two years "Tough Tony," as he was known on Broadway, became the team's leading scorer.

The turnabout for the Rangers from chronic losers to consistent winners didn't happen overnight, but Leswick went a long way to pumping fighting blood into the post-war team. He not only led them in scoring during the 1946-47 campaign but was just as useful as the supreme needler of the opposition and "shadow" of the leading scorers until traded to Detroit in 1951-52.

More than anyone else, the fabulous Rocket Richard of the Montreal Canadiens had the life annoyed out of him by Leswick. Once, at the Montreal Forum, Leswick needled The Rocket, and Richard swung his stick at Leswick. The referee sent Richard to the penalty box with a two-minute minor. Leswick didn't stop there and pestered The Rocket throughout the match. With just a minute remaining, Richard blew up again, and again the referee sent him to the penalty box.

At game's end, Richard bolted from the penalty box and charged Leswick, whereupon the two of them brawled for several minutes while teammates and officials attempted to separate the pair. The Richard-Leswick feud continued for several years.

Of course, Richard wasn't Leswick's only target. Once, in a playoff game against the Detroit Red Wings, he was given a two-minute penalty, followed closely by a two-minute penalty to teammate Nick Mickoski. The timekeeper, whose duty it was to wave inmates back onto the ice when their penalty time had expired, became Leswick's target.

"Tony chattered and argued about

the time he was to return to the ice," said Rangers' publicist Stan Saplin, "and so confused the timekeeper that he was allowed back in the game long before his penalty was up."

Robert Blake Theodore (Ted) Lindsay

Born: Renfrew, Ontario, July 29, 1925

Position: Left Wing, Detroit Red Wings, 1944-57, 1964-65; Chicago Blackhawks 1957-60; General Manager, Detroit Red Wings, 1977-1980

Awards: Art Ross Trophy, 1949-50; All-Star (First Team), 1947-48, 1949-50; 1950-51, 1951-52, 1952-53, 1953-54, 1955-56, 1956-57; All-Star (Second Team), 1948-49; Hockey Hall of Fame, 1966

One of the most determined and fearsome skaters in National Hockey League history, "Terrible Ted" Lindsay is best remembered as the left-winger on the Detroit Red Wings' Production Line with center Sid Abel and Gordie Howe.

The son of Bert Lindsay, himself a splendid player and inventor of the collapsible hockey net, Ted Lindsay skated in the NHL for 17 years, most of the time with the Red Wings. Lindsay was not especially big (five foot eight inches, 163 pounds), but he was regarded as totally tough. "By my definition," Lindsay said, "there is one helluva lot more to being a tough guy than getting into a few phony fights where there aren't even any punches thrown. To me being tough includes wanting to win so badly that you give it everything that you got on every shift, going into the corners without phoning ahead to see who is there, backing up your mates when they are in trouble and stepping into guys, even if they are bigger than you."

One of Lindsay's more devastating bouts involved the Bruins' William (Wild Bill) Ezinicki. The fight, at Olympia Stadium in Detroit, took place on January 25, 1951. When it was over Ezinicki had lost a tooth, acquired a couple of black eyes, a broken nose and 19 stitches. Lindsay only needed five stitches above the eye, but was treated for badly scarred and swollen knuckles on his right hand.

It was episodes such as that which caused Lindsay to become one of the all-time penalty leaders with 1,808 minutes in 17 seasons with Detroit and later Chicago. He could score, too, and finished his career with 379 goals, was named the All-Star left wing nine times and also made "trouble" in areas outside the rink itself.

Lindsay was a leader in the formation of an NHL players' union in the mid-'50s. When Red Wings' manager Jack Adams discovered Lindsay's role with the proposed union, he had the left wing traded to the Chicago Blackhawks in the 1957-58 season. "The concept we had for the players' association," said Lindsay, "was not the creation for one household for all the players in the NHL. What we were aiming for was for the benefit of the game of hockey, not just the players."

Curiously, Lindsay finished his NHL career with the Red Wings in 1964-65, but remained in the hockey limelight. He was hired as color commentator for the NBC-TV network "Game of the Week" in 1972 and never hesitated to speak out on controversial issues. Lindsay was especially critical of the NHL Players' Association and its director, Alan Eagleson. "The Players' Association," said Lindsay, "had encouraged familiarity between the players. They are one big, happy family now. The coaches have no way of pushing players. They can't send them to the minors; they can't fine them because the Players' Association would raise hell."

Harry (Apple Cheeks) Lumley

Born: Owen Sound, Ontario, November 11, 1926
Position: Goalie, Detroit Red

Wings, 1943-44, 1944-50; New York Rangers, 1943-44; Chicago Blackhawks, 1950-52; Toronto Maple Leafs, 1952-56; Boston Bruins, 1957-60
Awards: Vezina Trophy, 1953-54; All-Star (First Team), 1953-54, 1954-55

Harry Lumley, an outstanding goaltender who labored for 16 years in professional hockey as one of the stingiest netminders around, had an inauspicious NHL debut in a two-game trial with the Detroit Red Wings, allowing 13 pucks to elude his flailing limbs.

Looking back on that embarrassing goal splurge, one can forgive Lumley if he was a bit awed by it all since the netminder was only 17 years old at the time. This was the 1943-44 season and World War II had decimated the ranks of the NHL, necessitating Lumley's adolescent awakening to the harsh realities of big-league hockey.

Lumley matured, though, into one of the NHL's most proficient puck stoppers. He remained with the Wings for six more seasons, guiding them to the playoffs each year and sipping Stanley Cup champagne in 1949-50, his last campaign with the Wings.

At the end of that season the Red Wings came up with another wonder without whiskers in 20-year-old Terry Sawchuk. Lumley was dispatched to a hapless Chicago Blackhawks' team where he spent two frustrating seasons. In 1952, Lumley hit the road once more, this time to his home province of Ontario and the blue and white of the Toronto Maple Leafs. It was in Toronto that Lumley enjoyed his best years as a pro, leading the NHL in shutouts for two consecutive seasons and copping the Vezina Trophy in 1953-54 with an amazing 1.86 goals against average in 69 games.

Nearing the end of his career, Lumley had a three-year stint with Boston Bruins and then played in the minor leagues until his retirement in 1960-61.

James Alexander (Jimmy) McFadden

Born: Belfast, Northern Ireland, April 15, 1920
Position: Center, Detroit Red Wings, 1947-1951; Chicago Blackhawks, 1951-54
Awards: Calder Trophy, 1947-48

Jimmy McFadden was the first — and last — native of Belfast, Northern Ireland, to win the Calder Memorial Trophy (1947-48) as the NHL rookie of the year. Since McFadden was 27 at the time of the honor it was considered terribly unique and McFadden was hailed as a senior wunderkind. A chunky, little (five-foot-seven, 178-pound) guy, McFadden played some of his best hockey for the Ottawa Senators in the Quebec Senior League. Although he never quite duplicat-

ed the excellence of his rookie year (60 games, 24 goals and 24 assists for 48 points), McFadden played capably for Detroit, helping them win a Stanley Cup in 1950. He was traded to Chicago in 1951-52 and starred for the Blackhawks' surprise team in 1952-53, who nearly upset the favored Canadiens in the Stanley Cup semifinals. McFadden rounded out his big-league career in 1953-54.

Max McNab

Born: Watson, Saskatchewan, June 21, 1924
Position: Center, Detroit Red Wings, 1947-1950

Max McNab, frequently called the nicest guy in hockey (and not without validity) never quite made it to the big time the way the Detroit Red Wings had hoped for in the late '40s. A product of the Saskatoon Elks' Senior club, Max was groomed as the heir apparent to Sid Abel, who was the aging pivot on the Ted Lindsay-Gordie Howe Production Line. McNab led the United States League in goals in the 1947-48 season ringing up 44 in 44 games. The same season he was given a 12-game tryout with the Red Wings. McNab scored two goals and assisted on two others during his short stint. A year later he played 51 NHL games in Detroit and scored 10 goals with 13 assists. This encouraged the Red Wings' manager Jack Adams to keep Abel on the big line and, of course, Abel came through handsomely. The Wings gave McNab one more shot in 1949-50. McNab very simply failed with only four goals and four assists in 65 games. Injuries manacled his rise and McNab drifted to the minors. After his playing days he became one of the game's foremost executives.

Martin Nicholas (Marty) (Blackie) Pavelich

Born: Sault Ste. Marie, Ontario, November 6, 1927
Position: Forward, Detroit Red Wings, 1947-57

When the Red Wings' juggernaut ran over the opposition during the early '50s, Ted Lindsay and Gordie Howe captured most of the headlines among the Detroit forwards. But just as vital was defensive forward Marty Pavelich. Wings' manager Jack Adams knew it all the time. "Pavelich," said Adams, "was one of the four key men around whom we built our hockey club."

Pavelich came to Detroit via the Red Wings' Junior affiliate in Galt, Ontario. He played 41 games during the 1947-48 NHL season and remained a Red Wing regular through his final year, 1956-57. During that period Pavelich played on four Stanley Cup winners. "His scoring records never stood out," said Adams, "but he always had the toughest jobs — checking the great scoring right wings such as Maurice Richard. We practically had to put handcuffs on him to keep him off the ice." Pavelich, otherwise known as "Blackie," later became a business partner in Detroit with former teammate Ted Lindsay.

"Pavelich," Adams concluded, "was a real man and a real hockey player, one of the most popular ever to play in Detroit."

Rene Marcel Pronovost

Born: Lac la Tortue, Quebec, June 15, 1930
Position: Defenseman, Detroit Red Wings, 1950-65; Toronto Maple Leafs, 1965-70
Awards: All-Star (First Team), 1960-61; All-Star (Second Team), 1958-59

Of all modern day hockey players, Marcel Pronovost has the most claim to the unofficial trophy for the most injured man in hockey. Episodes of Pronovost's derring-do were legend around NHL rinks. He broke into big-league hockey with Detroit in the Stanley Cup playoffs of 1950 and was around to play a few games for the Toronto Maple Leafs in the 1969-1970 season. In between, Pronovost collected hundreds of stitches and innumerable broken bones. Once, in a game against the

Chicago Blackhawks, Pronovost sped across the blue line as two husky Chicago defensemen dug their skates into the ice, awaiting his arrival. They dared Pronovost to pass. "I decided that there was only one move," said Pronovost. "Bust through the middle." Even the most ironfisted hockey players shudder at the thought of crashing a defense, but Pronovost wasn't thinking about getting hurt. He never did. He eyed the two-foot space between the Hawks, boldly pushed the puck ahead and leapt at the opening.

It was too late. The crouched defensemen slammed the gate, hurling Pronovost headfirst over their shoulders. In that split second of imminent danger — when even the strongest of men shut their eyes — Pronovost looked and saw the puck below him. He swiped at it missed, and had to settle for a three-point landing on his left eyebrow, nose and cheek.

A few minutes later a doctor was applying ice packs to Pronovost's forehead as he lay on the dressing-room table. Pronovost's skull looked as though it had been a loser in a brawl with a bulldozer. His nose was broken and listed heavily toward starboard. His eyebrows required 25 stitches. "And my cheekbones," Pronovost recalled in a real deep tone, "felt as if they were pulverized." He was right, they were cracked like little pieces of china.

"What hurt the most," said Pronovost, whose face became as craggy as an alpine peak, "was that I had to miss the next two games. As for injuries, I didn't think twice about them." Pronovost always regarded his misfortunes casually. "To me," he said, "accidents are as common as lacing up a pair of skates. One of the prizes of my collection of injuries is a break in the fourth dorsal vertebra." In 1959, after Pronovost had broken his beak for the 13th time, he examined it with the air of a true connoisseur and said, "Frankly I was disappointed. After a few towels were put on I could see through both eyes. The first time I broke my nose in a hockey game, my eyes were swollen shut for three days.

Hubert George (Bill) Quackenbush

Born: Toronto, Ontario, March 2, 1922
Position: Defenseman, Detroit Red Wings, 1942-49; Boston Bruins, 1949-56
Awards: Lady Byng Trophy, 1948-49; All-Star (First Team), 1947-48, 1948-49, 1950-51; All-Star (Second Team) 1946-47, 1952-53

In the late 1940s and the early 1950s Bill Quackenbush was one of the best defensemen in the National Hockey League, first with the

Detroit Red Wings (1942-49) and then the Boston Bruins (1949-56).

Quackenbush was always in the thick of the action — sometimes on the wrong side. In the opening round of the 1952 Stanley Cup playoffs, when Rocket Richard scored the winning goal in the seventh game against the Bruins at the Montreal Forum, Quackenbush was the defenseman whom The Rocket circled to make the score possible. It broke a 1-1 tie and made the win possible.

Quackenbush played on some of the best Detroit Red Wing teams in history. "Ted Lindsay, Gordie Howe, Sid Abel — every forward on that great line back-checked," Quackenbush recalled. "It made it a hell of a lot easier on me. They took a lot of defensive pressure off the defenseman. There aren't too many players like there were on the Production Line anymore."

A classic defensive defenseman, Quackenbush was a cautious and remarkably clean-playing soul who won the Lady Byng in 1949.

Leo Charles Reise Jr.

Born: Stoney Creek, Ontario, June 7, 1922
Position: Defenseman, Chicago Blackhawks, 1945-46; Detroit Red Wings, 1946-52; New York Rangers, 1952-54

Awards: All-Star (Second Team), 1950-51

There are not many chips off the old block who are so identical in style and in ability than Leo Reise Sr. and Leo Reise Jr. The younger Reise also was a defenseman and a greatly-feared one at that. Although Leo Reise Jr. broke in with the Blackhawks in 1945-46, he was dealt to Detroit the next year and played his best hockey for the Red Wings through the 1951-52 season. His most memorable play was the sudden-death goal in the seventh game of the bitter 1950 Stanley Cup semifinals against Toronto. In 1952-53 he became a Ranger and, like his dad, finished his big-league tenure on Broadway (1953-54).

Although Gordie Howe, Ted Lindsay, and Red Kelly received much of the attention, it was Leo Reise Jr. who did much of the unheralded spadework for the first-place Red Wings in 1950 and 1951 when they won the Prince of Wales Trophy.

Terrance Gordon (Terry) Sawchuk

Born: Winnipeg, Manitoba, December 28, 1929
Position: Goalie, Detroit Red Wings, 1950-55, 1957-64, 1968-69; Boston Bruins,

1955-57; Toronto Maple Leafs, 1964-67; Los Angeles Kings 1967-68; New York Rangers, 1969-70

Awards: Calder Trophy, 1950-51; Vezina Trophy, 1951-52, 1952-53, 1954-55, 1964-65 (shared with J. Bower); Lester Patrick Trophy, 1971; All-Star (First Team), 1950-51, 1951-52, 1952-53; All-Star (Second Team), 1953-54 , 1954-55, 1958-59, 1962-63; Hockey Hall of Fame, 1971

One of the greatest and most tragic players of all time ever to grace a major league hockey rink was Terry Sawchuk. Quite possibly, Sawchuk was one of the best goaltenders ever to strap on the tools of ignorance. But he was also a moody, brooding figure who was a physical and mental wreck of a man when he met his untimely death in 1970.

Sawchuk's 20-year career in big-league hockey included tours of duty with the Detroit Red Wings, Boston Bruins, Toronto Maple Leafs, Los Angeles Kings and New York Rangers. He broke into the majors with the Detroit Red Wings, making first team All-Star during his maiden season and copping the Calder Trophy as the NHL's rookie of the year.

Incredibly, his goals against average never topped 2.00 during his first five full years with Detroit, a stretch that saw him rack up 56 shutouts. He finished his up and down career with an amazing total of 103 career shutouts, 65 more than his then closest challenger, Glenn Hall.

Sawchuk's early years were his great ones, but he insisted that the finest moment of his career came with the 1966-67 Maple Leafs, when he dramatically guided the Toronto team to an upset Stanley Cup victory.

It was said of Sawchuk that he wasn't a whole man, rather, he was stitched together — held in place by catgut and surgical tape. Sawchuk suffered a painful shoulder injury early in his career. Consequently, Sawchuk's ability to lift his stick above chest level became restricted. A full-page photo of Sawchuk once appeared in a national magazine illustrating each stitch that he had taken to his ruined face. The shocking picture could easily have passed for a horror movie's publicity shot.

An enigmatic, bitter man to the end, Sawchuk died as a result of injuries received in a scuffle with teammate Ron Stewart on the lawn of his Long Island home.

Victor John Stasiuk

Born: Lethbridge, Alberta,
             May 23, 1929
Position: Left Wing, Chicago
             Blackhawks, 1949-50;
             Detroit Red Wings, 1950-
             55, 1961-63; Boston
             Bruins,1955-61; Coach,
             Philadelphia Flyers, 1969-
             71; California Seals, 1971-
             72; Vancouver Canucks,
             1972-73

Vic Stasiuk, a hulking left-winger who liked to use his body in heavy checking, began his career in Chicago (1949-50), but his best hockey was played in Detroit (1951-55) and in Boston (1955-61). Stasiuk played his last three NHL seasons back in Detroit, finishing his big-league career in 1962-63.

Stasiuk could be intimidating as he was against the Rangers in the 1958 Stanley Cup playoffs. In that series Stasiuk skated the width of the ice to smash the Rangers' Red Sullivan with a jaw-breaking elbow. Vic was credited with turning the series in Boston's favor with the blow. However, Stasiuk was rewarded in turn when the Rangers' Andy Bathgate wasted him twice in fights during a later match. In time Stasiuk turned to coaching and handled the Philadelphia Flyers. During the 1970-71 season Stasiuk feuded with several players who opposed his direc-

tive ordering the Coke machine removed from the dressing room. In June 1971 Stasiuk was replaced by Fred Shero, but he remained in hockey in various capacities.

John Sherratt (Black Jack) Stewart

Born: Pilot Mound, Manitoba,
             May 6, 1917
Position: Defenseman, Detroit Red
             Wings, 1938-43, 1945-50;
             Chicago Blackhawks,
             1950-52
Awards: All-Star (First Team),
             1942-43, 1947-48, 1948-
             49; All-Star (Second
             Team), 1945-46, 1946-47;
             Hockey Hall of Fame,
             1964

If John Sherratt (Black Jack) Stewart is a name that gives you goose pimples, you can imagine what this husky, surly-looking defenseman did to opponents from 1938 through to 1952 in the National Hockey League. A Detroit Red Wing for most of his career, Stewart accumulated about 50 scars and 220 stitches, but never missed a minute because of it during his 10-plus years in the bigs. "Sew fast, doc," Stewart would tell the medics who were repairing his injuries, "I'm due back on the ice."

Stewart was as brave as any pro and

once played an entire season with a broken hand. A special device attached to his stick and wrist enabled him to have a firm grip. Red Wings' manager Jack Adams called him "one of the strongest guys I've ever seen in a hockey uniform."

Like the Rangers' Ching Johnson, Stewart took a joyous delight in body-checking. "He was a mean individual," said ex-Wing Ted Lindsay, "but when he was mean he had a big smile on his face. When he had on that smile, it was time for the opposition to look out. Once Gordie Howe and I decided we would take this old guy in the corner during practice and rough him up. Jack took his left arm and pinned me across the chest against the screen and then he lifted Howe off the ice by his shirt. Then, he just smiled at the both of us."

One of Stewart's toughest battles was with John Mariucci, the brawling Chicago defenseman. They warred for 15 minutes on the ice and in the penalty box. At the very worst, it was a draw for Stewart who rarely, if ever, lost a fight.

Norman Victor Alexander (Norm) Ullman

Born: Provost, Alberta, December 26, 1935

Position: Center, Detroit Red Wings, 1955-68; Toronto Maple Leafs, 1968-75; Edmonton Oilers, 1975-77
Awards: All-Star (First Team), 1964-65; All-Star (Second Team), 1966-67; Hockey Hall of Fame, 1982

While high-priced National Hockey League rookies and super-scoring centers captured the headlines, taciturn veteran Norm Ullman quietly did a steady job at center. Overshadowed by his flashier Toronto teammates, Ullman, nevertheless, consistently outscored them.

When the Maple Leafs released him in 1975, Ullman had scored 490 NHL goals, putting him in the exalted company of players like Gordie Howe, Alex Delvecchio, Jean Beliveau and other major point producers of his time.

Originally a member of the great Detroit Red Wings' teams, Ullman never played on a Stanley Cup championship squad. Perhaps this fact isn't so shocking when you examine Ullman's dossier. He came to the Detroit Red Wings as a rookie in 1955, the year after they had won the Cup. The Wings traded him to the Maple Leafs in the middle of the 1967-68 season, the year after the Leafs had won the cup.